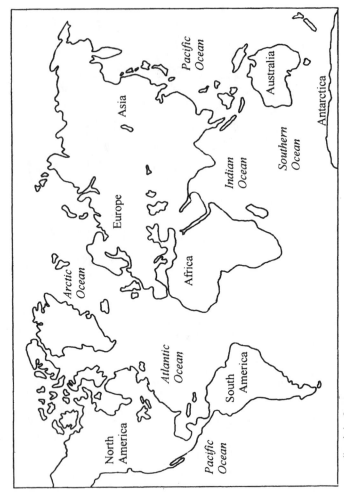

Pacific
Ocean

Asia

Australia

Antarctica

Southern
Ocean

Indian
Ocean

Europe

Africa

Arctic
Ocean

Atlantic
Ocean

South
America

North
America

Pacific
Ocean

Knowledge Quest

The Story of the World

The Story of the World: History for the Classical Child

Volume 2

The Middle Ages

From the Fall of Rome to the Rise of the Renaissance

By Susan Wise Bauer

Illustrated by Patty Martirosian and Jay Wise

Additional illustrations by Sharon Wilson and Lynn Hosegood

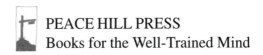

PEACE HILL PRESS
Books for the Well-Trained Mind

As noted, some of the blackline maps included in this book are adapted from originals drawn by Terri Johnson and are reprinted here with her kind permission. The maps have been altered to fit the content of this book. For a full selection of Terri Johnson's blackline maps of the Middle Ages, visit Knowledge Quest at knowledgequestmaps.com or write to Knowledge Quest, 7722 SE 282nd Ave., Gresham, OR 97080.

Publisher's Cataloging-in-Publication

Bauer, S. Wise
  The story of the world : history for the classical child. Volume 2, The Middle Ages : from the fall of Rome to the rise of the Renaissance / by Susan Wise Bauer.
  --1st ed.
  p. cm.
  Includes index.
  SUMMARY: Chronological history of the Middle Ages covering Africa, the Americas, Europe, and the Far East, from 400 A.D. to 1600 A.D.
  Audience: Ages 5-12.
  LCCN 2002108373
  ISBN 0-9714129-3-6

  1. Middle Ages--History--Juvenile Literature.
  2. Middle Ages--History. I. Title II. Title: Middle Ages

D118.B38 2003   909.07
                         QBI02-200542

Cover painting by Sarah Park
Cover design by Andrew J. Buffington

Printed in the U.S.A.

ISBN 0-9714129-3-6

Contents

Foreword

The hardest part of writing a world history is deciding what to leave out. In *The Story of the World,* I have tried to keep history simple and straightforward by highlighting the major events, personalities, and national stories of the world's cultures, in (more or less) chronological order. There's no way to simplify history without leaving out *something* important, so I encourage readers to use *The Story of the World* as a jumping-off point—a place of departure which can lead to further investigation of Mayan art, the French monarchy, English wars, or Native American cultures.

In writing this history, I have tried to keep my primary audience—young children—in mind. So although I describe major religious movements (the Reformation, the Counter Reformation, etc.) because of their historical importance, I have tried to tell these stories in a way that will allow parents to explain their religious significance. (I know, for example, that Catholic and Protestant parents will very likely choose to highlight different aspects of the Reformation and Counter Reformation, which are complex events in which both Catholics and Protestants behaved with courage and with cruelty.)

I have also chosen to ignore some events entirely. The Inquisition, for example, has historical importance. But its violence is impossible to treat in a way that would make sense to an eight-year-old, and its effects on Western history are not as pervasive as those of the Reformation.

I have made an effort here not to treat the West as an island; the stories of Japan, China, Korea, Africa,

India and Arabia are told, along with the stories of native peoples who lived in the Americas, in Australia, and in New Zealand. In selecting what episodes to include, I have tried to focus on what would prepare a child to understand today's world, rather than on the intricacies of past history. So I have given priority to those events and names which a child should know to be culturally literate, and also to those events which laid the foundation for the present day. So (for example) I spend a fair amount of time on the Emperor Justinian and his establishment of laws which are still foundational today—but not a great deal of time on the later Byzantine emperors.

Although maps are included, the Renaissance was a time of exploration, and the reader will need a globe to trace the paths of the adventurers who went all around the world.

Finally, I have chosen not to include dates in the narrative, since these are often meaningless to very young children. All important dates are included in an appendix, so that parents and older readers can locate these events on a timeline.

The Roman Empire at Its Largest Extent

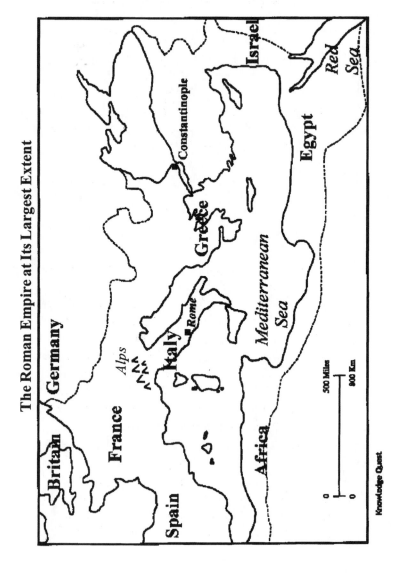

Chapter One
The Glory That Was Rome

Wandering Through the Roman Empire

What if you owned a magic carpet? You could use it to fly around the world—and back in time.

Let's imagine that you're going to fly back past the time that you were born, back to the days when people used horses to get around. Then you're going to fly back to the Middle Ages, back to the days of knights and castles. Then you're going to go back even farther, to the time of the Romans.

Your magic carpet stops. You're hovering high in the air, above the Mediterranean Sea. From your seat on the carpet, you can look down and see the Mediterranean. It looks a little bit like a duck flying.

You notice that the land all around the Mediterranean is glowing yellow! This is the land that belongs to the Roman Empire, the biggest, most powerful empire in the world. For hundreds of years, Roman soldiers have been attacking and conquering the countries around the Mediterranean Sea. Now, the emperor of Rome rules all of these conquered countries. They obey the laws of Rome, speak the language of Rome, and serve the emperor of Rome.

Your magic carpet swoops down towards the Mediterranean Sea, towards a piece of land that looks like a boot sticking out into the middle of the water. This is Italy, the center of the Roman Empire. And the most important city in Italy is Rome itself, right in the middle of the boot.

Your carpet dives down into the middle of the city. You're carried along paved streets, through crowds of people. They are wearing white robes, draped over their shoulders and caught up around the waist with belts of leather; they wear cloaks of red, blue, and other bright colors. Tall buildings rise up on either side of you—ancient apartment buildings, made out of concrete. On your right, you see an enormous circular wall curving away from you; it looms high over your head. On the other side of the wall, you hear the clash of metal against metal and the roar of an excited crowd. This must be the Coliseum, the huge amphitheater where gladiators fight to the death, chariot racers careen around a track, and lions battle with Roman soldiers for the entertainment of Roman spectators.

As your carpet takes you through the richest part of town, you see marble columns with the statues of great Roman generals and emperors on top of them. Slaves pass by you, staggering under the weight of litters—beds on which important Roman citizens lie to be carried through the city. You hear the sound of music, and a loud voice crying, "Clear the way! Clear the way for the Emperor!" A litter comes into view, draped in purple and surrounded by guards. On the litter lies a fat man wearing a gorgeous purple cloak and gold rings on his fingers. A green laurel wreath crowns his head. He is the ruler of all Rome!

You decide to get out of his way, and your carpet rises up above the city and carries you north, into the countryside. You're going to travel north up through Italy. The carpet follows a broad, smooth paved road, crowded with travelers and pack animals. You cross a bridge, built of tall stone arches, above a river that runs far beneath.

18

The road goes on and on and on. The Romans built hundreds of these roads to link the different parts of their empire together. None of the travelers on the roads seem worried about bandits or highway robbers. After

all, the Romans are careful to keep peace all over their kingdom. This *Pax Romana*, or Roman peace, means that all the parts of the Roman Empire obey the Roman laws. And the Roman laws are very strict when it comes to highway

Roman soldiers protected the Pax Romana.

robbery. Bandits who are caught are executed, or forced to fight in the gladiator shows!

After you've flown for hundreds of miles, mountains come into view ahead of you. Your carpet soars up above them. The air becomes very cold! Far below, you can see snow on the mountaintops. These are the Alps. When you come down on the other side of the Alps, you are in Gaul—one of Rome's provinces, or conquered countries. Throughout Gaul, you see Roman towns. And outside every Roman town is a garrison, or army camp. Soldiers cook meals over open fires, practice sword fighting, and exercise their horses, waiting for trouble. If the people who live in Gaul revolt, the soldiers will immediately go to war against them.

Your carpet flies you over a wide stretch of water to a huge island and hovers above the ground. You hope the carpet won't land—because below you are

19

crowds of fierce warriors, planning to attack the Roman army huddled on the shore. Now you're in Britain.

The fierce warriors below you are Celts. They are painted blue; their hair is greased with animal fat so that it sticks up in points all over their heads, and they carry great, two-sided axes and razor-sharp spears. The Pax Romana doesn't seem to be working very well here in Britain!

"Let's get out of here!" you tell the carpet. Instantly it whisks you back up into the air. You fly down the Atlantic Ocean, down through Spain, into the northern part of Africa. As you fly along the northern African coast, you see great trading cities down below: cities built by the Romans, with busy ports where ships sail in and out, carrying spices, silks, salt, lumber, and other goods. It is a peaceful scene. The Pax Romana must be back in action!

Up ahead you see the peak of a pyramid, jutting up from the sand of a desert. You sail overtop of the pyramids, half blinded by their white sides shining in the sun. Ahead you see a huge river, feeding into the Mediterranean Sea. It's the Nile River. Even Egypt, the land of pharaohs, pyramids, and mummies, is under Roman control.

The sun is starting to sink towards the horizon, but you've only gone halfway through the Roman Empire. "Hurry up!" you say to the carpet. In just moments, you swoop through Arabia, Syria, and up into Asia Minor. As soon as you fly across Greece, you'll be back in Rome.

Thanks to your flying carpet, Roman roads, and the Pax Romana, you've traveled around the Roman Empire in less than a day. But in the days of Roman power it would take months to get all around Rome. No wonder that Rome was called "The Ruler of the Whole World!"

The Fall of Rome

The emperors of Rome were called "The Rulers of the Whole World." But they had a problem: The world was too big to rule!

The Roman Empire was so large that the army couldn't protect its borders. And there were plenty of people outside the Roman Empire who wanted to come in and take parts of it away.

Imagine that you're standing in an orchard filled with apple trees. Ripe, juicy apples hang from every branch, and hungry animals are roaming in herds all around the edges. Three starving deer rush in and start to eat the apples on one side. You run at them, waving your arms and shouting. The deer dash off—but while you're chasing them, two enormous cows start snatching apples from the other side of the orchard. You turn around and charge at them, yelling, "Don't eat my apples!" The cows back slowly away—but now five squirrels are right in the middle of the orchard, and each squirrel has an apple in his mouth and another in his paws.

All alone, you'll never keep all of these animals out of the orchard. And that's just how the Roman rulers felt about their empire. Wandering tribes from other parts of the world wanted to come into Rome, conquer Roman villages, use the Roman roads, eat the Roman crops, and share in the Roman wealth. The Romans called these wandering tribes *barbarians*. The barbarians didn't live in houses like the Romans did, or take baths like the Romans did, or cook their food. Instead, they lived in tents, fought on horseback, and ate their food raw. The Romans thought that these barbarians were no better than animals.

21

Thousands of these barbarian invaders—called Huns, Vandals, Goths, Visigoths, and Ostrogoths—swept down on Rome's borders. The emperors sent their armies to protect the borders, but there just weren't enough soldiers to guard all the sides of the Roman Empire. And Rome had other problems too. In some places, food was running short and Roman citizens were going hungry. A terrible sickness called the *plague* killed many of Rome's strong fighters. And many of the emperors who inherited the job of ruling Rome weren't very good at running an empire. One of them went mad and tried to make his horse into a government official!

Finally, an emperor named Diocletian came to the throne. He decided that the empire was too big for one ruler and one army to protect. So he divided the Roman Empire into two parts. He kept the eastern part—the part on the right-hand side of your map. He gave the western part to another emperor, a man named Maximian. From now on, there would be two Roman Empires and two Roman Emperors.

Diocletian hoped that the Roman Empire would be easier to protect, now that it was smaller. But he was wrong. Two hundred years after Diocletian's death, the Western Roman Empire was finally conquered by barbarian tribes. They burned Rome and

Roman buildings crumbled.

carried away all of its treasures. Nothing was left but the Roman roads and bridges. And slowly, even those began to crumble away into dust.

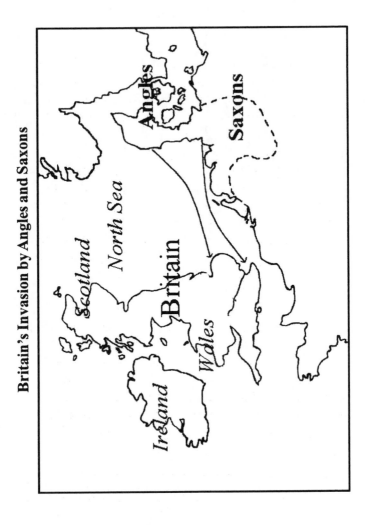

Britain's Invasion by Angles and Saxons

Angles

Saxons

North Sea

Scotland

Britain

Wales

Ireland

Chapter Two
The Early Days of Britain

The Celts of Britain

After the Western Roman Empire fell, all of the countries that had once belonged to Rome were free of Roman rule. One of those countries was Britain. Do you remember flying over Britain on your magic carpet? The Roman soldiers in Britain were fighting fierce, dangerous warriors who were painted blue.

These warriors were called Celts. The Celts lived in Britain before the Romans invaded the island. They weren't happy to see the Romans arrive! And even though the Romans set up camps and towns in the south part of Britain, they never managed to conquer all of the Celts. When the Western Roman Empire fell, the Celts drove the last Roman soldiers out of their country. Now Britain was theirs again.

The Celts were proud of their fighting strength. They praised men who had courage in battle. They sang songs and told stories about great warriors. Specially trained singers called *bards* learned stories about the chieftains and battle heroes of long ago. The stories weren't written down; instead, bards learned them from each other and memorized them so that they could be told again and again. These stories told Celtic children that it was good to be strong and warlike.

A Celtic warrior's emblem

One story told around the fires of the Celts was of Craith and his companions, three warriors with special powers. The story might have sounded something like this...

One day the warrior Craith said to himself, "I am a great fighter and have never lost a battle—but I am lonely. I want to marry a woman with hair as black as a raven's wing, skin as white as snow, and cheeks as red as blood. But the only woman as beautiful as all that is held prisoner by the great Giant Fovor of the Mighty Blows, at the end of the world."

So Craith set off to fight the giant Fovor and rescue the beautiful woman who was the giant's prisoner. As he walked along the road, he saw a warrior standing at the roadside with a rock in his hand.

"What are you doing with that rock?" asked Craith.

"See that bird, sitting on the topmost twig of the tree at the end of the world?" the warrior said, pointing. "I'm going to throw this rock and knock it off and eat it for my dinner."

Craith squinted, but he could see nothing. "You'd better come with me," he said to the warrior. "I could use a companion with eyes as good as yours."

And so the two men walked along. Soon the two of them saw a warrior lying on the ground with his ear pressed into the dirt.

"What are you doing?" Craith asked.

"Oh," the warrior said, "I am listening to the grass grow, down at the end of the world."

"You'd better come with us," Craith said. "Your hearing might help us in our quest.

And so the three men walked along. Soon they heard a noise behind them...*thump, thump, thump.*

They turned and saw a warrior coming up fast behind them. He was hopping on one foot, and his knee was bent so that his other leg was tied up behind him.

"Why don't you untie your other leg?" Craith asked.

"Oh," the hopping warrior said, "if I did that, I would run so fast that I would soon be at the end of the world; and then where would I go?"

"Come with us," the three said. And they walked on towards the end of the world.

Soon the castle of the giant Fovor of the Mighty Blows came into sight. The warrior Craith and his three companions stood beneath the walls and called up, "Giant! Giant Fovor! We've come to rescue the woman with hair like a raven's wing, skin like snow, and cheeks like blood. Set her free!"

When the giant heard them calling, he laughed. "Bring me three bottles of water from the well at the other end of the world!" he shouted out his window. "Then I'll let her go, I swear!"

"Go and get the water!" Craith said to the hopping warrior. The warrior untied his leg and set his foot on the ground. Instantly he was gone. No more than a moment passed; and he was at the well, all the way on the other end of the world. He filled his bottles and started back.

But halfway there, he thought, "I'm going so fast that I'll be back before they can blink! I might as well sit down and rest a moment."

He sat down under a tree to rest, the bottles of water by his side. But the sun was warm, the turf beneath him was soft, and soon he fell fast asleep.

Back at the giant's castle, Craith was growing restless. "Where is he?" he asked his other companions. The warrior with the keen ears lay down and pressed his ear against the ground. "I can hear him snoring, halfway around the world!" he said. "Here, you with the eyes; throw a rock to wake him up!"

So the warrior with the sharp eyes peered halfway around the world and saw his friend dozing by the roadside. He lifted a rock and threw it. The rock flew through the air for hundreds of miles until it hit the sleeping man—*ping!*—right between the eyes. He woke up with a start.

"I've been asleep!" he exclaimed. "I'd better go back with this water!" And he scooped his bottles up and began to run. A moment later, he was at the giant Fovor's castle, with the water from the well at the world's other end.

The giant Fovor was furious to see that his task had been done. But he had given his word, and so he had to free the beautiful woman with hair black as the raven's wing, skin like snow, and cheeks like blood. And Craith married her, and they lived happily ever after. And always after that, the three warriors with the keen eyes, the sharp ears, and the quick feet lived with Craith, and went with him into battle; and together they could not be defeated.

Barbarians Come to Britain

The Celts who lived in Britain didn't all belong to the same kingdom, and they didn't all obey the same king. Britain was full of different tribes of Celts. And each tribe followed a different king.

Old, old stories tell us that one of these kings was named Vortigern. Vortigern ruled a wealthy, power-ful tribe of Celts in the middle of Britain. His people obeyed him, and the warriors who fought for him followed his commands. But Vortigern still wasn't happy. Other tribes of Celts from up north kept attacking his kingdom, and Vortigern was tired of fighting them off! He wanted help.

Vortigern sent a message across the North Sea, to barbarian tribes called the Angles and the Saxons. "Come and help me fight against my enemies!" he said. "If you do, I'll give you land to live on, here in Britain."

So the Angles and the Saxons came across the North Sea, into Britain, and helped Vortigern fight his enemies. They liked Britain, so they settled down and stayed there. They sent word back to their friends: "Come live in Britain with us! There's plenty of room here." So more and more and MORE Angles and Saxons sailed across the North Sea to Britain. The whole middle part of Britain filled up with Angles and Saxons.

The Celts didn't like all these barbarians in their country. But there were so many Angles and Saxons that they couldn't drive them all out. Soon, the south and east part of Britain was completely occupied by Angles and Saxons. They divided the land into seven kingdoms. Today, we call this part of Britain *England*, a name that comes from the word *Angle*. We call the people who lived there *Anglo-Saxons*.

Poor Celts! First the Romans attacked them. Now the Anglo-Saxons had driven them out of their own land. Some of the Celts decided to make the best of it. They married the Anglo-Saxons and lived with them in peace. But other Celts retreated up into the north and west of Britain, to live by themselves. Today, we call the countries where the Celts lived Scotland, Ireland, and Wales.

Do you remember that the Celts told stories to each other, rather than writing them down? The Angles and the Saxons didn't do very much writing either. They didn't write down their history. They didn't write down their stories. And they didn't keep records of what they did every day. So although we know that the Angles and Saxons lived in England for a long time, we don't know what they did during all those years!

This time in England is called the *Middle Ages* or the *Dark Ages*. It is a "dark" time to us because we can't read about what happened in the seven Anglo-Saxon kingdoms. The only stories that we have from this time are stories that were passed down from one bard to the next by word of mouth.

Beowulf the Hero

The Anglo-Saxons told stories about their heroes, just as the Celts did. One of these stories was about a monster named Grendel and the great warrior who conquered him—Beowulf. The story of Beowulf is one of the oldest stories in the English language. It may have been told and retold for years before it was finally written down. The story was written in poetry, because poetry was easier to remember and perform for other people.

The whole story of Beowulf is long and complicated. But here is a shorter version of the story for you to listen to.

Hrothgar was king of a whole host of men,
Who fought for King Hrothgar again and again.
Their strength and their courage was well-known to all,
So Hrothgar decided to build them a hall.
It was hung all with tapestries, roofed all with slate,
Heated by fires enormously great.

Each night of the week, his men gathered there,
To feast and to sing and to put away care.
Then they unrolled their blankets, slept next to the fire,
While torchlight streamed out from the hall's highest spire.
Now, this hall of the king stood on high solid ground,
With safe friendly fields and great houses all 'round.
But far, far away, over swampland and heath,
Lived a monster named Grendel, with sharp claws and teeth.
He was hairy and hideous, tall as two trees,
The biggest of men only came to his knees!
He crawled up to the hall while the weary men slept,
Eased open the door, and through it he crept.
He picked up a warrior and ate him right there,
Then seized fifteen more and ran off like a hare.
The men tried to follow his tracks on the ground,
But soon came to a river where none could be found.
In the morning, the warriors mourned their dead friend,
And swore they would bring these attacks to an end.
But although in the daytime they wanted to fight,
Their courage all trickled away in the night!
Again and again, Grendel broke through the door,
Pounced into the crowd and ate up some more
Of the men gathered there. And day after day,
Hrothgar's warriors failed to keep him away.
They were tired and frightened, and lost all their pride,
As news of their troubles spread out far and wide.
Then Beowulf, mightiest man in the earth,
A fierce famous fighter, of very great worth,
Heard that Grendel attacked Hrothgar's hall every night,
And that Hrothgar's strong fighters were too scared to fight.
He gathered his clan, with their sharp swords and spears
And set off for the hall where the men nursed their fears.
Hrothgar was glad to see all those strong men!
He thanked them for coming again and again.
He said to them. "Welcome, Beowulf and all!
Tonight all of *you* can sleep in my hall.

When the monster arrives with his heart set on sin,
He will find you in there with all of your kin.
You can fight with him then. Do you need anything?
Sharper swords?" But Beowulf said to the king,
"Don't worry! We'll stay here with never a care.
As a matter of fact, it wouldn't be fair
To use swords to conquer this beast from the heath,
He doesn't have weapons—just claws and his teeth.
So I'll take off my armor and leave off my sword,
And fight with bare hands. Otherwise I'd be bored!"
Beowulf and his men then lay down on the floor,
Turned out all the lights, and locked the great door.
They waited for Grendel, pretending to sleep.
Then out of the darkness, so thick and so deep,
Came the sound of the monster, approaching the hall.
He howled and brought fear to the hearts of them all.
The door, made of iron, was closed, locked, and barred,
But the monster destroyed it without breathing hard.
He grabbed a plump warrior, got ready to feast—
But Beowulf seized the arm of the beast,
And started to twist it with all of his might.
So then Grendel turned on him, ready to fight,
But Beowulf twisted the arm yet again,
While Grendel howled out with the terrible pain.
He screamed and he howled, but he still couldn't flee—
Beowulf's muscles were something to see!
Then Beowulf pulled once again on the arm,
And it popped off at once—causing Grendel great harm!
Yelping, he galloped right out of the door,
Leaving his arm lying there on the floor.
When the warriors saw what their leader had done,
They cheered. Then they followed where Grendel had run.
The monster's great tracks led them down to a pool,
Where the dank mists had settled, all slimy and cool,
O'er the water's black surface. Engulfed there, they found
The body of Grendel, who'd jumped in and drowned.

"He is dead!" they rejoiced. "Let's have a great feast!
No more will we dread the approach of the beast!"
So with mirth and great glee they brought food to the hall,
And they hung Grendel's arm way up high on the wall,
And they ate, drank, and sang till the evening grew old,
Then Hrothgar gave Beowulf armor of gold,
And a bard lauded Beowulf, mighty of hand,
And his fame was eternally sung in that land.

Beowulf faces Grendel.

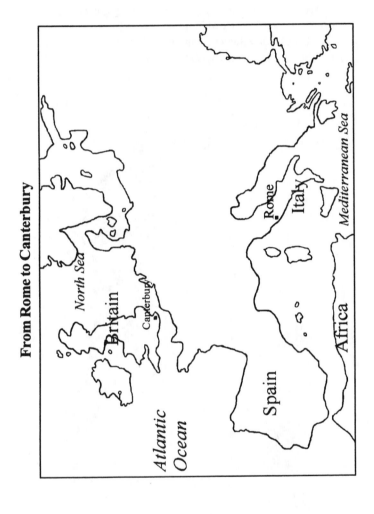

From Rome to Canterbury

Chapter Three
Christianity Comes to Britain

Augustine Comes to England

In the last days of the Roman Empire, one religion—Christianity—spread all through the countries controlled by Rome. The Roman Emperor himself became a Christian. He told his subjects that they should be Christians. Christianity was popular!

Then the Roman Empire was destroyed. The time after the fall of the Roman Empire was known as the Middle Ages. During the Middle Ages, even though the Roman Empire was gone, Christianity survived. Many people were still Christians, in all the different lands that had once been ruled by Rome. And many of these Christians in the old Roman empire followed a man called the pope. The pope was the leader of the Christian church in the city of Rome. Many people believed that God had given him the job of taking care of Christians all over the world.

One day, the pope was walking through the marketplace near his home when he saw slaves for sale. Men and women were being sold for large amounts of money, so that they could work for their masters for the rest of their lives! The pope shook his head over this evil. He walked over to look more closely at the slaves. Three of the slaves—just boys, not much older than you—had very blond hair. And their skins were white as paper. The pope was used to seeing only dark-haired people around him; in those days, fair hair was unusual and strange.

"Where did those boys come from?" he asked one of the slave traders.

"From the island of Britain," the slave trader answered. "We sailed over there and kidnapped them. All the British look like that."

Now, the pope had never heard of the island of Britain. "Are the people of Britain Christians?" he asked.

"Oh, no," the slave trader said. "They've never even heard of Christianity!"

The pope bent down to talk to the blond boys. "What are your people called?" he asked.

"We're called Angles," the oldest boy said. "And we want to go home!"

"Angles? You look more like angels!" the pope exclaimed. And he bought the boys so that they would not have to be slaves. He took them back to his home, fed them, sent them to school, and taught them about Christianity.

The first words of Genesis in medieval Latin.

Then he sent for another Christian, named Augustine, and told him about Britain and about the handsome Angles who lived there. "Augustine," he said, "I want you to go to Britain. Take these boys back to their homes, so that they can tell their families about Christianity. And I want you to stay in Britain and teach these people more about our faith. Build churches in Britain. I will make you the archbishop of England, and you can take care of all the Christians in the country."

Augustine agreed to go to Britain. He took forty men with him, and they set off on their journey to the island.

When they reached England, they were greeted by the most powerful king in Britain—Ethelbert, who ruled the whole southern part of country. Ethelbert had heard that strangers were coming to do magic in his kingdom. He met Augustine and his companions on the shore.

"What strange powers do you have?" Ethelbert demanded. "I won't let you into my palace until I can be sure that you won't try to lay a spell on me."

"We aren't here to lay spells on you!" Augustine said. "We are here to tell you about Christianity." And then he and his companions told Ethelbert all about the Christian faith."

"Hmm," Ethelbert said. "This sounds interesting— but it's all very new to me, and I don't want to give up my old ways. But you've come a long way, and you seem to be quite polite and harmless, so I'll give you permission to tell the people of my kingdom all about your God. You can live in Canterbury, and no one will bother you as long as you behave yourselves."

So Augustine and his companions settled down in the town of Canterbury. They built a church and preached to the Anglo-Saxons. Eventually, many of the Anglo-Saxons became Christians. They learned how to read and how to write. They built churches and monasteries, where men could live and worship God. And Augustine himself became the first Archbishop of Canterbury—the leader of all the Christians who lived in England. [1]

---

[1] There are three possible areas of confusion when it comes to Augustine's mission to Britain. **First:** There are several different versions of this story, including one where Ethelbert converts immediately; this version is from Bede. **Second:** There are two famous Augustines in history. The first, generally known only as St. Augustine, lived from 354 to 430 and was the Bishop of Hippo in Africa. This St. Augustine is the author of the famous *Confessions* and *The*

Medieval Monasteries

Augustine and the men who went with him to Britain were monks—men who had promised to spend the rest of their lives praying, working, and studying the Bible, rather than marrying and having children. Monks lived together in special buildings called *monasteries*. They went to church eight times a day to pray and worship God. During the day, they worked in the monastery garden, helped with the cooking, cleaning, and laundry, and did other jobs that the abbot, the chief monk, gave them to do.

There were monasteries all through the old lands of the Roman Empire—in Italy, Spain, Africa, and all the other countries that had once belonged to Rome. When the Anglo-Saxons learned about Christianity, some of them wanted to be monks too. So they built monasteries in England and in Ireland, where they could live just like other monks did.

Brother Andrew is a monk in an Irish monastery. His job is to build furniture in the monastery workshop; the monks make all their own chairs, tables and beds. This morning, Brother Andrew is working on building a new table for the refectory (the large room where the monks eat together). He is rubbing oil into the table's top

---

City of God. The second Augustine, St. Augustine of Canterbury, is the one we discuss in this story. He lived in the sixth century and headed up a monastery in Rome before he was sent to England by Pope Gregory. He became Archbishop of Canterbury in 601. **Third:** There is some evidence that Christianity reached Britain centuries before Augustine, but Augustine's mission is nevertheless the first *organized* effort to bring Britain into the fold of the Church.

to finish it, but he keeps stopping to blow on his fingers. He's cold! The workshop is in a stone shed, and there's a fireplace in one wall. But the December wind is blowing around the windows and in under the door. And it's still very dark outside, because the sun hasn't risen yet. He is working by candlelight, and his eyes hurt.

Brother Andrew hopes that the bell will ring soon to summon him to the refectory. He got up at two o'clock this morning for the early morning service, and then went on to his workshop to get started on the day's tasks. It must be nearly five o'clock by now, he thinks. Almost breakfast time!

Finally the bell rings. Brother Andrew puts on a heavy cloak and hood and walks toward the refectory. On his way, he passes a line of sick and hungry people who have already formed outside the monastery gates. Brother James knows a lot about herbs and about healing sickness; he is the only doctor within three days' journey, and villagers from several small villages nearby come up to the monastery whenever they get sick. The monks cook food for the hungry too, and serve it even before they eat themselves.

The sun is just beginning to come up when Brother Andrew steps into the refectory. He can smell the fresh wheat bread that's been baked for breakfast! The monks aren't allowed to eat butter on their bread, unless it's Christmas or another special day. And the rules of the monastery say that no one can eat the meat of a four-legged animal, so sausage, bacon and beef are never on the breakfast table. But he likes the thick, crusty brown bread. And this morning, there are cooked beans and peas and a few sweet, withered apples—the last of the fall harvest, kept in a cool dirt cellar until now.

Monks aren't allowed to talk at meals. Instead, Brother John reads to them from the Bible while they eat

39

in silence. But Brother Andrew whispers to the monk next to him, "How did your pupils behave yesterday?"

"Terrible!" the monk whispers back. He teaches in the monastery school, where village children are sent to be educated. "They don't want to learn how to write. Every time I turn my back, they whisper and giggle to each other. They don't pay any attention to me at all! And they drew a rude picture of me on the slate when I had to go out for a few minutes."

Brother John hears the whispering and glares over at them. Brother Andrew finishes his breakfast and waits until the abbot, the monk who runs the whole monastery, prays. He goes back to his workshop to finish his table. It is a beautiful piece of furniture! He knows he shouldn't be proud of it, but he carves, "Andrew, his work" on the underside of the table, in tiny, tiny letters. Maybe one day, someone will see the letters and know that the table is his work!

Writing Books by Hand

A few lessons ago, we learned that the years after the fall of Rome are called the Middle Ages, and that in England these years are also known as Dark Ages. Do you remember why we call this time the Dark Ages? Most people in England couldn't read or write, so they didn't write down stories and histories.

When Augustine and his companions came to England, they told the Anglo-Saxons about Christianity. But they also taught them how to read and write. They wanted these new Christians to be able to read the Bible.

Monks in monasteries also thought that reading and writing were important. After all, they spent a large part of every day reading the Bible and books written by religious men. But back in the Dark Ages, books weren't as easy to make as they are today! Bookmaking was a long, complicated process. And only the monks were skilled enough to make beautiful books.

In the Dark Ages, you couldn't just go to a store and buy paper. So the monks began by making a special paper, called *parchment,* out of animal skin. They put cow or sheep skins in running water, such as a stream or river, for several days. Then they soaked it again, in a barrel filled with water and lime (a chemical that loosened the hair on the skin) for several days more. Finally, they would stretch out the skin, scrape the hair off with a knife, and then attach it to a frame so that it could dry. But that wasn't all! Once the skin was dried, the monks would take it off the frame, wet it again, and rub it with a rough stone. One medieval book tells us that the best way to wet the skin was to take a mouthful of beer and then spit the beer all over the skin.

When the skin had been dried all over again, it was time to make the ink by mixing soot with water and the sap of trees. The monk had to prepare quill pens by pulling feathers out of a goose's or swan's wing, soaking the feathers in water, and scraping the tips. Then the parchment had to be cut into rectangles, folded over to make pages, and stitched together to make booklets.

Finally, it was time to write out the words. All books were written out by hand. The monks worked all day in special rooms called *scriptoriums.* They made copies of the Bible and other important books by copying them out, one letter at a time. Each letter was carefully written in the monk's best handwriting.

The books copied by the monks weren't just black letters on white pages. The monks decorated the pages of their books with beautiful colors. They made paints by mixing their colors with egg whites. Often real gold and silver, beaten into sheets so thin that they could float on the air, were attached to the page as part of the picture. Sometimes a picture took up an entire page. Sometimes it was painted just in the margin, or at the top of a page. And sometimes, just the first letter on a page was painted and leafed with gold.

Writing out long books by hand was hard, slow work. An expert monk might copy out two or three books in a year, working eight hours every day! So there weren't very many books in the Middle Ages. And books were valuable. After all, they took months of labor! Often, books were chained onto library shelves so that people could only read them standing up. And you certainly couldn't check them out.

Monks weren't supposed to talk in the scriptorium. They were supposed to pay close attention to what they were doing. But monks got bored! We can still read some of the books written by hand in the Middle Ages—and we can see that sometimes monks wrote messages to each other and even drew silly pictures in the margins of their books. "I'm cold," one monk wrote. "I wish we had a bigger fire, but Brother John won't let us." Another monk wrote, "I wish I were finished. I have to go to the bathroom!" And a third monk drew a little mouse on the edge of his book and wrote "Curse that mouse!" Maybe the mouse had stolen some of his dinner!

The Byzantine Empire

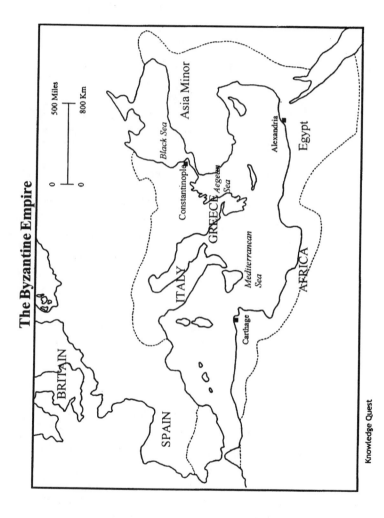

SPAIN

BRITAIN

ITALY

GREECE

Constantinople

Black Sea

Asia Minor

Aegean Sea

Mediterranean Sea

Carthage

AFRICA

Alexandria

Egypt

0 — 500 Miles

0 — 800 Km

Chapter Four
The Byzantine Empire

The Beauty of Constantinople

Several chapters ago, we read that the Roman
Empire got too big for one emperor to rule all alone. So
the Roman Empire was divided into two parts. The part
of the Roman Empire that still had Rome in it was called
the Western Roman Empire, and the rest of the empire
became known as the Eastern Roman Empire. Its
capital city was called Constantinople.

When the barbarians flooded into the Roman Empire,
the Western Roman Empire fell apart. And the Eastern
Roman Empire lost land to the barbarians too. It shrank
until the Eastern Roman Emperor only ruled the land
near Constantinople, right around the Aegean Sea.

But the Eastern Roman Empire survived.

Today, we call this last surviving part of the Roman
Empire the *Byzantine Empire.* We call its people
Byzantines, and their emperor the *Byzantine emperor.*
The Byzantine Empire was small at first, because the
invaders had taken so much of its land away. But then,
strong, warlike emperors began to reconquer some the
land that had once belonged to Rome. Eventually, the
Byzantine Empire spread all around the Mediterranean
Sea. Constantinople, the capital city of the Byzantine
Empire, became the biggest city in the world. It was
larger and richer than Rome had ever been!

Imagine that you're walking through the streets of
Constantinople. The road beneath your feet is smoothly
paved; the Byzantines know the Roman art of making
good roads out of rock and cement. People push and

jostle you from every side. There are almost a million people in this one city! Many of the people are dressed like Romans, in togas (white robes draped over one shoulder and belted around the middle) You pass beautiful shops selling silks, jewelry, and all kinds of food— peaches, almonds, peanuts, grapes, fish, bowls of hot lentil soup, and cups of white kidney beans cooked with sage and onion. The smells of fruit, meat, and soup mix together and float out into the street. Suddenly, you're feeling very hungry.

You don't see many children on the streets. "Where are all the children?" you ask a woman passing by. She is wearing a beautiful blue wool cloak, edged with gold thread.

"They're in school, of course," the woman answers. "We have schools for all children—even the poor ones! The little ones are working on their reading and writing, and the older students are reading the great books written by the Greeks and Romans. Our children have better things to do than run around in the streets! Excuse me, I've got to go. I'm a lady in waiting to the empress, and I've got to get to her palace right away."

"Where is the palace?" you ask.

The woman laughs. "What do you mean, *the* palace? We have fourteen palaces in Constantinople. The Emperor and his court have five. The ladies of the court have six more, of their own! And we even have three palaces for people who work for the emperor! But you can't go inside them because you're just a commoner. If you want to see a beautiful building, go visit our biggest church, the Hagia Sophia. It's right up there."

She points to a huge marble dome up ahead of her, and hurries away. You walk towards the dome. The top of the Hagia Sophia shines bright white in the sun, and the walls glow red. The dome in the middle is surrounded by smaller domes all around it. You make your way through the main door. Sunlight is everywhere; the church has high windows all around the top of the walls. And the whole ceiling is covered with pure gold that glitters in the sun. The stones of the walls are all different colors—purple, green, crimson, and white. Columns rise up all around you. Even Rome never had a building as beautiful as this!

Justinian, The Just Emperor

Powerful rulers made Constantinople great. And one of the most powerful rulers of all Byzantium was Justinian, the Just Emperor.

Justinian's parents weren't important people—they were just peasants, who lived hundreds of miles away from the great city of Constantinople. They grew crops and tended animals for a living. But Justinian didn't want to be a farmer. He wanted to be a great, educated man. He learned how to read, and he spent every spare minute studying law, music, poetry, and religious books. He begged his family to send him to Constantinople so that he could go to school.

Finally, Justinian's parents agreed. They packed his clothes and books. His mother cooked him bread and meat to eat on the journey. And Justinian began the long, long journey to the city of Constantinople.

When he arrived in the city, he was over-whelmed. The buildings were the biggest he had ever seen. People swarmed everywhere! And his studies were difficult. He had to memorize fifty lines of Greek poetry every day. He had to learn how to make convincing speeches in public. The teachers at the school gave him hours of homework every day in math, music, and astronomy (the study of the stars).

When he finished school, young Justinian joined the army. He was brave and full of energy, and he spent hours helping the officers keep records, order supplies, and plan their campaigns. Soon, more and more people agreed: Justinian would make a good emperor. When the emperor died, Justinian was named ruler of the Byzantine empire.

When Justinian became emperor, Byzantium wasn't very big yet. But Justinian decided to change that. He had read many books about the greatness and glory of the old Roman Empire. And he wanted that empire back.

So Justinian recruited more and more men into his army. He set off on campaigns to reconquer the countries that used to belong to Rome—Italy, North Africa, Spain, and the countries all around the shores of the Mediterranean. He even took Rome away from the barbarians who were living there, but the war to recapture Rome destroyed what was left of the old city. Justinian was left with nothing but ruins.

Did Justinian recapture *all* the land that used to belong to Rome? No, but he made the Byzantine Empire bigger than it had ever been before. And now that he ruled all of these different countries, Justinian had a problem. Each country had its own laws! Something that was against the law in one country might be perfectly fine in another country. A thief might be put to death in one part of the empire—but only told to pay a fine in another part. It was very confusing to rule an empire full of different laws.

So Justinian set out to make one set of laws for *everyone* in his empire. It was a huge job. Hundreds of scholars helped him to collect all the laws of the ancient Romans and Greeks, so that a new law could be written. Finally the new set of laws, the Code of Justinian, was finished. Everyone in the Byzantine Empire was supposed to follow these laws.

Here are some of the laws from the Code of Justinian.

THE SEA AND THE SEASHORE BELONG TO EVERYONE. EVERY PERSON IN MY EMPIRE IS ALLOWED TO GO TO THE BEACH. NO ONE CAN TELL THEM, "I OWN THIS PART OF THE BEACH! GET OFF IT!"

⊰⊱

RIVERS BELONG TO EVERYONE. EVERYONE IN MY EMPIRE CAN FISH IN THE RIVERS, WITHOUT BEING TOLD TO STOP.

⊰⊱

IF YOU FIND A JEWEL OR OTHER TREASURE WASHED UP ON THE SEASHORE, YOU CAN KEEP IT FOR YOURSELF.

⊰⊱

YOU ARE ALLOWED TO OWN SLAVES AND MAKE THEM WORK FOR YOU WITHOUT PAY. BUT YOU CAN'T BEAT OR MISTREAT YOUR SLAVES UNLESS THEY ARE DISOBEDIENT.

⊰⊱

A THIEF WHO STEALS SOMETHING VALUABLE MUST PAY THE OWNER FOUR TIMES WHAT THE STOLEN OBJECT IS WORTH.

⊰⊱

IF YOU ARE TRIMMING A TREE NEAR A ROAD, BE SURE TO CALL OUT TO ANYONE COMING BY, "BE CAREFUL! LIMBS MIGHT FALL ON YOU!" IF YOU DON'T CALL OUT A WARNING, AND A LIMB

FALLS ON A TRAVELER AND HURTS
HIM, IT'S YOUR FAULT. BUT IF YOU
CALL OUT A WARNING AND THE
TRAVELER WALKS UNDER YOUR TREE
ANYWAY, IT ISN'T YOUR FAULT IF A
LIMB FALLS ON HIM AND HURTS HIM.
HE SHOULD HAVE PAID ATTENTION TO
YOUR WARNING.

WHEN A BISHOP, PRIEST, OR PASTOR IS
PRAYING OR PREACHING, HE HAS TO
SPEAK LOUDLY ENOUGH FOR EVERY-
ONE TO HEAR. IF HE DOESN'T, GOD
WILL PUNISH HIM—AND SO WILL THE
EMPEROR!

Do you think these are fair laws? Would you change
them?

The Empress Theodora

Justinian was a powerful emperor, but he didn't
rule the Byzantine Empire all alone. His wife, the
Empress Theodora, was a brilliant, energetic woman who
helped him make his decisions.

Theodora wasn't always an Empress. Her
parents ran a circus at the Hippodrome, a huge arena in
Constantinople. Her father was the circus bear-trainer.
Little Theodora used to sit in the warm sand of the arena
and watch him work with his bears. Sometimes she fed
the bears apples and honey to reward them for doing
their tricks!

When she grew a little older, Theodora got to
work as a clown in the circus. She painted her face
white and pretended that she couldn't speak. The

Little Theodora with her father's bear.

audiences loved Theodora's act. Soon Theodora was acting in plays as well, and attracting hundreds of fans. They came to see her shows, threw flowers to her, and applauded her performances. Theodora was a success! She got to travel all around the Byzantine Empire, staying in the best inns, eating the best food, and drinking the best wine.

But one day Theodora heard about Christianity and decided to become a Christian. "I can't go on being an actress, going to parties every night and doing whatever I please," she thought. "I need to have a different kind of life. A quiet, peaceful life."

So Theodora left her job as an actress, moved to Constantinople, and became a wool spinner. She spent her days quietly making wool thread out of sheep's wool and selling it to the merchants of Constantinople.

One day, Theodora was walking to the market with a basket full of yarn when she heard, "Make way! Make way for the soldiers of the royal army!"

She stepped out of the street and craned her neck to see the soldiers. Justinian hadn't become the emperor yet; he was still serving in the army. So he was riding with the other soldiers, wearing a red cloak over his shining armor, with his sword hanging by his side. Theodora thought that he was the most handsome man she had ever seen.

Justinian saw Theodora standing by the side of the road. "Who is that beautiful woman?" he asked the soldier beside him. The other soldiers only shrugged. "I must find out," Justinian thought to himself. "I want to know who she is at once!"

After a long search, Justinian found Theodora's home. He was overcome by her beauty—and charmed by her intelligence. He fell in love with her and married her. And when he became the Emperor, Theodora became the Empress. The two of them ruled side-by-side, and Justinian rarely made a decision without consulting his wife.

Five years after Justinian became Emperor, the people of Constantinople rioted. They wanted Justinian to get rid of two men who worked for him—two men who were very unpopular. When Justinian refused, the crowd became more and more angry. They charged through the streets of the city, overturning merchant's stalls, wrecking walls, and burning buildings. They even set fire to the Hagia Sophia. They killed policemen and gathered around the emperor's palace, shouting, "Victory! Victory!"

Justinian was terrified. "If they break into the palace, they'll kill us both!" he exclaimed. "Let's leave Constantinople at once."

"If you run away, they'll take the throne away from you," Theodora warned him. "You'll never be emperor again."

"That's better than dying!" Justinian retorted.

"You can run if you want to," Theodora said. "You have plenty of money, and you can always sail away in the royal ships. But I never want to give up my royal purple cloak and my crown. How can someone who has once been Emperor agree to become a wandering refugee? If you run away, you will soon wish that you had died instead."

Finally, Theodora convinced Justinian to stay. He ordered his generals to lead the army against the rebels. The fight was long and hard, but Justinian's men won. Justinian kept his throne, and rebuilt the damaged city. He made the Hagia Sophia even bigger and more beautiful than ever. And for the rest of his life, he was grateful to Theodora for keeping him in Constantinople. The Empress had saved the Emperor's throne.

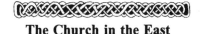

The Church in the East

After the riots that nearly frightened him out of Constantinople, Justinian ordered the burned buildings rebuilt. The Hagia Sophia, Constantinople's biggest church, had been almost completely destroyed. So Justinian decided to hire two very famous architects to design and build a new church. This new Hagia Sophia had great domes, big windows, and huge open spaces. Inside, it was decorated with paintings and *mosaics.*

Mosaics were pictures made by arranging colored pieces into a pattern. These pieces were called *tesserae.* Tesserae could be made out of stone, marble, glass, wood, clay, or even gold and silver! By setting the tesserae close together, artists could make beautiful patterns. And they could even make pictures of people and animals. Some mosaics were whole scenes, like a man feeding a donkey, or an emperor and his whole court. [1]

Making a mosaic was slow and careful work. First, the artist would cover the wall or ceiling with a thin layer of plaster, which was thick, white and sticky like glue. Then, the artist would carefully and slowly begin to put tesserae into place. In a shop or house, the tesserae might be little pieces of colored glass, stone, clay, or wood painted different colors. But in a beautiful church or palace, the tesserae were more likely to be bits of marble or pieces of silver. The mosaics in the Hagia Sophia are especially bright and shining, because the artists who made them covered glass cubes with gold and made the backgrounds of the mosaic pictures out of these glittering tesserae. Each glass cube was set into the plaster at a slightly different angle. So when the sun shines on the golden mosaics of the Hagia Sophia, light bounces off the pictures in all different directions. The pictures seem to glow in the light!

Many people saw the mosaics in the Hagia Sophia, because this church became the center of a whole group of Christians. Remember: after the fall of Rome, many Christians in the lands that had once belonged to the Roman Empire believed that the pope was their leader. They believed that God had given him the job of looking after all Christians.

But not all Christians agreed. Those Christians who lived in Constantinople (as well as many Christians who lived in Africa, Asia, and in the eastern part of the continent of Europe) didn't believe that the pope should

---

[1] The mosaic of a man feeding a donkey is found on the floor of the Great Palace at Istanbul; the Basilica of San Vitale in Ravenna has a mosaic picturing the emperor with his whole court.

be able to make decisions for the whole church. Instead, they thought that the leaders of the churches in Jerusalem, Rome, Constantinople, and two other important cities should join together to make decisions—and that Christians everywhere would join in saying, "Yes, those decisions are right." This was a very different way to think about the Christian church! And as time went on, the pope (who was in the west of Europe) and the leaders of the Christian church in the east disagreed more and more about how the church should be led. Finally, the Christian church divided into two groups. Those who continued to believe in the authority of the pope became known as *Roman Catholics*. The Christians further east, including those in the Byzantine Empire, became known as *Orthodox* or *Eastern Orthodox*. Orthodox Christians called their leaders *patriarchs*. They had their own prayers and their own *rites* (ways of worshipping God). [2]

The Eastern Christians liked to tell stories about Christians from the past who had been faithful to God. One of these Christians was called Nicholas. Here is one story that the Christians of the Byzantine Empire told about Nicholas:

Nicholas lived in Asia Minor. His parents were Christians, but they died when Nicholas was very young, leaving him lots of money.

Now, in those days a girl could not get married unless her father gave a gift of money to her husband. In the village where Nicholas lived was a very poor family with

---

[2] The formal breach between the Eastern Orthodox and Roman Catholic Churches occurred in 1054, when the patriarch of Constantinople defied the Pope; this is known as the Great Eastern Schism.

three daughters. Each girl was in love with a young man and wanted to get married. But their father had no money to give them.

One cold, snowy night, Nicholas was walking by the house of this poor family when he heard a girl weeping. He stopped and came closer. There in the window sat one of the daughters, crying and crying. He came even closer, until he could hear what she said.

"Oh," the girl wept, "I will never be able to marry the man I love. My sisters and I will live here in poverty for the rest of our lives, and all because my father has no money!"

Nicholas couldn't bear to hear such sadness. He ran quickly home and gathered as many gold coins as he could find into a bag. Then he ran back through the snow to the house where the girl sat weeping. He didn't want anyone to know who had brought the gold, so he drew his arm back, aimed carefully, and threw the bag up into the top of the chimney.

A moment later he heard the girl exclaim, "Look! Something has fallen into the fireplace! What is it?" And he crept away, satisfied that he had given the girl and her father money enough to arrange for her wedding.

But later that night, he thought, "What about her two sisters? Suppose they wish to get married too. Who will pay the money for them?"

So the next evening, Nicholas returned with another bag of gold. Again, he threw the bag down the chimney, into the fireplace. And the next night, he came back with a third bag of gold and did the same thing.

The next spring, all three daughters were married. They wore beautiful gowns stitched with gold, and wreaths of white flowers on their heads. Their father and mother danced together with joy at the wedding feast. And Nicholas watched, happy that his gift—given in secret—had brought so much happiness.

As time went on, the story of Nicholas was told and retold by the Christians in the Byzantine Empire. Soon, Nicholas was called a *saint*—a person who has a special relationship with God. The Emperor Justinian built a cathedral to honor St. Nicholas, in Constantinople. And his story spread all over the world. In many countries, children get gifts on St. Nicholas's special day, December 6th. Sometimes, they put their shoes next to the door. In the morning, the shoes are filled with chocolate coins wrapped in gold foil—to remind them of the gold St. Nicholas gave to the three poor girls.

     Do you know that St. Nicholas has another name? Sometimes he is called Santa Claus! The story of Santa Claus comes from the story of St. Nicholas, a Christian from the Byzantine Empire.

The Gupta Empire of India

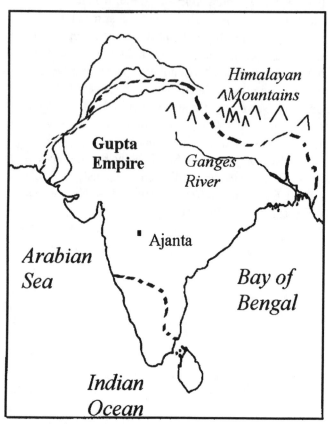

Himalayan Mountains

Gupta Empire

Ganges River

Ajanta

Arabian Sea

Bay of Bengal

Indian Ocean

Knowledge Quest

Chapter Five
The Medieval Indian Empire

A King Named Skandagupta

If you were traveling during the Middle Ages, you'd have to be careful where you went! Barbarian tribes had settled in many of the lands that used to belong to Rome. There was no king or emperor to keep the peace. Instead, many different war leaders ruled over little pieces of land—and these war leaders were always fighting with each other. You might be riding innocently along, going to visit your cousins far away, and get caught in the middle of a battle between war bands.

But travel in the Byzantine Empire was much safer. You could ride your horse along the roads in peace. Justinian and the other emperors made sure that their subjects obeyed the laws. And the soldiers of the Byzantine army helped protect the people from robbers and invaders.

You could also feel safe traveling down into India. Like Byzantium, India had a king who ruled over a large, peaceful empire.

Imagine that you decide to leave Byzantium and go south. (Remember, south is *down* on your map.) You ride for days and days. Slowly, you begin to see a line of mountains ahead of you—mountains that seem to touch the sky. These are the Himalayas, the highest mountains in the world. Mount Everest, the tallest peak in the Himalayas, juts up almost into space. Up on top of Mount Everest, the air is too thin to breathe! And snow and ice stay on the mountains all year long.

As you begin to come down the other side of the mountain range, you see villages, tucked into the rocky slopes. The people who live here are tough and strong. They raise mountain sheep and make warm clothing from their fleece.

You ride further south, veering a little to the west. (West is *left* on your map.) The air grows hotter and hotter. The ground becomes sandy and flat. Your horse stumbles in the deep sand. Sweat rolls down your face. When the wind blows, sand whirls up from the ground; it gets into your mouth, your eyes, and your clothes. This is the Thar Desert, where it hardly ever rains! You decide you'd better get out of the desert, so you head east. (East is *right* on your map.) Slowly, you begin to see trees and grass. The sand gives way to dry dirt, and then to rich, black soil. Ahead of you, you can see the blue gleam of a river. You've come to the Ganges, the most important river in India. Every year, the Ganges overflows and leaves damp, black silt all over the ground. This silt is like fertilizer—it makes crops grow. Houses are all around you. Thousands of people live here, near the river.

In your journey, you've seen mountains, deserts, and river-villages. But this is only a small part of India! If you were to keep on going south, you would cross over more mountains and rivers. And eventually you would come to the coast of India, where palm trees grow in tropical jungles along the edge of the sea, and where villagers hunt tigers and ride elephants.

India has many different parts to it. So for hundreds of years, the Indian people lived in many small, different kingdoms. But a man named Chandragupta wanted to make all of those kingdoms into one large Indian empire. At first, Chandragupta only ruled a little kingdom near the Ganges River. But he managed to conquer a few of the little kingdoms nearby. His son conquered a few more. And his grandson conquered even more. Eventually, Chandragupta's descendents ruled over the whole upper part of India. Chandragupta had founded a *dynasty* (a family that rules over one area of the world for many years). Listen to the names of some of the kings in this dynasty: Chandragupta, Samudragupta, Kumargupta, and Skandagupta. All of these kings were part of the *Gupta* dynasty!

Under the Guptas, India became peaceful and rich. Indian poets and playwrights wrote great works in the Indian language, Sanskrit. Artists painted and sculpted in copper and iron. Scholars wrote learned books about mathematics and astronomy. Indian doctors even learned how to reattach ears and noses that had been cut off! This is often called the Golden Age of India.

But then the barbarians came!

Barbarian tribes called the Huns had already attacked Rome and Byzantium. Now they swooped down into India. If the people of India had still been divided into many small kingdoms, the Huns might have been able to destroy them. But the king of India, Skandagupta, rallied all his people together into one strong army. And with Skandagupta to lead them, the Indians managed to drive the Huns away from their empire.

Skandagupta's people praised him for saving them. They made coins with his picture on them. They carved his portrait into rock. "Skandagupta has been embraced by the goddess of wealth and splendor!" they exclaimed.

India had survived the barbarian attacks. But fighting off the Huns had made India poorer—and weaker. Slowly, the different parts of the empire began to divide into separate small kingdoms once more. The Golden Age of India had ended.

Monks in Caves

Do you remember the monks of England? Instead of having families, they lived together in monasteries and spent their lives working and praying. India also had monks. These monks were followers of a man called the Buddha. The Buddha was an Indian prince who had left his palace, many years before, to live the life of a beggar. He taught that anyone, no matter how poor, sick, or miserable, could find happiness by leading a good life. [1]

In England, the monks lived in buildings made of wood or stone. But the Indian monks who lived near the mountains carved their monastery right out of the sides of cliffs! They had large caves where they met and ate together, around tables made out of stone. Small, bare caves called *cells* surrounded these large caves. In their cells, the monks could go to be alone, to sleep, or to think about the teachings of the Buddha. Passageways and stone bridges connected the caves together.

The monks worked for years to build their monastery. They didn't have dynamite or explosives to carve out the caves. Instead, they hacked long trenches into the rock with iron tools. Then they put logs into the trenches and filled the trenches with water. The logs soaked up the water and began to swell. As they swelled, they pushed against the sides of the rock—and cracked it into bits.

---

[1] The historical origins of Hinduism and Buddhism and the caste system in India are covered in Volume 1 of this series.

When the caves were dug out, the monks started to decorate them. They carved away at the walls with tiny, sharp chisels, just a little wider than your thumb. Bit by bit, beautiful sculptures emerged from the stone walls. Some of the stone figures show scenes from the life of the Buddha. Other figures seem to act out stories that the Buddha told. Stone elephants, as large as life, stand at the entrances to several caves. In one of the caves, the rock ceiling is carved to look like the wooden rafters in an old temple. A huge statue of the Buddha sits beneath the rafters, on an enormous rock throne.

In other caves, the monks painted *frescoes*. They covered the rough stone walls and ceilings with fresh plaster, and then painted on the plaster while it was still wet. When the plaster dried, the painting dried with it and became part of the wall. Frescoes stay bright and colorful for years, but painting on fresh plaster is like painting on pudding. If the painter makes a mistake, he can't wipe it out. He has to paint perfectly the very first time!

These caves are called the *Ajanta Caves*. The monks lived in them for years and years. But slowly, they moved away to other monasteries. The caves were used less and less. Most people in India forgot they were there. Only a few pilgrims remembered the Ajanta Caves.

Hundreds of years later, two soldiers were out hunting. They tracked a tiger into a deserted valley, filled with trees and shrubs. They were searching through the brush for tiger-tracks when they found the entrance to the Ajanta Caves. Inside the caves, the stone elephants, the carved Buddha, and the colorful paintings lay undisturbed, just as they had been since the monks left.

The officers told everyone they knew about the caves. More and more people came to see the sculptures and frescoes. Soon, hundreds of people were visiting the caves every day. Some of the visitors began to take away parts of sculptures to put in museums. They even cut the heads off some of the paintings! But before the sculptures and paintings could be destroyed, the government of India ordered wire screens to be put up around them. Now the Ajanta Caves are safe. And visitors can still see the art created by the monks of India, more than a thousand years ago.

The Birthplace of Islam

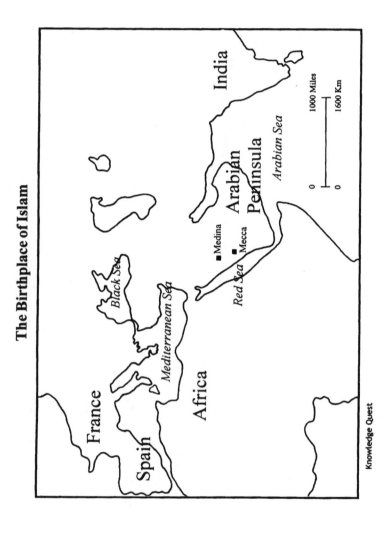

France

Spain

Black Sea

Mediterranean Sea

Africa

Red Sea

Medina

Mecca

Arabian Peninsula

Arabian Sea

India

1000 Miles

1600 Km

0

0

Knowledge Quest

Chapter Six
The Rise of Islam

Muhammad's Vision

Far, far away from Rome and from Constantinople, a hot, dry desert lay under the blazing sun. This desert, on the *Arabian Peninsula*, has water on three sides of it. But even though water is all around it, the Arabian Peninsula is parched and sandy. During the day, the sun beats down on the desert with blistering heat. Sand blows through the air; sometimes, the blowing sand is so thick that you can hardly breathe. Little clumps of palm trees dot the burning sand. The clumps are called *oases*. If you dig deep enough, you can find water in an oasis—but not very much!

A desert is a hard and dangerous place to live! But strong, determined tribes of people called *Bedouins* managed to live in the Arabian Peninsula and even build cities there. One of these cities was called Mecca.

Over a thousand years ago, an orphan boy named Muhammad [1] lived in Mecca. He lived with his grandfather and uncle. Although they had little money, Muhammad learned that a Bedouin should always help the poor, give food and lodging to strangers if they needed it, and take care of the sick. He helped his uncle herd his flocks of sheep. He worked hard. Soon he became known as *Al-Amin*, which means "The Trustworthy One."

---

[1] This name is often spelled Mohammed; there is no one single accepted spelling for most Arabic names, so spellings will vary significantly.

But when Muhammad looked around him, he saw other Bedouins treating the poor and sick badly. The men around him drank too much. They gambled their money away instead of buying food for their children. And they worshipped many different idols.

Muhammad spent more and more time alone. He liked to go into the desert, away from the crowded, noisy city of Mecca, to think and pray in a dark, quiet cave. He wondered: What would make men change their ways? How could they become better?

One day, something odd happened to Muhammad in his quiet cave. Here is the story as Muhammad's followers tell it:

Muhammad sat alone in his cave. The sun had set; the hot desert sand was cooling in the night air. A breeze blew gently into the cave. He closed his eyes. Silence was all around him.

Suddenly he heard a faint musical sound. It grew louder and louder, as though bells were ringing all around him. He opened his eyes, but he could see nothing but rock and sand.

Then a voice came out of the darkness. "Read!" it ordered.

"But I can't read!" Muhammad cried out.

"Read!" the voice repeated. Suddenly Muhammad saw a silk scroll, floating in the air. Words were written on it in letters of fire. And although Muhammad had never learned how to read, suddenly he knew what the words said!

Terrified, Muhammad ran out into the desert. But the voice spoke to him again.

"Muhammad!" it said. "Muhammad, you are the messenger of Allah, the one true God! And I am the angel Gabriel!"

Muhammad looked up. Above him, he saw the angel Gabriel, like a huge shining man with his feet set on the edge of the sky. Light came pouring down from Gabriel. And as Muhammad watched, Gabriel disappeared into the sky.

What do you think Muhammad did next?

Muhammad Flees to Medina

After his vision, Muhammad ran home. He told his wife and his family what had happened to him. "The most important thing I have learned," he said, "is that all of these idols the Bedouins worship are false. There is only one God, and he is called Allah."

"You are a prophet!" Muhammad's wife exclaimed. She believed Muhammad's story. So did Muhammad's cousin, his servant, and three others. These six people were the very first Muslims. Muhammad's teachings became known as Islam, and those who followed his teachings were called Muslims.

At first, Muhammad only talked about Allah to these six followers. But after several years went by, he began preaching to others in Mecca. He walked through the city, proclaiming, "There is only one true God, and his name is Allah! He created the universe, and he rules it! At the day of judgment, Allah will look at your life, and reward or punish you. So share with the poor. Don't be greedy and spend all your time trying to make money. Stop worshipping idols! Only worship Allah."

Many poor people in Mecca liked what Muhammad was saying. But the rich people were worried when they heard his teachings. "Share our money with the poor?" they said to each other. "We don't want to do that! And what will happen if people stop believing in the idols of Mecca? They won't come here to the city to worship any more. They won't buy food and drink, or special clothes to wear at the temple. We won't make any more money selling these things!"

So the rich and powerful people of Mecca started to persecute the poor slaves and workers who had converted to Islam. They threw stones at them, forced them to leave the city, or put them in jail. And no one would sell food to Muhammad and his family. He had to send friends to buy food secretly. They brought the food to his house in the middle of the night, so that no one would see them.

Things in Mecca grew worse and worse for Muslims. Soon, more and more Muslims began to leave the city. They went to a nearby city, Medina, which welcomed them. The leaders of Medina even invited Muhammad to come and preach to them. "Come to Medina," they told him, "and we will promise to worship only Allah. We won't steal any more, or tell lies. We'll do anything that you tell us!"

Muhammad would rather have stayed in Mecca. He didn't want to leave his home! But most of his followers had gone. Soon he and one friend, Abu Bakr, were the only Muslims left in the city.

One night, Muhammad and his friend Abu Bakr were sitting in Muhammad's home, eating their supper, when someone hammered frantically at the door. "Muhammad!" the visitor hissed. "Muhammad, you must let me in!"

Muhammad went to the door. He peered out, but he didn't recognize the man who stood there. "Who are you?" he asked.

"A friend," the stranger answered. "There is a plot to kill you! The leaders of the town are sending soldiers, right now, to murder you in your home. If you want to live, leave Mecca at once." And then he slipped away into the night.

Muhammad and Abu Bakr left their plates and cups on the table and ran. They hurried through the dark empty streets of Mecca, to the city gates. As they ran, they heard shouting behind them. The soldiers had found Muhammad's house empty!

"Quick!" Muhammad said. "To the mountains! We'll hide in a cave there."

They hurried down the road, hearing the soldiers behind them. Soon they found a small, dark cave and crept into it. They waited there, hardly breathing, hoping that the soldiers would pass them by.

Muslims say that when the soldiers got to the cave, they paused, wondering whether to search it or not. Then one of them noticed a spider web, stretching all across the cave's front. He poked at it. The strands were thick and old, covered with dust, and flies were caught in it. "Look," he said, "this spider web has been here for days. If Muhammad and Abu Bakr had gone into this cave, they would have broken the web. They can't be here."

So the soldiers moved on. When Muhammad and Abu Bakr finally came out of the cave, the soldiers had passed them by.

They traveled to Medina, two hundred miles away. When the Muslims of Medina heard that Muhammad, the Prophet, was arriving, they poured out of the city to greet him, cheering and praising Allah.

Muhammad's journey from Mecca to Medina has a special name—the *Hegira*. The Hegira is so important to Muslims that they count their years beginning from the Hegira.

Do you remember what B.C. and B.C.E. mean?

71

They mean "Before Christ" or "Before the Common Era." And A.D. and C.E. both tell us that a date came after the birth of Christ.

For Christians, the year Jesus was born is the first year of the new calendar. So the year A.D. 2000 came two thousand years after the birth of Jesus. But Muslims don't count their years from the birth of Jesus. Instead, they count their years from the Hegira. So the year that Muhammad went from Mecca to Medina is called A.H. 1, or "The first year after the Hegira."

The Koran: Islam's Holy Book

Muhammad stayed in Medina for many years. He went on teaching his followers about Allah. He taught them to be loyal to each other, to be generous to those with less money, and to treat their wives and families well. He also told them that they shouldn't drink any alcohol, gamble, or mistreat their slaves.

Not all of Muhammad's followers could read. So they would carefully memorize his teachings, word for word. Other Muslims wrote these sayings down on whatever they could find—bits of paper, pieces of leather, even palm leaves! Finally, Muhammad's friend Abu Bakr decided that all Muhammad's words should be gathered together in one place. He ordered Muhammad's followers to bring him every single word spoken by Muhammad. "Bring every word," he said, "whether it is written on leaves, bits of leather, bones, pieces of stone, or simply written in your mind."

All of these scattered teachings were written down in a single book. Then, the bits and scraps were destroyed. Now, all of Muhammad's teachings could be found in one place. Today, we call this book the Koran.

It is the holy book of Muslims all over the world.

The Koran tells Muslims that their lives are built on "Five Pillars." The Five Pillars are the five duties every Muslim should do. The Koran says that a life built on five pillars is a strong, good life!

Here are the Five Pillars of Islam. Each Pillar has a special name:

First Pillar: Shahadah, or Faith

Each Muslim must believe that Allah is the one true God. Muslims say, "There is no god but Allah, and Muhammad is his prophet." They say this to each newborn baby, before praying, and at other special times, every day.

Second Pillar: Salah, or Prayer

Muslims pray to Allah five times every day. Before the prayer, they must wash themselves, put on clean clothes, and face towards the city of Mecca. Muslim children are expected to begin praying when they are seven. By the time they are ten, they too must pray five times every day!

Third Pillar: Zakat, or Giving

Muslims must give away part of their money every year to those who need help.

Fourth Pillar: Sawm, or Fasting

During one month of the year, called Ramadan, Muslims do not eat or drink anything all day long! They can only eat and drink before the sun comes up, and after the sun sets at night. Young children don't have to fast—but by the time Muslim children are ten years old, they must fast during Ramadan, just like grownups. Going without food is supposed to remind Muslims of those who are poor and suffer from hunger all the time.

❧Fifth Pillar: Hajj, or Pilgrimage❧

Every Muslim tries to go to Mecca at least once during his or her life. Mecca is a very important city to Muslims because Muhammad had his first vision there.

Do you think the Five Pillars are difficult? Do they help people to live good lives?

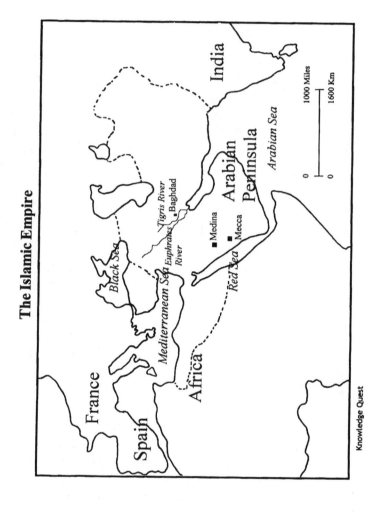

The Islamic Empire

France

Spain

Black Sea

Mediterranean Sea

Africa

Red Sea

Tigris River

Baghdad

Euphrates River

Medina

Mecca

Arabian Peninsula

India

Arabian Sea

0 1000 Miles

0 1600 Km

Chapter Seven
Islam Becomes an Empire

The Fight for Mecca

Muhammad lived in Medina for two years. The Muslims who had come to Medina from Mecca obeyed Muhammad's teachings and did whatever he commanded. And soon, so did the people who had always lived in Medina! They came to him with their difficulties and their questions. "Muhammad," one man might say, "I promised to pay my neighbor two pieces of gold for his camel. I gave him the gold and he gave me the camel. I took the camel home, but the next morning, it was dead! He sold me a sick camel. Shouldn't I get my money back?" Then Muhammad would decide whether the man would get his money back.

Now Muhammad was more than just a prophet. He was also the ruler of a city. He had to be a judge and a king as well as a preacher. And the people of Medina followed the laws that Muhammad made. "Be kind to your parents," he ordered his followers. "Be loyal to other Muslims. Always watch out for them! Don't drink wine or eat pork—those things are bad for you. And take care of your families!"

Muhammad's new laws made life in Medina peaceful. But the city of Medina had other problems. There was barely enough food and water in Medina to take care of the people who had always lived there. And now Muhammad's followers—all the Muslims who had fled from Mecca—needed food and water as well. Soon, people in Medina began to go hungry.

So several of the city leaders went to visit Muhammad. "Prophet," they said, "our children are hungry. There's barely enough water to keep us alive. What will we do?"

Muhammad thought for a long while. Finally, he said, "Go out to the high road, and wait until you see a caravan of camels taking food and supplies to the city of Mecca. Then attack the caravan, and take the food! Bring it back here to Medina, and share it with those who are hungry."

So Muhammad's followers armed themselves with short, curved swords and round shields. They went out to the road and stole from the caravan headed for Mecca, just as Muhammad had commanded.

For weeks, the Muslims raided the caravans headed for Mecca. Soon the leaders of Mecca grew angry. "What will happen to us here in Mecca?" they complained. "The caravans are empty when they arrive at our walls! If we don't stop Muhammad and his followers, we'll begin to go hungry ourselves."

So the army of Mecca marched out towards Medina. When Muhammad heard that Mecca's army was on its way, he gathered his own army together and marched out to meet them. The two armies met in a dry riverbed and fought until the Meccans admitted defeat. The army of Mecca retreated, and Muhammad declared victory.

But the quarrel between Mecca and Medina didn't end. The two cities fought with each other for seven more years! Meanwhile, Muhammad and his men convinced more and more Arabian tribes to become Muslims. Now Muhammad had many allies, willing to fight with him. And Muhammad declared Mecca to be a holy place.

"From now on," he told his followers, "you must always pray, facing towards the city of Mecca. This will show that you turn only to Allah Himself when you pray."

Now the Muslims wanted to conquer Mecca more than ever. Finally, Muhammad and ten thousand Muslim followers marched towards Mecca. When the weary, battle-scarred Meccans saw Muhammad's huge force, they surrendered. The Muslims entered Mecca triumphantly. They burned all the idols in the city and declared it the Holy City of Islam. "Only Muslims will be allowed to enter Mecca from this day on." Muhammad declared. "Any unbelievers who enter will be put to death!"

Mecca is still the Holy City of Islam today. Do you remember the Fifth Pillar of Islam? Every faithful Muslim tries to visit Mecca at least once during his lifetime.

The Spread of Islam

Now Muhammad ruled in Mecca. Soon, Muhammad and his followers ruled most of the Arabian peninsula too. More and more Arabian tribes became Muslims. And Muhammad went on telling them what Allah wanted them to do. Now Islam wasn't just a religion followed by a few tribes in the Arabian desert. Islam had its own empire—an empire as big as Arabia!

Muhammad was the leader of this empire. But one day, Muhammad complained that he had a headache. He lay down to rest—and never got up again. The Prophet was dead!

Now what would happen to the empire of Islam? Muhammad was the prophet of Allah! Who else could tell the people what Allah required? The Muslims of Mecca gathered together to ask each other what they should do next. And many of them began to panic. "Can anyone else lead us?" they asked. "What if Islam vanishes, now that Muhammad is dead? What if our whole nation falls apart!"

But Muhammad's friend Abu Bakr stood up. Do you remember Abu Bakr? He was with Muhammad in Mecca, when the leaders of the city were trying to kill Muhammad.

"Friends," Abu Bakr said, "Muhammad is only the messenger of Allah. We follow Allah alone! Muhammad may be dead, but Islam lives!"

When the Muslims heard Abu Bakr's words, they became calmer. But they still needed a strong leader to govern the empire that Muhammad had built. So they chose Abu Bakr to be their new leader, or *caliph*. The caliph of the Islamic empire ruled over all the people who believed in Allah.

Abu Bakr wasn't a big, powerful man. He was small, thin, and dressed in shabby clothes. He was gentle and soft-spoken. But Abu Bakr, the first Islamic *caliph*, kept Islamic rule over Arabia strong. He ordered Muslim soldiers to attack and conquer any Bedouin tribes who rebelled against Islamic laws.

But this was only the beginning for the Islamic empire. The caliphs who came after Abu Bakr attacked the Byzantine Empire and took away some of its land. They spread Islam all the way up to the Caspian Sea. They conquered the land to the east of them, almost all the way over to India. And they took over North Africa—the part of Africa closest to the Mediterranean Sea.

Islam had started as the religion of one man, Muhammad. But now it had become much more.

Hundreds of thousands of people now worshipped Allah. And Islam wasn't just a religion. It was an empire.

The caliphs of the Islamic Empire built a new capital city on the banks of the Tigris River. The city was round, with three walls surrounding it. The caliphs called it Baghdad.

Mecca was still the holy city of Islam. But Baghdad, the Round City, became the center of the empire. The caliph lived there, in a splendid palace. Ships sailed to Baghdad from far away to trade silks from China, spices from India, and gold and gems from all over the world. Baghdad became one of the busiest and most beautiful cities in the world.

The City of Baghdad

The city of Baghdad was known for its beautiful buildings, its running water, its public libraries, and its thinkers. Philosophers, scientists, astronomers, and writers came to Baghdad to study, to learn, and to write books.

One of the most famous Islamic books, *The Thousand and One Nights,* takes place in the palace of the caliph in Baghdad. In the book, sailors, soldiers, and explorers tell the caliph all about their adventures. One of the sailors is named Sinbad. Sinbad tells this story about himself:

When I was a young man, I had more money than the king. I bought myself the best food, the finest drink, and the most beautiful clothing. I did nothing but eat, drink, and go to parties with my friends!

But one day I discovered that my money was almost gone. And I had done nothing all my life but enjoy

81

myself. I thought, "Before it is too late, I want to have an adventure and make a name for myself. When people hear my name, they will think, 'Sinbad was a great explorer, braver than a lion!'"

So I sold everything I had left, even my fancy clothes. I used the money to buy clothes for traveling, and food for a long journey. Then I went down to the harbor and set sail with a group of merchants, heading for foreign lands.

We sailed over the sea for weeks and weeks, stopping at one island after another to trade and to buy. We were tired of sailing and weary from our trading when we saw, ahead of us, the most beautiful island in the world. It looked like Paradise! Tall green trees shaded soft, lush meadows. Flowers grew blue, yellow, and scarlet along the edges of clear running streams.

"Land!" called out the captain. "Let's sink our anchor here and rest for a while!"

So we all left the ship anchored on the shore, and wandered through the dim cool gardens and sunny fields. Some of the men built fires on the shore and roasted meat for a feast. Others swam in the sparkling streams and washed their clothes. I walked in the grass, for it had been a long time since I had felt solid ground under my feet! I could smell the roasting meat on the breeze, and the scent of food made me hungry. I thanked Allah that he had brought us to this beautiful place, where we could rest and eat.

Suddenly I heard frantic shouts coming from the shore. The captain had climbed back aboard our boat, where it lay up against the sand. He was screaming, "Run! Run for your lives! Leave your clothes and food and get on board! Allah save us. This is no island—it's a fish!"

And when I looked around me, I saw that he was right! A great fish, as big as a mountain, had settled in the middle of the sea. It had been there so long that sand washed up on it, and trees grew in the dirt. Covered with ground and grass, the fish looked like an island. But when our sailors built fires on the shore, the fish felt the heat and began to move. I could feel the ground shaking beneath my feet as the fish shuddered and twisted! Dirt began to fall away from the fish's gigantic back. Beneath my feet, I could see glittering, moss-grown scales. A huge eye rolled up at me. The fish was awake—and angry!

Men were fleeing back to the ship, leaving their pots, their food, and their clothes on the heaving sand. But I was too far away! I was still running across the sand when the fish shook itself and leaped high into the air. Trees, grass, flowers, and streams all flew away in a cloud of destruction. And then the fish hit the surface of the water with a thundering crash. Water sprang up all around it, high as a mountain, as it dived down into the surging sea.

Waves swept over me! My eyes and mouth were filled with water. I kicked frantically, seeing only the glitter of green sea all around me. I could hear the shouts and cries of my fellow sailors, also struggling in the sea.

I thought that I would drown, but Allah sent my way a wooden tub, washed from the island. I climbed into it and huddled in the bottom while the waves tossed me this way and that. And as I watched, our ship disappeared into the distance! The terrified captain was sailing away as fast as he could, ignoring the shouts of the men stranded in the sea.

Night came. All that night and all the next day, I sailed in my wooden tub, pushed about by the wind and waves. I suffered terribly from thirst and hunger. The sun beat down on me. When I dangled my feet over the tub's edge to cool them in the seawater, fish rose to the surface and nibbled at my soles!

But as dark began to close around me again, I saw that the tide was carrying me towards a mountain island, with trees bending from its sides almost down to the water's surface. My tub washed beneath a tree, and I grabbed its branches and pulled myself up onto land. My legs were numb and cramping, and I had not slept since the fish-island dove into the deeps beneath me. So I threw myself down on the shore and slept like a dead man until the next morning.

When I awoke, I managed to get to my feet and look about me. I found trees that bore sweet figs and apples, and springs of fresh sweet water. So I ate until I was full, and drank until I was no longer thirsty. I thanked Allah for sparing my life, and began to explore the island. Birds sang sweetly in the trees above me. The soft smell of flowers drifted past me. But I could not see any sign of man! Was I alone on this island? I climbed a tall tree, so that I could look around in all directions. But I saw nothing but sand, trees, the sky, and the mountain rising above me.

I looked and I looked for some sign of life. Surely I could not be the only man on this island! Finally, I saw, far away on the other side of the mountain, some great white thing in the middle of the trees. It was too smooth to be a rock. Perhaps it was a building!

I noted its direction, climbed down from the tree, and began to walk towards it. I struggled through the underbrush and over rocks for hours, until my feet were cut and bleeding. Finally, I arrived at a clearing in the trees. In the center of the trees, a huge white dome rose to the sky.

I walked all around it. But there was no door or window in any wall! I beat on it with my fists, but it was not made of stone; the thick white walls were warm and hard, and I could not make any dent in them. I tried to climb up it, but the sides were so smooth and slippery that I could only get a few feet off the ground before I slid off and fell.

By now, the sun was sinking towards the sea. Dusk was creeping up around me. I thought that I should find myself a place to sleep. But as I turned away to look for shelter, I saw the sky grow suddenly dark. The light of the sun was blotted out. The air grew cold around me. I thought that a cloud had come over the sun—but then I saw that an enormous bird, as wide as a cloud and as tall as a mountain, had swooped down over my head! So large was this bird that it blotted out the sun.

I was so amazed that I fell down on the ground, hoping that the bird would not see me! And I remembered that I had once heard a sailor tell of a huge bird called a "roc," that lives on far away islands and feeds elephants to its babies. Then I knew that the enormous dome was the roc's egg!

Sinbad in the Valley of Snakes

The gigantic bird settled down on the dome, spread its wings over its head, and fell asleep. So I got carefully up, unwound my turban from my head, and made a rope from the cloth. Then I tied the cloth around my middle, crept up to the roc, and tied the other end to its thick, scaly leg. For I thought to myself, "If the bird flies away, maybe it will take me to a land where there are people and cities, and then I will escape from this island!"

85

I was afraid to go to sleep. What if the roc flew away while I was sleeping? So I spent the whole night sitting with my back against the roc's egg, my waist tied to its foot, waiting for it to wake up. When the first light of the sun glowed red in the sky, the roc stirred. It spread its wings and rose up off its egg, carrying me with it! We rose so high into the sky that I thought we would leave the earth altogether and travel into the darkness of the air beyond! And below me, the island and its dome were the size of grains of salt, scattered on the blue of the sea.

Finally, the roc flew over land. Little by little it began to descend, coming closer and closer to earth. As soon as my feet touched the ground, I began to untie myself. I was shaking with fear! What if the roc took off again? Or what if it saw me, and pecked me up from the earth like a grain of corn?

But the bird never spotted me, and as soon as I was free, I ran away from it as quickly as I could. Soon I saw it snatch something from the ground with its enormous claws, and rise back up into the air. It carried a snake, as long as a tree and as big around as a man!

I kept walking, until I found myself at the edge of a valley. Through the valley ran a river too wide to cross, and tall mountains stood all around the valley's sides. Then I thought to myself, "I should have stayed on the island! At least there I had fruit to eat and water to drink! Here I have no food, and no water, and I can never cross those mountains!"

Soon I recovered my courage, and began to climb down into the valley. As soon as I put my feet to the ground, I saw that it was studded with diamonds, as big as my fist. I filled my pockets, my turban, and my cloak all full of diamonds. "Perhaps I can make a raft," I thought, "and float down the river until I come to a city."

But as I came close to the river, I saw that the shores were swarming with snakes as big as palm trees, that would swallow an elephant in one gulp! I was too afraid to go further. "What can I do?" I cried out. "I will never escape this place! And where can I sleep to be safe from the snakes?" For night was beginning to fall.

Sinbad in the Valley of the Snakes

As I staggered along, weary and frightened, I saw ahead of me a flat place with a cliff rising up above it. Eagles circled around it. As I watched, a piece of meat fell from the cliff onto the ground, and an eagle swept down and seized the meat.

I looked up. There, far above me, were men! They were throwing down large pieces of meat into the valley below. And then I saw that this was how the men of this land got diamonds out of the dangerous valley of the snakes. When they threw pieces of meat down on top of the diamonds, some of the precious stones would stick to the meat. Then an eagle would swoop down, seize the meat and carry it back up to the land above. As soon as the eagle settled to eat, the men would run at it waving sticks and shouting, to scare it away. Then they would take away the diamonds that had stuck to the meat, and leave the meat itself for the eagle to eat.

As soon as I understood this, I ran and grabbed

hold of one of the pieces of meat, and held it up over my head. An eagle swooped down on it and seized it with his claws. Then he flew back up out of the valley with me dangling beneath him, holding on to the meat with all my strength!

As soon as my feet touched the mountainside, I let go of the piece of meat and ran towards the men at the cliff's edge. They were disappointed to see that they had caught only another man, rather than a handful of diamonds!

But I said to them, "Don't worry. I am an honest man, and Allah has delivered me from the valley of the snakes! Out of gratitude, I will give you some of the diamonds I have brought with me!"

Then I gave handfuls of diamonds to all of them. When I told them my story, they were amazed. For no one before had ever come alive from the valley of the snakes!

China in the Early Middle Ages

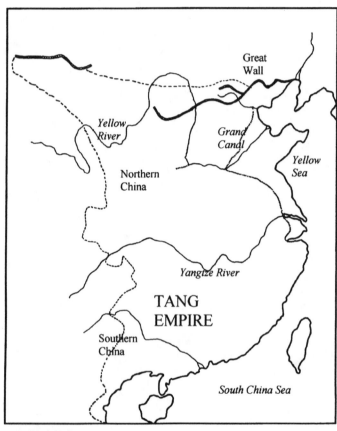

Knowledge Quest

90

Chapter Eight
The Great Dynasties of China

Yang Chien Unites North and South

The Muslim empire spread up from Arabia, over towards the land that used to belong to Rome. It spread down to Egypt and North Africa. It became an enormous empire. But far to the east was an even bigger empire: the empire of China.

In ancient times, China had been ruled by one emperor. But over time, China had divided into two different countries—the North and the South. People in the North and the South didn't like each other. Southerners insisted that the Northern king wasn't a real king—only an imposter. And Northerners thought that people in the South were ignorant and crude. One Northerner wrote, "The South is hot and infested with bugs. People and animals live together, like frogs and toads in the same hole. People in the South like the company of fish and turtles, but they don't know anything about art and music!" [1]

Yang Chien was a general in the Northern army.[2] He thought that China should be one country again. So he led the soldiers of the North down to attack the Southern king and his army. The South fought back, but the Northern army was too strong to resist. Soon, Yang Chien controlled both North and South. He became the new emperor of China and founded a new

---

[1] This quote is adapted from Patricia Ebrey's translation in *Chinese Civilization: A Sourcebook.*

[2] Yang Chien is sometimes spelled Yang Jian.

dynasty. Do you remember what a dynasty is? It is one family that rules a country for years and years. Yang Chien founded the *Sui dynasty* to rule over one, united China.

Yang Chien

Yang Chien and his descendents in the Sui dynasty wanted to keep northern and southern China together. But they had a problem: In China, wide, deep rivers run from the sea in the west, all the way over into the east. Travelers who wanted to go from the north down to the south had to cross the Yellow River. And anyone who wanted to go from the south up the north had to cross the Yangtze River. These rivers were hard to get across, especially in the spring, when floods made them even wider and wilder.

The Sui emperors knew that if people from the North and people from the South couldn't meet, talk to each other, and trade with each other, China might divide again. So they decided to dig a new "river" that ran from north to south, between the Yellow and the Yangtze Rivers. This new "river" would be called the Grand Canal.

The Grand Canal took years to dig by hand. The Sui emperors needed money to build it, so all of the families in China had to pay their taxes ten years ahead of time! The emperors also forced millions of people to work on the Canal. Every man between fifteen and fifty had to spend months digging and building. And every family had to send one woman, one child, and one old man to work on the Canal too.

Finally, the Canal was finished. The emperor, Yangdi, decided to go for a ride on it to celebrate. He took his family and all the members of his court with him. It took 62 boats to hold them all! And since Yangdi didn't want to row, he forced workers to pull his boat with ropes. It took 80,000 men to pull all of those boats!

The Grand Canal did make it easier for the people of China to go from South to North and back again. Now merchants could sail up and down the canal with rice, pottery, and other goods. Some families even lived on boats! They ate and cooked and slept on boats. The mothers of these canal families tied bamboo life-jackets onto their babies until they learned how to swim.

But the Grand Canal also made the people of China angry with the emperors of the Sui. Many people died building the canal, because they had to work hard without much food, in cold and in damp, all year long. Families had become poorer, because men had been forced to build the canal instead of tending their farms and doing their own work. And everyone hated the extra taxes.

Finally, the Chinese people rebelled against Yangdi and killed him. He was the last Sui emperor. The dynasty founded by Yang Chien had kept China together—but lost its throne.

The Tang Dynasty

Yangdi, the last Sui emperor, treated the Chinese people like his slaves. He forced them to pay high taxes and to work on the Grand Canal without pay. The next king of China, Li Yuan, didn't make the same mistake.

Li Yuan knew that an emperor who rules hungry, unhappy people won't last for very long! He wanted the Chinese people to be prosperous and content. So he spent money on making cities stronger and cleaner. He decreed that the people of China could follow any religion they wanted to. He encouraged merchants in China to trade with the people of India and Byzantium. Li Yuan founded a new dynasty—the *Tang dynasty*. The Sui dynasty only lasted for forty years. But the Tang dynasty lasted more than three hundred.

A statue of a Tang warrior from about 650

Do you remember the Golden Age of India? The Indian Golden Age was a time when India was rich and at peace, and when the people of India created beautiful art, music, and stories. The three hundred years of the Tang dynasty were the Golden Age of China. The Chinese learned how to print books by carving the words into wooden blocks and dipping the blocks in ink. That way they could print the same pages over and over again, instead of writing each page out by hand. Chinese jewelers made beautiful, delicate jewelry with green jade, creamy pearls, and gold strands beaten so fine that they were no thicker than threads. Artists painted beautiful pictures on silks and sculpted graceful figures from pottery. They learned how to drain the sap from special trees called *lacquer trees,* color it black, red, gold, and green, and paint it onto wood and cloth. The lacquer dried into a hard smooth surface—like a beautiful, medieval kind of plastic!

The Chinese people became wealthier. Babies of rich people ate out of lacquer bowls with lacquer spoons! Many families were rich enough to eat fancy food, like ice cream made from rice and milk, and twenty-four different flavors of dumplings. In the early Middle Ages, most other people ate with their fingers, but the Chinese ate with carved and lacquered chopsticks. They dressed in silks trimmed with jewels. The sleeves of men's coats were so wide that the tailors had to sew weights into the cuffs, so that the sleeves wouldn't flap around and get in the way. And the richest women of all wore skirts made out of the feathers of one hundred different birds.

Chinese scientists thought that China could become even richer if they could learn how to make gold. So they spent years combining different metals and chemicals, trying to figure out how to create gold. They never succeeded, but they made another discovery by mistake. When they mixed charcoal with two chemicals called saltpeter and sulfur, they ended up with a black powder that exploded! The Chinese had invented gunpowder. Soon they learned how to use it in rockets made out of hollow bamboo tubes.

No wonder that the Tang emperors became richer and more powerful! They built four long walls around their beautiful capital city, Xi'an. Each wall had three gates in it. Only the emperor could use the middle gate in each wall.

The palace of the emperor had twenty thousand musicians and entertainers living in it. One Tang emperor even brought one hundred dancing horses to his court! The horses wore gold and silver halters and had jewels woven into their manes. When musicians played, the horses bent their legs up and down, nodded their heads in time to the music, and reared up and down. One Chinese writer tells us that, after the emperor's reign was over, the dancing horses were sold to the army. One day, the soldiers decided to have a party out in the stables. When they started to play music, the horses began to dance. The soldiers were terrified. They thought that the horses were possessed by evil spirits—and chased them out of the stable with brooms!

China, Korea, and Japan

Chapter Nine
East of China

The Yamato Dynasty of Japan

India had many small kingdoms, but the Gupta dynasty united them into one. China had two parts, but the Sui dynasty united them into one. And exactly the same thing happened in the country of Japan. The dynasty that united Japan was called the Yamato dynasty. It is the oldest dynasty in the world. The first Yamato emperor ruled in Japan almost two thousand years ago—and a Yamato emperor is still on the Japanese throne today!

If you put your finger on the map, right in the middle of China, and then move *right* or *east,* you'll come to the Pacific Ocean. The country of Japan is made up of four long, thin islands in the Pacific, just east of China. Japan isn't very wide, but it is so long that there are frozen plains of snow at the north end of the island—and coral reefs and warm, sunny beaches at the south end! The four big islands that make up Japan have almost four thousand small islands all around them.

At first, Japan was ruled by many different *clans,* or families. Each clan had its own territory and its own government. But one clan in the middle of Japan, the Yamato clan, grew stronger than all the rest. The Yamato leaders conquered all of the other clans, one by one. It took over two hundred years! But finally, the

Yamato leaders could call themselves the emperors of Japan.

The Yamato emperors told stories to prove that they deserved to rule over Japan. These stories announced that the Yamato emperors were living gods, descendents of Amaterasu, the Sun Goddess. Here is one of these legends:

In the beginning, the world was full of sky-spirits who created the islands of Japan. These spirits had children of their own. The strongest and most beautiful of the daughters was Amaterasu.

Amaterasu was given the entire sky to rule over. But her brother Susano, who had been given the Sea, was jealous. "The sky is larger than the sea!" he complained. So he mounted a war against Amaterasu to throw her out of the sky.

But he lost the fight and had to flee from the sky, down to earth. He ran until he was weary and had to rest by a stream. As he rested, he saw a pair of chopsticks drifting by him on the current. "There must be people around here!" he exclaimed. And he set off upstream to find them.

Soon he heard weeping and wailing. Just around a bend in the stream, he saw an old woman, an old man, and a beautiful young girl on the shore. All three were mourning.

"What's the matter?" Susano asked.

"An evil serpent with eight heads has come to our land!" the old man wept. "Every year for the past seven years, he has eaten one of our daughters. We had eight daughters, but all have been eaten except for our youngest. And today the serpent will come and eat her as well!"

Susano looked at the beautiful girl and fell in love with her at once. "I will save her," he said "if you will give her to me in marriage."

"Anything!" the old man cried.

So Susano turned the lovely girl into a comb and hid her in his hair. Then he laid out eight bowls of rice wine for the serpent, and hid in the bushes. Soon he heard the serpent approaching. It roared and thrashed its eight heads around, looking for its prey. But then it saw the wine. The eight heads dipped down and drank the eight bowls of rice wine. And then the serpent, full of wine, rolled over and went sound asleep!

Susano came out of the bushes, drew his sword, and chopped the serpent into eighty pieces. Inside the serpent, he found a great magical sword. He sent this sword to his sister Amaterasu for a peace gift. Then he took the comb from his hair and turned it back into the beautiful girl. He built a palace with eight walls and lived there with his lovely wife. Together, they had eighty fine sons.

Their youngest son was named Okuninushi. He settled down in the center of Japan and ruled over a plain covered with reeds. But his kingdom was an unhappy one! All over it, men fought with each other. And Okuninushi's seventy-nine brothers were constantly trying to overthrow his rule. The Reed Plain became so noisy and full of battle that the plants, rocks, and trees started sending up complaints to the heavens!

Up in the sky, Amaterasu heard the complaints. She decided to send her favorite grandson, Honingi, to bring peace to the Reed Plain. So she called him before her throne and gave him three sacred objects: the string of beads she wore in her hair, the mirror in which she had first seen her own reflection, and the great sword that Susano had found inside the eight-headed serpent.

"Honingi," she said, "I want you to go down to the islands below and rule there. Establish peace and order, instead of chaos. Your descendants will reign as long as heaven and earth endure!"

So Honingi went down to the Reed Plain in the center of Japan and began his reign. In time he had children and grandchildren of his own. His descendents were the Yamatos, and the blood of the goddess Amaterasu runs in their veins. And when each Yamato emperor comes to the throne, he is given copies of the three sacred objects of Honingi: the magic sword, the string of beads, and the mirror of Amaterasu.

Susano retreated into the darkness and chose it as his kingdom. From then on, Susano was the Moon God who ruled the dark, and Amaterasu was the Sun Goddess who ruled the day. Because of their old quarrel, the two never met again—just as the sun and the moon never meet in the sky.

A Tale of Three Countries: Korea, China, and Japan

The Yamato emperors of Japan had a big job: They had to rule over many different clans who were used to having their own way! Claiming that they were descended from the goddess Amaterasu gave the emperors some power. But they knew that they also had to be good rulers if they wanted to keep control of Japan.

So the Yamato emperors borrowed ideas about how to run their country from two other countries: China and Korea.

Korea is a *peninsula* (a piece of land surrounded by water on three sides) that juts out into the Pacific Ocean from the eastern side of China. The

Korean people have lived on this peninsula for thousands of years. But back in the days when the Roman Empire was still powerful, Chinese war leaders invaded Korea and ruled over part of it. The Korean people didn't want to be ruled by China, so they fought back. Eventually, the Chinese had to retreat until they only ruled the very northern part of the *peninsula*. The rest of Korea was divided into three parts called "The Three Kingdoms." These three Korean kingdoms ruled themselves.

Now the Korean people no longer had to obey the Chinese. But the Koreans had learned Chinese writing and Chinese customs from the invaders. They had learned about Buddha, and many Koreans had become followers of Buddhist ways. So even though they weren't ruled by China, the people of Korea had become like the Chinese in many ways.

The kingdom on the western side of Korea was called Paekche. The king of Paekche hoped that he could conquer the other two kingdoms and add their land to his own. So he decided to make friends with Japan. After all, Japan was right across the water! And the armies of Japan could help the kingdom of Paekche become stronger than the other kingdoms of Korea.

So the king of Paekche sent members of his court across to the island of Japan. "We'd like to be friends," he said, "and if we decide to fight with our neighbors, we'd like you to come and fight on our side." To convince the emperor of Japan to be his friend, he sent presents, too—silks, tea, jewels, and a book with Chinese letters in it.

The Japanese court liked the silks, tea, and jewels. But they had never before seen a book with Chinese letters in it! They were fascinated by these letters. The emperor sent a message back across the water to Korea. "I want my son, the prince, to learn how to read and write these letters!" he said. "Can you send someone to teach him?"

The king of Paekche agreed. According to ancient stories, he sent the prince a tutor named Wani. Wani taught the prince how to read and write Chinese letters. Soon, the whole court learned how to read and write in Chinese!

The Koreans also taught the Japanese about the Buddha. Soon, many people in Japan became Buddhists as well. Japanese emperors gave their noblemen titles that were like Korean titles. They kept their chronicles and their court records in Chinese

A pagoda (Japanese Buddhist temple), Pagoda Kofuku-ji

characters, just like the Korean court did.

Soon, all of the important people in the Japanese court spoke Chinese. Only the common people used Japanese. Japanese noblemen sent their sons to study in China. These young men came back to Japan with Chinese ideas, Chinese games, and even Chinese hairdos! New cities in Japan were laid out just like Chinese cities.

Korea and Japan copied many things from the Chinese. But that didn't keep China from wanting to rule over Korean and Japanese land! And although it was difficult for the Chinese army to march into Japan

104

because of the water that lay between China and the Japanese coast, it was much easier for China to invade Korea. During the Tang dynasty, the Chinese marched back into Korea again. They wiped out the Paekche kingdom. And although the people of the other kingdoms eventually drove the Chinese soldiers back out of their country, it took them six long years of difficult fighting.

Japan saw what had happened to Korea—and didn't want to be next! The Japanese enjoyed many of the Chinese customs, but they didn't want to become Chinese. They only wanted to be equals. The Japanese called themselves "The Land of the Rising Sun" and China "The Land of the Setting Sun." This was their way of saying that Japan was just as important as China.

But it was very difficult to be equal with a country as large as China! China was like a big, old beech tree with beautiful leaves and long, shady limbs. A huge beech tree casts so much shade that other plants can't grow beneath it. The tree chokes out all smaller trees. The Japanese felt a little bit like a small pine, trying to grow underneath a huge sprawling beech.

So, four hundred years after the Yamato prince learned how to write in Chinese, the Yamato emperor broke off all ties with China. Japan would no longer send its young men to China. Instead, the Japanese began to write, to paint, to dress, and to think in their own, unique, Japanese way.

Australia and New Zealand

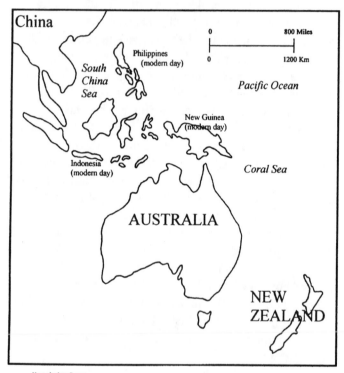

Knowledge Quest

Chapter Ten
The Bottom of the World

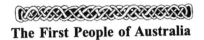

The First People of Australia

We started our story of the world with the fall of
Rome. If you have a globe, put your finger on Rome, in
Italy, and move *east* (right). You'll come to the Byzantine
Empire. Go *south* (down) from the Byzantine Empire,
and you'll find yourself on the hot sandy peninsula of
Arabia, where Muhammad gathered his followers into
the Islamic Empire. Go *east* again from Arabia, over into
India, and you'll be in the land that once belonged to the
Gupta dynasty. Keep going east, and you'll be in China.
Go all the way over to the Pacific Ocean, on the far side
of China, and you'll find the most eastern countries of
all—Korea and Japan.

Now go south from Japan, down into the Pacific
Ocean. You'll bump into an enormous island called
Australia. This island is so big that we call it a *conti-
nent* (a large land mass). There are seven *continents*,
or huge areas of land, in the world: North America, South
America, Antarctica, Africa, Europe, Asia, and Australia.
On most maps, the continent of Australia is down near
the bottom of the world.

When the Guptas were ruling in India and the
Tang were ruling in China and the Yamatos were ruling in
Japan, *no one* was ruling in Australia! The people of
Australia were *nomads*. Instead of living in houses and
villages, with one king ruling over them, they lived in
small groups that moved from place to place, hunting
food and gathering plants. No one knows where these
nomads came from. But their own legends said that they

had been in Australia from the beginning of the world. Today, we call these Australian nomads *aborigines,* because the Latin words *ab origine* mean "from the beginning."

Let's imagine the life of an Aboriginal boy, more than a thousand years ago. Rulu lives in a *clan* (a group of people related to each other) in the south of Australia. Rulu calls all of the men in the clan "father" and all of the women "mother." He has thirty-six grownups who can tell him stories at bedtime—and spank him when he puts mud into his sister's hair!

The clan fathers began to teach Rulu how to hunt a year ago, when he was seven. At first, they taught him how to fish in the ocean. Rulu loves fishing! The last time he went fishing, he helped to catch two huge sea cows. Rulu's mouth still waters when he remembers those fresh slices of raw meat with chunks of blubber balanced on top.

But now the clan has moved inland, away from the water. It is the dry season, and food is getting scarce. Late one night, Rulu catches a bat, and he and his sister cook it over a fire along with a handful of moths. Roasted moths are Rulu's favorite snack; they taste like crunchy, furry nuts! But there aren't enough moths to fill his stomach. In the morning, he is hungry again—and so is the rest of the clan.

So Rulu and two of the "fathers" start out very early in the morning to hunt for food. Before they leave the camp, they coat themselves with a paste made out of mud and the ashes of last night's fire. The paste will cover up their human scent so that the kangaroos won't be able to smell them. Then they start off for the nearest waterhole.

When they get there, they find kangaroo tracks all around it. But the waterhole is almost dry, and Rulu knows that they'll need water before the hunt is over. So he helps the fathers dig down beneath the waterhole. He scoops mud and dirt with his hands until his hole is so deep that he has to lie on his stomach and reach down into it. Finally his fingertips brush against something hard and cool. Rulu whoops with joy. He has found a water-frog! He wrestles the round, dark frog out of the hole. In the rainy season, the water-frog soaks water into its skin and swells up—and then buries itself deep into the sand until the dry season passes. This frog is almost as big as Rulu's head! He holds it up and squeezes water from its skin right into his mouth. Now he's ready to go hunting.

Rulu and the fathers track the kangaroos through a forest of scrub and brush. Soon they glimpse movement. The kangaroos are in the brush ahead of them, nibbling the tender leaves from the low branches. So the hunters dig a deep pit in the hard, red earth and cover it over with branches and leaves. They search out the freshest, newest leaves, cut them and pile them on top of the pit. Then they back away into the bushes to hide. Rulu crouches on the ground without moving for hours. Sweat runs down the back of his neck. His left foot goes to sleep. But he knows that he must stay very still. Nearby, the fathers are standing motionless, holding branches in front of them. They look almost exactly like trees!

Rulu holds his breath. He can hear the rustle of a kangaroo. The big brown animal hops slowly into sight. It pauses, sniffs the air, and then bends its head down. It sees the fresh leaves. It takes another hop towards the food, and crashes down into the pit below.

Rulu and the fathers haul their catch back to the camp. Another hunter has trapped an emu. The women have been working hard all day and have caught a whole potful of lizards and snakes. There will be a feast tonight! Soon the rich warm smell of roasting kangaroo meat and cooked snake fills the air. Rulu eats and eats until he is so full that he can barely move. He curls up near the fire and listens to the fathers of the clan tell stories of the Dreamtime—that long-ago age when spirits still lived on earth. But Rulu has walked miles and miles today, hunting kangaroos and water-frogs, and he can't keep his eyes open. Slowly he drifts into sleep. In the morning, there will be cold snake meat for breakfast!

The Long Journey of the Maori

Australia may be near the bottom of the world, but if you put your finger on Australia and keep going down, you'll bump into two islands that are even closer to the bottom of the world. Today, these two islands belong to the country of *New Zealand*.

Aborigines have lived in Australia for as long as anyone can remember. But the first people of New Zealand, the *Maori,* came to their islands for the first time during the Middle Ages. By the time the Maori arrived in New Zealand, *Beowulf* had already been written, Justinian and Theodora had finished their reigns, and the Gupta dynasty had already driven the barbarians out of India. By the time the Maori arrived in New Zealand, the Aborigines of Australia had already been in *their* country for thousands of years.

Although we don't know for sure, we think that the Maori sailed to New Zealand from far out in the Pacific Ocean. If you go east (right, on your map) from Australia, you'll find a little scattering of islands so far away that they are halfway to North America. These

110

are the Polynesian Islands. And the people who lived here were great explorers. They built canoes from enormous trees, and made sails from coconut fibers (the tough, white strings on the insides of coconut shells,

woven together into cloth). On these canoes, they sailed out into the Pacific Ocean. They ventured out into the deep ocean—so far out that they could no longer see their home. They fished for sharks and for other huge fish that live in the deep

Maori warriors of New Zealand painted their faces and bodies to frighten enemies.

ocean. And they searched for new islands. They packed their canoes with pigs and chickens, with fruits and vegetables, and looked for new shores where they could settle and live.

Usually, the Polynesian islanders settled on islands that were only a few days' journey away. But one day, a group of these explorers just kept on sailing. They sailed until the Polynesian Islands disappeared into the distance. They sailed for weeks, with nothing but empty ocean in front of them. The pigs grew restless. The chickens got seasick. The fruits and vegetables got eaten! The men and women on the canoe strained their eyes to see into the distance. "Surely," they said to each other, "we will reach another island soon!"

One morning, as the sun rose, they saw something long and white lying on the water far ahead of them. "It must be a cloud!" they exclaimed. But as they drew nearer and nearer, they saw that the white cloud was actually two huge islands, bigger than any islands they had ever seen before. They landed on the shores of the northern islands, and decided to stay. From then on, the Maori called their new home *Aotearoa*—"Land of the Long White Cloud."

As the Maori explored the northern island, they discovered mountain after mountain, jagged rough valleys, and deep gorges cut down into the earth. They told this story to explain the shape of their new country.

Once upon a time, a great hero was born into a big family. His name was Maui. Although he was brave and strong, he was the youngest of many brothers. And his brothers didn't want to play with him!

"Take me hunting with you!" Maui would plead.

"No," his brothers would answer. "You're too little."

"Take me swimming with you!"

"No. You're too little."

"Take me fishing with you!"

"No. You're too little."

One day Maui got so tired of this answer that he climbed aboard his brothers' canoe with his fishing pole and hid. When the canoe was out in the middle of the ocean, he popped out of his hiding place.

"Here I am!" he announced. "Now I can fish with you! Give me some bait!"

His brothers looked at each other, annoyed. "No!" they said. "No bait! You can't fish with us. You're too little!"

But Maui was determined to fish. So he threw his hook over the side anyway. And while his brothers caught little, useless fish, Maui hooked the Most Giant Fish of All—a fish who lived at the bottom of the ocean, a fish so huge that when he began to pull it up, the sea began to boil and heave in protest.

"What are you doing?" his brothers yelled. "Are you trying to kill us?" And they leaped to their feet and began to hack and chop at the giant fish with their *meres*—their sharp-edged wooden clubs. As the giant fish rose up to the surface and the sun shone on it, its body became earth. Because the brothers had chopped and gouged it, the earth was full of mountains and valleys. And this new earth became known as "The Fish of Maui"—in the language of the Maori, "Te Ika-a-Maui."

"Te Ika-a-Maui" is the Maori name for the northern island of New Zealand. And although the story of Maui and his enormous fish is just a fairy tale, New Zealand *did* "rise up out of the sea." The islands of New Zealand were formed when volcanoes rose up out of the sea bed below, spewing lava and hot ash. The lava hit the seawater and cooled into stone. As time went on, soil collected on this stone and formed an island. Te Ika-a-Maui still has three active, smoking volcanoes on it, along with hot springs (water heated by under-ground lava streams) and hot pools of mud that bubble, pop, and steam all year long. Perhaps the Maui people were trying to describe this eruption from beneath the sea when they told the story of the Fish of Maui!

The Height of the Frankish Empire

Chapter Eleven
The Kingdom of the Franks

Clovis, The Ex-Barbarian

Now we're ready to travel back to the west. At the beginning of the last chapter, you put your finger on Rome and then moved it east and south, all the way down to New Zealand. Rome used to be the strongest empire in the ancient world. But at the beginning of the Middle Ages, barbarians invaded Rome. Rome became weaker and weaker, and other civilizations became stronger and stronger.

Let's imagine a journey from New Zealand, where the Maori live, back through some of these civilizations. Start by finding New Zealand on your map. Now paddle your canoe *north* (up, on your map) and *west* (left). You should see the coast of Australia just ahead of you! You'll need to paddle along the coast, still going north. Keep your eyes open, and you might see Aborigine canoes, out fishing for sea cattle.

You have a long journey ahead of you, up through the Pacific Ocean. Go on paddling! After many weeks, you'll find yourself approaching the islands of Japan, the "Land of the Rising Sun." Beach your canoe on the shores of Japan and wander across the country, and you'll see Chinese clothing, Chinese books, and Chinese buildings. Remember, China lent Japan its language, its architecture, and its customs, until Japan decided to break free!

Cross over the water between China and Japan (you'd better hire a boat!) and come ashore at the Chinese mainland. If you're feeling adventurous, you can hike south, into Korea, which sits between China and Japan. But you might stumble into the middle of a battle, because China and Japan are fighting to control Korea, which sits between them.

Find a sturdy mountain pony, hop on, and start your long journey west through Asia. If you take a little detour to the south (remember, south is *down* on a map or globe), you'll find yourself in India, where the Gupta kings ruled. Now travel west again. You'll need a boat, because you're going to sail through the Indian Ocean, across to the peninsula of Arabia. The Islamic Empire began here, following the lead of Muhammad. Climb out of your boat, rent a camel (you're going to have to plod through hot, sandy, deserts), and start your journey back north (up, on a map or globe).

Keep traveling north, and you'll arrive at the borders of the Byzantine Empire, the land once ruled by Justinian the Just Emperor, and his wife, the empress Theodora. The Byzantine Empire was once the eastern half of the old Roman Empire—until the Roman Empire split in two. Now go west (left) one more time. Are you swimming in the Mediterranean Sea? The land all around the Mediterranean used to belong to Rome. Swim over to Italy (the *peninsula* that looks like a boot), climb ashore, and walk up through Italy. Now you're standing on the top of an icy mountain range: the Alps.

Take a good look around! The land all around you was ruled by Rome until barbarians invaded. But a funny thing happened to these barbarians. When they came into Roman territory, they began to learn Roman customs. They built houses, like Roman houses, and lived in them, instead of roaming around on horseback. They discovered Roman customs, like shaving and taking baths. Missionaries taught them about Christianity. They learned to speak Latin. They became *civilized*. And

116

these ex-barbarians began to establish their own kingdoms, all over the land that once belonged to the Romans.

The land of Gaul, just north of the Mediterranean Sea, was invaded by barbarians called the Franks. The Franks were made up of several different tribes. And they didn't regard *themselves* as barbarians. As a matter of fact, they claimed that they were descended from the ancient inhabitants of the great city of Troy!

The Frankish tribes settled down in Gaul next to the Roman citizens who were already living there. Other barbarian tribes, called the Burgundians and the Allemani, settled in Gaul too. Now many different people lived side-by-side in Gaul. And they didn't like each other very much!

But even though the Romans and the Franks and the Burgundians and the Allemani were enemies, they became allies, just long enough to fight off the Huns. Do you remember that the Huns helped destroy Rome and invaded countries all the way over to India? The Huns were a frightening, savage warrior race. And the people of Gaul decided that although they hated each other, they hated the Huns even more!

So they united into one army under the leadership of a great fighter named Merovius. Merovius was the chief of a Frankish tribe. He led his army against the Huns—and defeated them! The Huns retreated from Gaul. And as soon as the Hun threat had vanished, the people of Gaul divided again into their warring tribes.

But Merovius's grandson, Clovis, always remembered the days when his grandfather had briefly made the Franks into one people. When Clovis was twenty, he inherited the leadership of his tribe. And he set out to make all of Gaul into one empire.

So Clovis married a princess from one barbarian tribe—Clotilda, a Burgundian. He fought other tribes and forced them to accept him as a leader. He defeated the last Roman soldiers left in Gaul. He convinced other Frankish chiefs to swear allegiance to him. And eventually, he ruled over all of Gaul. His empire became known as the Frankish Empire. Today, we call this part of the world *France*, after the Franks.

While he was conquering his empire, Clovis became a Christian. According to a medieval book called *The Chronicle of St. Denis,* Clovis converted to Christianity because he wanted God to help him defeat his enemies. Clovis's wife, Clotilda, was already a Christian. And she wanted her husband to become a Christian too. But Clovis refused, until he fought a great battle against the Allemani and saw that his men were being slaughtered. So he looked up to heaven. "God," he said, "I will serve you forever, if only you will give me the victory!"

The medieval story tells us, "Instantly, his men were filled with burning valor, and a great fear smote his enemies, so that they turned their backs and fled the battle." The Allemani leaders surrendered, and Clovis won the day.

As soon as he got home, Clovis went to find a bishop and asked him to explain Christianity. The bishop did, and Clovis agreed to be baptized. Now Clovis, the ex-barbarian, was an emperor—*and* a Christian. [1]

---

[1] There are several conflicting accounts of the conversion of Clovis in medieval chronicles, but all agree that his conversion took place during a battle (perhaps in imitation of Constantine's similar experience).

Four Tribes, One Empire

Clovis managed to unite the battling peoples of Gaul into one empire: the Franks. But could he *keep* them together?

Clovis decided that three things would help make the Franks, the Romans, Burgundians, and the Allemani into one people. First, he established a capital city at a place called Lutetia Parisiorium—an old Roman fortress, built on a hill near the river Seine. It was easy to defend, because anyone who attacked it would have to climb uphill while fighting! And there were already good, smooth, Roman roads leading to Lutetia Parisiorium. Clovis had a wall built around the hill and named his new city Paris. Now, all of his people could call Paris *their* capital city.

Second, Clovis decreed that everyone in his empire should become a Christian. When he was baptized, he had three thousand of his fighting men baptized at the same time. Do you think all of those men were Christians? Probably not! But Clovis knew that people who follow the same religion are less likely to attack each other. So he made Christianity the official religion of the Franks. And he built an enormous cathedral in Paris, called St. Genevieve.

Now Clovis had one religion in his country, and one capital city. But he needed one more thing to keep his country unified: One law.

The Franks and the Romans and the Burgundians and the Allemani all had different laws. Like Justinian, Clovis knew that a strong, peaceful country needs *one* set of laws that *everyone* follows.

So he had his scribes and clerics issue a new set of laws called the Salic Law.

These laws tell us quite a lot about the kingdom of the Franks! Here is one of the Salic Laws:

> ℃ If a Roman attacks a Frank and steals from him, he will pay twenty-five hundred denars.

This was a lot of money! A man would have to work for at least three months to earn 2500 denars. But then the law goes on:

> ℃ But if a Frank attacks a Roman and steals from him, he will pay fourteen hundred denars.

A Frank who attacked a Roman would pay a much smaller fine than a Roman who robbed a Frank. So although the Romans were part of the Frankish empire, they weren't given the same protections as the Franks. Does this seem fair to you? Here is another law:

> ℃ If a man calls another man "Fox," or "Hare," he will have to pay 120 denars.

Calling names was against the law! If you called someone a "fox," you were calling them sly and untrustworthy—like a spy. And if you called a man a "hare," you were saying that he was cowardly and anxious to run away from a fight. Loyalty to their country and bravery in battle were very important to the Franks!

> ℃ If anyone wants to move to another village, and even one person in the village doesn't want him there, he cannot move. If he does anyway, the people of the village must warn him three times

to leave. After the third warning, the people of the village can summon the king's men to come and take the offender away.

Clovis may have brought the Franks, Romans, Burgundians, and Allemani together into one empire—but it sounds as though some of them still didn't want to live close to each other! What if a Roman wanted to move into a Burgundian village? The people who lived there could refuse to accept him. The empire of the Franks was united, but it was not peaceful.

The Height of the Islamic Empire

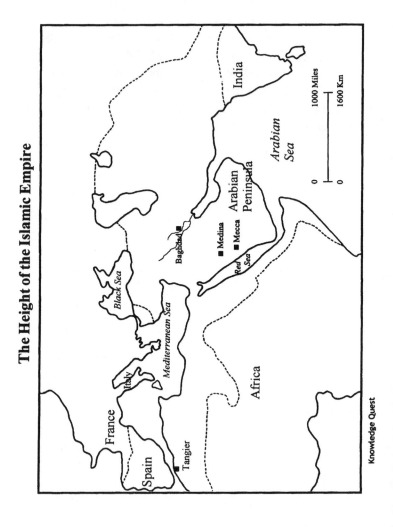

Knowledge Quest

122

Chapter Twelve
The Islamic Invasion

Just west of the Frankish empire, another tribe of barbarians had settled down in the land of Spain. The Visigoths had once stormed through the ancient world, creating havoc and spreading terror. But now they too had a kingdom of their own. They had adopted Roman customs. They had become Christians. And they had a king.

But when their king died suddenly, the Visigoths quarreled over who would be king next. Some of them wanted the king's sons to rule. But the strongest noblemen insisted that a warrior named Rodrigo would be a better king. They put Rodrigo on the throne and forced everyone to accept him.

The sons of the dead king were furious. They wanted to rule! So they sent messengers down to North Africa and asked the great fighter Tariq Bin Ziyad to bring his armies up and help them drive Rodrigo out.

That was a big mistake!

You see, Tariq was a Muslim commander. And his armies were the armies of the Islamic Empire. Do you remember how the Islamic Empire began? Followers of Muhammad, who preached that Allah was the one true God, took over the cities of Mecca and Medina. Then they took over most of Arabia. Then they attacked the Byzantine Empire and took some of *its* land. They conquered Egypt, and then they spread across North Africa, just beneath the Mediterranean Sea. They built holy cities in North Africa. And they added twelve thousand North African men, called *Berbers,* to their army.

One of these Berber men was Tariq. He was only a slave. But when the Islamic armies captured Tariq's home town, he converted to Islam and joined the conquerors. He fought willingly in the front lines of every battle! Soon Tariq's bravery became known to his commanding officers. He was promoted again and again until he became a general.

Under Tariq's leadership, the Islamic army charged through the rest of North Africa, all the way over to the city of Tangier. Look at your map, and you'll see that Tangier sits right at the edge of the Mediterranean Sea—the sea that looks like a flying duck. Tangier is on the "beak" of the duck. And just across the water is Spain. Once Tariq and his forces were in Tangier, it was a very short trip over to Spanish land!

So when Tariq got a message *inviting* him into Spain, he was happy to oblige. But he didn't go over to Spain to help the king's sons get their throne back. He went to capture Spain for Islam.

He organized seven thousand fighting men into small groups. One hot May morning, each group got onto a ship. The ships sailed in a long procession across the water to the coast of Spain. Tariq was in the first ship. He leaped over the edge of the ship, into the water, and waded ashore. He climbed up to the top of a huge rock nearby and watched as each ship came up to the Spanish sand. And as soon as all of his men had come ashore, he ordered, "Burn the ships!"

"But sir!" his soldiers cried. "Why are you doing this? How will we ever return home?"

Tariq glared down at them.

"We haven't come here to return," he said. "We will either conquer—or perish!" And with that, he led his armies into Spain.

The Visigoths, divided by their quarrel over the throne, couldn't resist Tariq's fighting men. Soon Rodrigo and the king's sons and the rest of the Visigoths were all under Islamic rule. And Spain remained a Muslim country for many years. Spanish followers of Islam became known as *Moors*. They built great mosques all across Spain

A Moorish mosque and fountain.

and decorated them with delicate, complicated patterns. They designed magnificent gardens and cool, open buildings for the hot Spanish cities. They planted new crops in Spain: cherries, apples, almonds, and bananas. Cities in Spain became great centers for philosophy, poetry, and music. Spanish mathematicians used the numbers that we still use today; we now call these "Arabic numerals."

The rock where Tariq stood to watch his ships come in became known as *Jabal Tariq,* the "mountain of Tariq." Over many years, *Jabal Tariq* became pronounced *Gibraltar.* Today, that rocky hill is still known as *the rock of Gibraltar.*

The Empire of Charlegmagne

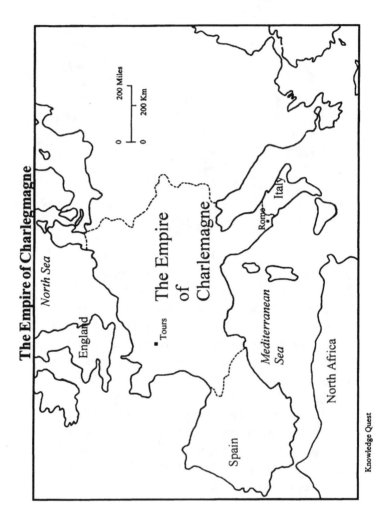

200 Miles

200 Km

North Sea

England

The Empire
of
Charlemagne

Tours

Rome

Italy

Mediterranean
Sea

Spain

North Africa

Knowledge Quest

126

Chapter Thirteen
The Great Kings of France

Charles the Hammer

After the Islamic army invaded Spain, they didn't want to stop. The Muslim fighters planned to charge right up into France and conquer the kingdom of the Franks as well. "We are like a mighty wind!" they boasted. "No one can stop the wind when it blows. And no one can stop the armies of Allah."

But then the wind met a hammer.

The "hammer" was Charles Martel, the new king of the Franks. Charles had a hard time becoming king! Not everyone wanted him to inherit the throne. He was even thrown in jail to keep him from claiming the crown.

But Charles escaped from jail. He gathered together an army, and he led his men into battle against his enemies. He fought so hard, and he was so persistent in "hammering" the armies of his foes, that he gained the nickname *Martel*—which, in the language of the Franks, meant "The Hammer." He won the throne of the Franks through sheer determination. And he didn't intend to give it up to the Islamic empire! When he heard that the Islamic armies had blown through Spain and were approaching his borders, he gathered his men together and went to meet them. The Franks and the Muslims met at the city of Tours. Here is how one medieval Arab chronicler described the battle:

When the Muslims came into the land of the Franks, they passed through it like a desolating storm.

They laid waste the country and took captives without number! All the Franks trembled at the terrible army. They ran to their king, Charles, and told him that the Muslims were making havoc in their land.

"Be of good cheer!" the king told them. And he got on his horse and led a numberless host of soldiers towards the city of Tours.

Now, the troops of the Muslims were camped outside the walls of the city of Tours. They had gathered so much wealth, and food, and clothing, and horses, and gold that they were weighed down with spoils. Their general looked over the camp. "My men are not ready to fight!" he thought. "They are more worried about their plunder than about the coming battle! I should order them to abandon everything except their scimitars and their war-horses."

But he was afraid that his soldiers would revolt against him if he ordered them to give up their booty. So he decided to let them keep it. And when they insisted that they were ready to attack the city of Tours, and to steal from it all of the wonderful riches inside, he agreed—even though he knew that Charles, the king of the Franks, was approaching with a great army to defend it.

So the army of the Muslims prepared to attack the city walls. But as they were besieging it, Charles himself came into sight, with his army behind him. The horsemen of Islam charged out to meet him, and the two armies fought all day, until night came and they could no longer see each other. As soon as the grey light of dawn came, they began to fight again.

But when the Muslims saw that Charles was coming closer and closer to their tents, they began to think of all the wealth inside. "The Franks will plunder our camp!" they cried. "We will lose our wealth!" And instead of fighting, they rode back to protect their tents. Their general tried to rally them back to the front lines— but he was surrounded by Franks and killed. And when he fell, the whole host fled before their foes. [1]

The Franks had won the day! And Charles Martel had hammered his enemies, once again.

The Greatest King: Charlemagne

Clovis, the first ruler of the Frankish empire, was a great king. Charles Martel, also known as Charles the Hammer, was an even greater king. But Charles's grandson, also named Charles, was the greatest Frankish king of all. In the Middle Ages, many people thought he was the greatest king in the whole world. He became known as "Charles the Great"—in Latin, *Charlemagne*.

Charlemagne was worried about his kingdom. He was afraid that the Franks were beginning to return to their old, barbarian ways. They were forgetting about Christianity; they weren't going to church or having their children baptized. And the children weren't taught to read and write.

So Charlemagne set out to make his kingdom prosperous—and Christian. He paid hundreds of monks to copy out manuscripts of the Scriptures. He built new roads and bridges so that teachers and priests could travel easily through the land of the Franks. He put a famous monk named Alcuin in charge of starting schools

---

[1] This story of the battle is a retelling of an account by an unnamed Arab historian, quoted in Edward Creasy's *Fifteen Decisive Battles of the World*. The Battle of Tours is also known as the Battle of Poitiers.

for boys all over the kingdom. And he tried to make the Franks cleaner and more civilized. He taught them better ways to farm. He ordered them to bring their children to church. And he even scolded them for treading grapes into wine with their dirty bare feet!

But most of all, Charlemagne fought wars. He spent thirty years fighting wars to make his kingdom bigger. He led his soldiers into battle himself, brandishing his great golden sword *Joyeuse* over his head. And when he won, he was ruthless. He forced his prisoners to be baptized as Christians—or die! Charlemagne's kingdom grew and grew. He fixed up the old, crumbling Roman roads, so that they ran all through his new empire. He ordered new bridges and churches built. And he told his builders to copy the Roman arches and columns in his new buildings. By the time Charlemagne was as old as your grandfather, he ruled over an empire that contained Roman buildings, Roman roads, and almost half of the land that used to belong to Rome.

One Christmas, when he was almost sixty, Charlemagne traveled to Rome to visit the pope. On Christmas morning, he put on the clothes that a wealthy Roman man would wear, and went to the Church of St. Peter for the Christmas service. He knelt down in front of the altar to pray. Suddenly the pope took out a golden crown, covered with glittering jewels, and placed it on Charlemagne's head. "You are the great and peace-bringing Emperor of the Romans!" he declared. And the whole congregation shouted out, "Hail to Charles, crowned by God the great and peace-bringing Emperor of the Romans!" [2]

---

[2] Charlemagne accepted the title of "Roman Emperor," but the word "Holy" did not become part of this title until 1155.

Of course, the Roman Empire had fallen apart long ago. But people still remembered that the Roman emperors had made the ancient world safe for a little while. They remembered that Rome had been a rich, comfortable empire. They remembered the Pax Romana, the peace that the Roman rulers kept all through their territory. And they hoped that Charlemagne would bring this same peace and wealth to the medieval world.

Charlemagne was a great ruler, but his empire was never as powerful as the ancient empire of Rome. And although he wanted to be as educated and civilized as Julius Caesar and the other emperors of Rome,

Charlemagne had never been taught how to read and write properly. He hired teachers to show him how to make his letters.

Scholars in Charlemagne's day wrote letters that look like these.

Until he was an old man, he kept a writing tablet under his pillow. Whenever he woke up at night, he would sit up in bed and practice making letters on his tablet. But he never really learned to write. As a matter of fact, *you* probably write better than Charlemagne—Charles the Great, the Roman Emperor of the Middle Ages.

Viking Lands

Greenland

North Atlantic Ocean

North America

Newfoundland ("Vineland")

Iceland

Scandinavian Peninsula

Norway

Sweden

Denmark

Rhine River

Franks

Seine River

North Sea

England

Normandy

Spain

Italy

Mediterranean Sea

Islamic Empire

0   500 Miles

0   1000 Km

Knowledge Quest

132

Chapter Fourteen
The Arrival of the Norsemen

The Viking Invasion

Charlemagne, the king of the Franks, ruled an empire that stretched all through Europe. His people called him the "Roman Emperor," because they said, "Charlemagne's kingdom is like the old Roman Empire, rebuilt. We can live in peace and prosperity, just like the Romans of old!"

But do you remember what happened to the old Roman Empire? Barbarians attacked it. And soon the empire of the Franks had its own "barbarians" to fight off. Fierce warriors arrived by ship from the north. They attacked cities along the coast—and even sailed down the Rhine and the Seine rivers into the middle of Frankish land. These invading warriors were called North-men or *Norsemen.*

Look on your map, up above the kingdom of the Franks, and you'll see the North Sea, a cold, grey sea often covered with clouds of mist. A *peninsula* reaches down into the North Sea. (Remember: A peninsula is a piece of land surrounded by water on three sides.) This peninsula is called *Scandinavia.* The Norsemen came from the kingdoms of Norway, Denmark, and Sweden, on the Scandinavian peninsula.

Most Norsemen didn't fight for a living. They were farmers who could no longer find good land to farm in Scandinavia. So they built ships and set out to find new homes. In the language of the Norsemen, a man who went adventuring by sea was said to have gone "i viking." So sometimes these Norsemen were also called *Vikings.*

The Viking ships were long and narrow, with fearsome dragons' heads on their fronts to frighten enemies. The ships were built with unusual, flat bottoms. Boat builders in other countries made boats with round

A Viking longship

bottoms that jutted down beneath the water. With a round-bottomed boat, you could only sail in deep water. Otherwise, the bottom of your boat would scrape against the bottom of the sea. But the flat-bottomed Viking boats floated right on the water's surface. They could sail right into shallow water—and right up onto the sand of a beach!

Imagine that you've come down to the banks of the Rhine River with your water-buckets. It's a cool, foggy morning. Your farm is right up the road, and you have cows waiting to be milked and grain waiting to be hoed. But first you need to haul water up from the river. The Rhine is shallow here, so you wade out knee-deep and bend down to scoop water into your buckets. Little waves splash gently around you as you pull your buckets through the calm, clear surface. But another sound is mingling with the splash of the waves. Could it be the muffled sound of oars? You strain your eyes to see into the mist. Long, dark shapes are moving indistinctly in the fog. Suddenly a carved dragon's head springs out of the mist. It is the front of a Viking longship! The ship is propelled forward, right onto the sand of the beach. You spring aside as Viking warriors pour over its edges, waving battle-axes and double-edged swords. Three more longships loom into view through the mist. You've been invaded by Vikings!

While Charlemagne was king, the Vikings only invaded the kingdom of the Franks occasionally. Charlemagne wasn't afraid of the Vikings. He called them "worthless scamps"! And his army was so well-organized that the Vikings couldn't conquer it.

But after Charlemagne died, his empire was divided between his three grandsons. Now the Franks no longer had a strong, united army. And the Vikings were ready to invade! They sailed into France again and again with their flat-bottomed boats. They burned cities and stole treasure. They raided the western part of France so often that the king of the western Franks finally gave them a piece of it for their very own. Now the Vikings had a new homeland. The Franks called it Northmen's Land. Soon it became known as *Normandy*.

Do you remember what happened to the barbarians who settled down in Rome? They became more and more like Romans. The same thing happened to the Vikings. After they settled down in Normandy, they learned to speak and dress like the French. Many of them converted to Christianity. And they no longer went "i viking." The Vikings had become *Normans*.

Eric the Red and "Eric's Son"

The Vikings sailed down the coast of Europe all
the way to Spain. They sailed into the Mediterranean
Sea. And they sailed west, into the Atlantic Ocean.

One Viking family sailed west all the way over to
Iceland, a small island in the cold North Atlantic, and
settled there. They had to leave Scandinavia because
the father of the family, Thorvald, had killed a man in a
fight. And soon it became clear that Thorvald's son Eric
had inherited his father's temper! Eric grew to be a
fierce, broad-shouldered man with bright red hair. His
friends called him Eric the Red.

One day Eric the Red got into a quarrel with his
neighbors. The argument grew louder and louder and
soon turned into a fight. By the time it ended, two of
Eric's neighbors were dead! The other Vikings in
Iceland ordered Eric the Red to leave Iceland. So Eric
sailed west again, looking for a new home. Soon he
came to the shores of a brand new land. It was an icy,
rocky, bleak place, so far north that during the summer
the sun never set. And during the winter, night lasted all
day long for three whole months! Who would want to
live in such a place?

Eric the Red didn't know. So he named his new
land *Greenland*. He hoped that this cheerful name
would encourage other Vikings from Iceland to come
with him. And the name worked; he convinced twenty-
five boats full of settlers to come with him to Greenland.

But on the long, dangerous sea voyage, eleven of
the boats were destroyed. And when the cold, wet,
unhappy Vikings climbed out onto the shores of
Greenland, they didn't find any green. They found a

136

huge island covered with thick, rough ice. Only a small, narrow strip along the coast had any grass or trees on it.

For years, the unhappy colonists lived in Greenland. They raised their skinny cows and hunted whales and seals. But they couldn't plant fields of grain or grass, because of the ice that covered their island. So they learned to collect sealskins, polar bear furs, horns from reindeer, and ivory walrus tusks, and to trade these to visitors in exchange for grain. But even with this extra grain, the colony did not have enough to eat. They had so little food that the children did not grow to be very tall. Archaeologists who have dug up the graves of these Viking settlers on Greenland have found that the skeletons of grown women are only four feet tall—and most of the men are shorter than five feet!

In this unhappy place, Eric the Red had a son. This son also had red hair. He became known as Leif Ericsson: Leif, Eric's son. And he was determined to find a better place to live.

When he was a teenager, Leif used to sit around the campfires at night and listen to the tales told by the older men. One of these men, an explorer named Bjarni, told a story about his adventures in the North Atlantic. "I was sailing home from a fishing voyage," Bjarni explained, "when I saw a shore off in the distance. It had hills covered with trees. I don't know what land that shore belonged to, and I didn't have time to go explore it. And I've never had a chance to find it again." As Leif listened, he thought to himself, "When I grow old enough, I will go and find that mysterious new land."

So when Leif became a man, he bought Bjarni's boat from him and decided to go and find this new country. He begged his father Eric to come with him, but Eric refused. "I am now too old to go exploring," he protested. "I don't want to sail in an open boat across the icy ocean. It will hurt my old bones!"

But Leif insisted. "You will bring good luck to us!" he said.

Finally Eric agreed to go. On the morning of departure, Eric and Leif set off on horseback for the harbor. But on the way, Eric's horse stumbled and the old man fell off. Leif leaped down to help his father. But Eric had broken his foot.

"Go without me," Eric said. "I am no longer meant to discover new lands."

So Leif set off with thirty-five followers. They sailed across the icy northern oceans in open boats. For days, they could not eat any hot food or sleep under shelter. They were soaked by waves and rain. But they kept on sailing until they found Bjarni's mysterious land— a land of hills, with plenty of grass and trees, and with clear streams running down into the ocean.

Leif and his men landed and began to explore. But soon they found that one of their men was missing! Leif set out to find the missing man, and discovered him in the middle of a patch of wild grapes, eating as fast as he could. "Now," Leif said to his men, "we will gather these grapes, and take them back with us to our friends at home."

So with their ships full of grapes, Leif and his men set off for Greenland. Leif called the new land he had discovered *Vineland*, the Land of the Grapes.

Other Greenlanders followed Leif's path back to this new land of grapes and grass. But when they arrived, they were met by native tribes which were ready to defend Vineland from these Viking invaders. The Greenlanders called these native tribes *Skraelings*, which probably meant "screechers," because of the terrifying battle yells the natives used when they attacked! The Greenlanders built huts and tried to defend themselves against the Skraelings, but eventually they were forced to give up their settlements in Vineland and return to Greenland.

So where was this new land—this Vineland? Leif had discovered North America! The Skraelings were Native Americans, defending their tribal lands. Today, archaeologists have found remains of Viking houses, jewelry, and wood carvings in Newfoundland, on the Canadian coast. Some historians think that the Vikings also explored down into what is now the United States. Archaeologists have found a rock in Maine that has carvings in its surface which look like Viking letters, or *runes*. And some people claim that similar carvings have been found as far inland as Minnesota!

Historians continue to argue about whether these runes were really made by Vikings. But even if they didn't go all the way to Minnesota, the Vikings were in North American a thousand years ago—hundreds of years before Christopher Columbus journeyed across the ocean.

The Norse Gods

The Vikings believed that there were many gods and goddesses, and that they lived in a land above the sky called Asgard. Asgard was connected with earth by a rainbow bridge, but only the gods could walk on the rainbow bridge. The Vikings believed that Odin, the king of the gods, lived in a great feasting hall called Valhalla. After great battles on earth, Odin would send warrior-maidens called Valkyries down the rainbow bridge to gather up the souls of dead warriors and bring them to Valhalla.

Thor, the thunder-god, was one of the most warlike of all the Viking gods—and so he was one of their favorites! He was a short-tempered god, always getting himself into trouble for no reason, just like thunderstorms that blow suddenly up out of the middle of a hot afternoon. This is one of the stories that the Vikings told about Thor.

Thor and the Giant King

One fine afternoon, the gods were feasting in Asgard. They ate, drank, and told stories. But as night came on, the mead ran out. There was nothing left to drink, and no kettle left to brew more mead in. The gods began to sulk.

"No mead!" they complained. "We might as well go home and go to bed."

But Thor rose up from his seat. "I'll go and get mead for the feast!" he said. "The giant Skymer has a kettle a mile wide, full of the most delectable, golden, honey-flavored mead I've ever tasted. I'm off to take his kettle *and* his mead!"

So Thor leaped into his goat-drawn chariot and drove it down the rainbow bridge to earth. He thundered along in his chariot until the sun had set and dark covered the land. Off to the side of the road, he saw the lights of a humble peasant house. He yawned.

"I'm tired of traveling," he said to himself. "I'll stop for the night."

So he drew his chariot up to the low stone house, tied up his goats, and swaggered in. As soon as the wife of the house saw him, she dropped her clay bowl of bran on the floor.

"One of the gods is in my house!" she wailed. "And I have nothing to feed him but bran and water!"

"Never mind," Thor said. "We'll eat my goats." So he walked out to the chariot, killed his goats, skinned

140

them, and gave them to the woman to roast. He put the goatskins down beside the table.

"Eat as much as you like," he said to the woman and to her husband and her children. "But don't break the bones, and put them all back on top of the skins when you're finished. Tomorrow I will need them."

So the poor family ate and ate and ate until they were full. Thor collected the bones in the skins, tied them up, and then lay down next to the fire to sleep. Soon his snores were shaking the house.

The oldest son of the family, Thialfi, was kept awake by the snoring. By midnight he was hungry again. Remembering the delicious goat meat, he licked his lips. Finally he crept down to the goatskins, slid a thigh-bone out from underneath Thor's arm, cracked it open, and sucked out the marrow.

In the morning Thor woke up, stretched, and bounded to his feet. He swung his giant hammer overtop of the goatskins. Immediately the goats stood before him, whole and alive.

"Let's go!" Thor shouted. He drove the goats towards the door. But then he saw that one was limping. In anger, he shouted, "Who broke my goat's leg?"

The woman and her husband and children fell down on the ground in terror. But the son, Thialfi, stood up, even though his knees shook with fright. "I did, O Thor," he said bravely.

"Then you will come with me as my servant," Thor ordered, "and together we will journey to the land of the giants to steal the mead kettle that belongs to Skymer."

So together the two set off. Soon Thor yawned again.

"Time for a nap," he said. "Look around for a place where I can rest undisturbed."

He halted the chariot, and Thialfi scurried off. Soon he returned. "There is a cave just around the next curve, O Thor," he reported. "It has five dry, warm caverns. We can sleep there."

Thor followed the boy around the bend in the road. Sure enough, a cave with five smaller rooms in it was just visible through the trees. He lay down in the nearest cavern, pulled his cloak over his head, and drifted off to sleep. But a terrible roaring and thundering woke him up.

"What is that noise?" he demanded. "I am the only god who can bring thunder!" He scrambled out of the cave and followed the sound of the snoring. On the other side of the forest, he saw an enormous man stretched out asleep. His fingers were longer than Thialfi was tall, and even lying down, his stomach was higher than Thor's head.

Enraged, Thor swung his mighty hammer and struck the snorer between the eyes. Such an enormous blow would have driven a tree right into the ground like a matchstick! But the giant snorted and reached up to flick at his forehead.

"Dratted flies," he muttered. His eyes opened, and he saw Thor with the hammer in his hand, ready to strike. The giant sat up and chuckled, and his laugh shook the ground.

"Who is this little man with the tiny hammer?" he asked. "Can this be the mighty Thor, come to see me all the way from Asgard?"

"Who are you?" Thor demanded.

"Why, I am Skymer, the giant who lives in the castle just up there." The giant yawned and glanced around him. "Oh," he said, "I see you've found my glove. I wondered where I dropped it!" And with that, he picked up the cave where Thor had been sleeping, and drew it onto his hand.

When Thor realized that the five "caverns" had actually been the fingers of the giant's glove, he felt foolish. But he was determined to steal Skymer's kettle. "Well," he demanded, "aren't you even going to ask me in for a feast? Don't you know how to welcome the gods?"

"A feast?" Skymer said. "Certainly. Come on, little man." He leapt to his feet and strode across the ground, each step covering a mile. Thor whipped his goats into a gallop just to keep up with him! Thialfi was left far behind. Soon they arrived at gates that reached so far up into the sky that Thor could not see the tops. Skymer pushed them open and showed Thor into his feasting hall. Thor clambered up onto a bench and stretched his neck to peer up onto the table. There, he could see Skymer's kettle, and next to it an enormous horn filled with mead.

"I'd offer you some mead," Skymer sighed, "but my horn is too large for you to drink from."

"Nonsense!" Thor snapped. "Give it here!" He seized the horn and tipped it to his lips. He drank and drank and drank until he thought he would burst, but the mead in the horn remained at the same level. Finally he dropped the horn, gasping for breath.

"Dear me," Skymer said. "Is the horn too full for you? What else can I offer you? Perhaps you'd be better off playing with my cat."

He lifted his finger, and an enormous grey cat bounded into the hall. It patted at Thor with one enormous paw. Thor braced himself, but the cat licked him with its rough tongue and knocked him flat onto the floor.

Enraged, Thor leapt up, put his shoulders under the cat's belly, and did his best to heave it from the ground. But the cat arched its back and purred. All Thor could do was to lift one paw from the ground.

143

"You're even weaker than I thought," Skymer said gloomily. "I'll find you a playmate worthy of your strength." He opened a door at the end of the hall, and in shuffled an old, bent woman, so ancient that she could barely move, and so shriveled that she seemed more like a raisin than a human being.

"Here," Skymer said. "Wrestle with my old nanny."

Thor hurled himself at the old woman. But she raised one skinny arm, threw him to the ground, and pinned him there. He struggled and huffed and strained, but she put one old foot on his chest and kept him on the ground.

Skymer leaned down. "Well, Thor," he said. "Do you think you can steal my kettle now?"

Thor, humiliated, could only shake his head.

"Then let me tell you what you have done," Skymer said. "When you swung your hammer at my head, you struck the earth so hard that you opened a valley three miles wide and a mile deep. When you drank from my horn, you were drinking from the sea—and you drank so much that you lowered the surface of the ocean. I thought you would drink the sea dry! When you lifted my cat, you were lifting the Midgard Serpent—the world serpent that lies around the edge of the earth with its tail in its mouth. You should not have been able to budge it, but you lifted it almost to the sky.

"But despite your might, you could not beat the old woman, for she is Old Age. And no one can conquer Old Age. It brings even the strongest men to the earth, weak as children."

Thor roared out with fury over the giant's trickery. He jumped to his feet and swung his hammer over his head, ready to fight. But in a moment the giant, the old woman, the horn of mead, the cat, and the castle itself all shimmered into the air. And Thor stood alone in the middle of a lonely forest, swinging his hammer and shouting at emptiness.

England and Normandy

Knowledge Quest

Chapter Fifteen
The First Kings of England

The Vikings Invade England

The Vikings settled in Iceland, Greenland, and North America. They invaded France, took over part of it, and named their new kingdom Normandy. And they also invaded the islands of Britain.

Look at your map, just above Normandy, and you'll see Britain. The southern part of the largest island is called England; the northern part is called Scotland; and the western part is called Wales. The smaller island is called Ireland. Do you remember what we've already learned about the British Isles? The first people who lived there were called Celts. The Romans tried to conquer the Celts, but only managed to take over a small part of the island. After the Roman Empire fell apart, barbarian tribes named Angles and Saxons came into England and settled down there. Many of the Celts retreated into Scotland, Ireland, and Wales. And a few years later, a monk named Augustine came to England to preach Christianity to the Angles and the Saxons.

When the Vikings began to go "i viking," looking for new land to farm, they sailed down to British Isles and landed in Scotland and Ireland. They raided farms and monasteries and stole food and treasure. The Celts and the Anglo-Saxons were terrified of the Vikings! The Vikings weren't Christians, and they didn't pay any attention to the British custom of leaving priests and monks alone. Instead, they burned monasteries and churches, stole beautiful illuminated manuscripts, and kidnapped women and children to serve as wives and slaves! "Never before has such terror appeared in Britain as we have now suffered," wrote one Anglo-Saxon historian, a man named Alcuin. Another history that was written during the Middle Ages, the *Anglo-Saxon Chronicle*, says, "They lay waste everything in sight. They trample the holy relics under foot. They throw down the altars….Some of the monks they kill outright. Others they carry away with them. A great many they insult and beat and fling out naked."

Some of these Viking invaders took their treasure and went back home. But others decided that they liked Ireland and Scotland. They claimed some of the land as their own and settled down to farm it. And they sent messages back to their friends and relations in Scandinavia. "Come over to this new country!" they said. "There is rich land here, and no one to defend it!"

Why did the Vikings find it so easy to attack Britain? Because Britain did not have a strong king to fight back! In fact, England was divided into seven different kingdoms. Maybe, if they had all joined together under one leader, these kingdoms could have driven the Vikings out, just like Charlemagne did, over in the land of the Franks. But separately, the English kingdoms were too weak to resist. So the Vikings kept on coming. Soon, a huge band of Viking invaders called "The Great Army" landed in England. It was led by two Viking brothers, named Halfdan and Ivar the Boneless. Ivar the Boneless got his name because he was so long and skinny that he looked as though he'd been stretched out—like Silly Putty!

The Great Army marched through England, capturing kingdoms right and left. They spent ten years raiding English farms, fighting, and looting. Finally, they began to settle down. Ivar the Boneless went over into Ireland with his men, and Halfdan stayed in England and divided his conquered lands up among *his* men. Now the Vikings were living on farms of their own.

These Viking farms were in the middle of England. And there was still plenty of English land to the south, down in the kingdom of Wessex. The Vikings weren't done fighting yet. They wanted *all* of England, not just part of it. And without a strong king, the English could not defend themselves. "Why not keep going south?" the Vikings asked themselves. "We'll just conquer all of England right down to the sea!"

But the Vikings didn't count on meeting a strong English king, down there in the south! Soon, this king would lead the English against the Vikings—and defeat them.

Alfred the Great

The kingdom of Wessex, down in the south of England, watched the Viking invasion with fear. When the Vikings arrived at the borders of their kingdom, the noblemen of Wessex collected bags and bags of gold and went out to meet them. "Here," they said. "Take our gold and go away!"

The Vikings took the gold and left—for a little while. But soon one of Halfdan's commanders, a warrior named Guthorm, decided that he wanted Wessex after all. So he took a band of fierce fighters with him and headed back down south. "Give me more gold!" he demanded, "or I'll invade!"

The people of Wessex thought, "Soon we're going to run out of gold. We need a strong king to defeat Guthorm and his warriors!" So they appointed a nobleman named Alfred to be their leader.

Alfred knew that he needed time to collect an army. So he sent Guthorm a little more gold, just enough to convince him to leave Wessex alone for a few more months. Alfred started to train the farmers of Wessex to fight. But Guthorm decided to mount a surprise attack! He marched south with his warriors at Christmastime— during the winter, when armies usually stayed quietly in their camps waiting for warmer weather.

Alfred wasn't expecting an invasion. After all, he and the nobles of Wessex had just paid Guthorm to leave them in peace. When Guthorm's army came charging down on him, Alfred wasn't ready. His soldiers were still scattered all over Wessex, and he was celebrating Christmas with only a few bodyguards.

The English were terrified! Many of them left England and headed for France. They were sure that Alfred would be killed by Guthorm. And Alfred himself was forced to flee into the wild countryside of Wessex. There he hid, pretending not to be the king. According to one legend, Alfred stopped at a peasant's hut and begged for shelter. The peasant and his wife didn't know who this weary, mud-splattered stranger was. But they took pity on him and let him have food and a bed in exchange for help with the household chores. Alfred humbly did whatever he was told.

One day, the woman made some cakes out of oatmeal and water and put them on the stones of her hearth to bake. "I'm going to collect firewood," she told Alfred. "Watch the cakes for me and make sure they don't burn." And she went out to gather wood, leaving Alfred in front of the fire. But the king soon forgot about the cakes. He was worrying about Guthorm and the invading Vikings. The cakes began to smoke and blacken, but Alfred didn't notice. He was too busy wondering how he could defeat the Vikings!

150

When the woman came back with her armful of firewood, she dropped the sticks and ran to the fire. "What's wrong with you?" she scolded Alfred. "Don't you see that the cakes are burning? You'll eat them fast enough. Can't you even help cook them?" Alfred was too ashamed to tell her that she was scolding the king!

But soon Alfred managed to think of a plan. He

Alfred the Great

decided that he would stay in hiding until spring—so that his soldiers, who were all farmers, could plant their crops before they started fighting. After all, if he took his farmers away from their fields before they could plant their grain, there would be no food in the summer and fall. Even if they won the fight against the

Vikings, they might starve to death. So he hid all spring on a little hill, surrounded by swamps and briars. He sent out secret messages to all of his men: "Plant your crops and then come to my headquarters. We will collect an army to fight against Guthorm and his Vikings!"

Finally Alfred collected a big enough army to face Guthorm. And in the meantime, Guthorm's army had shrunk. Many of his warriors had gotten bored, waiting around to fight. They had settled down to grow crops of their own instead! By the time the two armies met, the English were as strong as the Vikings. They fought an enormous battle at a place called Salisbury Plain. And the English drove the Vikings right off the battlefield. The Vikings fled into a nearby castle and barred the gates. So Alfred and his men surrounded the castle and kept food and water from going into it. Soon Guthorm and his Vikings could no longer hold out. They surrendered! Guthorm agreed to go away. He traveled back north and settled down to raise crops. The warrior had become a farmer. And Alfred had truly become a king.

When Alfred died, he was buried in a cathedral in Wessex. But later his body was moved to another church, called Hyde Abbey. Hyde Abbey was destroyed, and a prison was built overtop of Alfred's grave. Then the prison was destroyed as well. Eventually the English forgot where Alfred's body lay. Just a few years ago, in 1999, archaeologists figured out that Alfred's grave was underneath a parking lot! They dug up the parking lot and found pieces of rock that belonged to Alfred's coffin. But the bones were gone. What happened to them? No one knows. Perhaps the prison inmates found Alfred's bones!

The Battle of Hastings

After Alfred died, the kings who followed had to keep fighting off Viking invasions. Alfred's son Edward was a strong, fierce leader who protected his kingdoms and even took some of the northern parts of England back from the Vikings. But the kings after Edward were not as successful. One hundred years after Alfred's death, his descendent Ethelred was defeated by a Viking king named Sweyn Forkbeard. Sweyn had a very long and bushy beard which he wore in two braids, like a fork! He became the king of England. And Ethelred, who had to flee to Normandy, got his own nickname. He was called Ethelred the Unready, because he wasn't able to keep the Vikings away.

After Sweyn Forkbeard, the descendents of the Vikings ruled England for many years. But all the time, the children of the Vikings and the children of the Anglo-Saxons were living side by side, trading with each other and marrying each other. England was becoming a mix of Anglo-Saxon and Viking. The English stopped thinking of themselves as Viking or Anglo-Saxon. They were just "English."

But soon a whole new race of warriors would invade England.

The trouble began when Edward the Confessor, who ruled England for over twenty years, began to get old. He had no sons, so his advisors decided that a nobleman named Harold should be the next king of England after Edward's death. Harold was a strong fighter with soldiers of his own who were loyal to him. And he was from Wessex, just like the great king Alfred.

But Edward's distant cousin William thought *he* should inherit the English throne. William wasn't even English. He was French, and he lived in Normandy, the French kingdom of the Vikings. But William was married to an English princess, and he *was* related to the king. He protested that he should be Edward's heir. But the English advisors refused to listen. They didn't want a Norman ruler!

One day, William heard a startling piece of news. Harold, sailing along the coast of Wessex, had been caught in a storm and blown off course. His ship had been driven by the winds all the way across the water between England and France—and had wrecked on the shores of Normandy.

William went down to the shore and rescued Harold from the wreckage. He took Harold back up to his castle, gave him dry clothes and a place to sleep, and planned a huge feast in his honor for the next night. At the feast, Harold was seated on a *dais* (a raised platform for an honored guest). He was surrounded by tables draped in scarlet and gold cloth, covered with meat and drink. Jugglers and acrobats entertained him.

But Harold was nervous. He knew that William wanted to be Edward's heir. And even though William was acting friendly, Harold was in William's castle—with the doors locked!

Sure enough, at the end of the feast, William asked Harold to put his hands flat on the table and swear to give William the English throne. Harold was afraid to defy William in his own castle, so he put his hands on the table and swore the oath. But then William whipped the tablecloth away. The "table" in front of Harold was a box with the bones of saints in it! Harold had sworn an oath on sacred *relics* (saints' remains, which were thought to have miraculous powers). Now he was bound to keep his promise!

William finally let Harold go back to England. Several years later, Edward the Confessor died. At once William sent messengers to Harold, demanding that Harold honor his sacred promise. But Harold refused. "I will be king of England!" he declared.

So the English noblemen held a grand ceremony to make Harold king. But they were nervous. A bad omen hovered on the horizon: Halley's Comet! Halley's Comet comes around every 76 years, but the English didn't know this. All they knew was that a giant light was moving through the sky. They were sure that this light had some terrible meaning. "Over England," one monk wrote, "is a sign in the skies such has never been seen before!"

And sure enough, just as Harold was crowned, bad news came. William and his army were ready to attack!

William had prepared carefully for his invasion. He landed his army far away from Harold's army, so that Harold would have to march a long way to face him. By the time Harold's soldiers arrived to fight William, they were exhausted. Harold had pushed them so quickly that many soldiers had been left along the way. But William's army was fresh and ready to fight.

Harold knew that his army needed a rest, so he camped for the night on a hill. He thought that William would wait for him to come down, rather than trying to climb up the hill to fight. But William decided that he would launch an attack, even though fighting uphill is very difficult. He told his troops, "Now is the time to show strength and courage! You fight not only for victory, but for survival!" The Normans charged up the hill towards the English camp, and the most famous battle in English history—the Battle of Hastings—had begun.

At first, the Norman attack seemed doomed to failure. The English army fought ferociously, and the Norman force began to weaken. William was knocked off his horse, and his soldiers began to shout, "The King is dead! The King is dead!"

But William struggled to his feet and yanked his helmet off. "I am still alive!"" he bellowed. "And by the grace of God, I will still conquer!" The relieved Norman soldiers threw themselves back into the battle. They surrounded the English army and overwhelmed it. Harold was killed, and the English surrendered.

Harold was buried in purple robes, with the name "Harold the Unfortunate" carved on his tombstone. But William was given a new name too: "William the Conqueror." He became the new king of England. And his fighters, who were French-speaking descendants of Vikings, were given land and castles in England. Once more, England had been invaded, and conquered, by a foreign people.

Part of the Bayeux Tapestry, a medieval tapestry showing the Battle of Hastings. This scene depicts the death of Harold.

Chapter Sixteen
England After the Conquest

The English Language

After William the Conqueror became king of England, the Normans poured into England and changed it forever. They changed the way the English lived. They changed the way the English built houses and farmed their land. And they even changed the way the English spoke.

The English that you are hearing right now is a mix of several different languages. English is a little bit like a greedy friend who keeps taking your toys. Imagine that your greedy friend sees your Play-Doh and decides that she wants it. After all, *her* Play-Doh is all brown and mixed up with other colors. So she takes your nice clean orange and green Play-Doh and mixes it in with her own Play-Doh. After a little while, you can't tell your Play-Doh apart. All of the Play-Doh has become hers!

That's just the way the English language works. Whenever English-speakers heard a useful word in another language, they would just take it and mix it in with all of their English words—and soon that word would *be* English.

The very first "English" was the language spoken by the barbarian Angles and Saxons, when they invaded England long ago. This "Old English" was very different from modern English. It even used different letters. Here are a few lines of Old English poetry for you to look at:

> Ða wæs on burgum   Beowulf Scyldinga,
> leof leodcyning,   longe þrage
>
> folcum gefræge   (fæder ellor hwearf,
> aldor of earde).

Do you see the strange letters? The letter that looks like a "p" with a tall stem and the letter that looks like a "D" with an extra line are both pronounced "th." The funny letter that looks like an "a" and an "e" stuck together is pronounced like a long "a." These lines are from *Beowulf,* the story we read earlier. These lines mean, "Beowulf was in the city of the Scyldings. He was a beloved ruler, and he ruled for a long time, famous to all folk, since his father went away from the world." Old English looks very strange to us, but we can recognize a few of its words. Do you see **wæs** in the first line? It means "was." The word **longe** means "long." And **fæder** means "father." *Man, house, sheep, dog, wood, field, work, drink, laughter, the, this, here, that*: all of these English words and many more come from "Old English."

When the Anglo-Saxons came, speaking Old English, they drove the Celts away from England into Ireland, Scotland, and Wales. And the language that the Celts spoke—the "Celtic language"—went with them. Today, this Celtic language is still spoken in Ireland, Scotland, and Wales. Here is a line of Welsh, the Celtic language spoken in Wales. As you can see, it is nothing like English!

Yn y dechreuad yr oedd y Gair; yr oedd y Gair gyda Duw, a Duw oedd y Gair.

This is a Welsh translation of the first line of the Gospel of John, "In the beginning was the Word, and the Word was with God, and the Word was God." These Celtic words probably do not look familiar to you at all! The Angles and the Saxons spent very little time talking to the Celts, so English did not borrow very many words from Celtic.

But English *did* borrow plenty of words from Latin and from Greek. Do you remember who came to England after the Anglo-Saxons? Augustine came, bringing Christianity with him. And when Christianity came to England, so did Latin and Greek words. The monks and priests who taught the Anglo-Saxons about Christianity also taught them Greek words like *apostle* and *pope, angel* and *baptize.* The Anglo-Saxons had no words for these Christian ideas, so they borrowed the Greek words for them straight from the New Testament.

They borrowed even more Latin words! Old English took the Latin words for *minister, nun, monk, gospel, sanctified,* and dozens more and made them English words. And Old English borrowed Latin words that didn't have to do with the Church too. *Fraternal* means "brotherly" in English; the Latin word for "brother" is *frater. Maternal* means "motherly"; can you guess what the Latin word for "mother" is? *Mater!*

By now, English had words from at least three other languages in it. But then another invasion came: the Viking invasion. The Vikings brought plenty of words with them from Scandinavia. Most of these words are short, plain, simple words. *Leg, skin, skull, angry, cut, crawl, die,* and *drown* are all Scandinavian words. (Angry, die, and drown sound like words that Vikings would use a lot!) So are *hungry, weak, egg, steak,* and *dirt.* And the days of our week are named after Viking gods. Tyr, the warrior-god, had Tuesday named after him. Odin, the king of the gods, is also called Woden; Wednesday is named after him. Friday is named after Odin's wife Frigg, and Thursday is named after Thor, the short-tempered thunder god.

When William the Conqueror and his noblemen settled in England, English went through the greatest change of all. Harold spoke English, but after he died, French-speaking kings ruled England for almost three hundred years! French was spoken by all of the rich and important people in England, and by all of the educated people—doctors, lawyers, and scientists. Most of the common people went right on using English. But they borrowed French words from the Normans. And the Normans married English men and women, brought up English children, and began to speak English. *Peace, curtsy, beef, chair, curtain, garden, castle, judge, jury*, *honor*, *courage*, and *rich* are all French words, borrowed from the Normans.

English still borrows words from Latin, French, and other languages today. In the twentieth century, English needed a word to describe something new—a movie that you could watch on your own television. Do you know what word we borrowed? *Video*—the Latin word for "I see."

Serfs and Noblemen

Before the Normans came, English people lived in small villages. Each family farmed its own little piece of land. Each village had a big open area, called the "common ground," where every family could put sheep, cows, or pigs out to pasture. Each village had its own *sheriff,* or police officer, who made sure that the law was kept. When there was fighting to be done, the farmers of England banded together to do it. And the king of England was their warleader, who led them into battle against invaders

But William the Conqueror had different ideas. William thought that the king was more than just a warleader. Instead, William believed that the king *owned* the land that he ruled. So when William was crowned king, he claimed all the land of England as his own! And he gave his favorite knights—the ones who had fought for him in the Battle of Hastings—pieces of England for their own. In exchange for this land, the knights had to promise to give William money to keep his army strong, and to serve in William's army whenever he called them to come and join him in a fight.

The wealthy knights who settled down on these pieces of land were called *lords*. And they gave smaller parts of their land away to other knights, who would fight for them, and to English farmers, called *peasants* or *serfs*. In exchange for these little farms, the peasants had to promise to give part of everything they raised to their lord.

So the peasants gave the lords food, and the lords gave the peasants land. The lords gave the knights land, and the knights promised to serve the lords. The lords gave the king service in his army and paid him taxes, and the king gave the lords land and castles. This way of living was called *feudalism*. Every person in England served someone else, and the person that they served had a duty to give them back something in exchange. Feudalism was a Norman way of life. And after the Norman invasion, it became an English way of life as well.

What would your life be like, if you were a serf? You spend your days caring for animals, working in the fields, harvesting fruit and nuts, mending harnesses, making tools out of wood and iron, and tending beehives. Every week, you send some of your animals, vegetables, fruit, nuts, and honey to the castle, for the lord and his family. The lord who owns your land can't ever force you to leave—you have the right to live there for the rest of your life! You live in a house with one room. The walls are made out of mud and twigs, and the roof is made of bundles of straw, called *thatch*. The dirt floor is spread with straw too, with a fireplace right in the middle of it and a hole cut in the roof to let the smoke out. Your bed is a pile of leaves near the fire. Your whole family sleeps in it with you. So do your pigs and chickens! They are too valuable to leave outside at night, so you bring them into the house when it gets dark. You don't get to eat meat very often, unless you can catch fish from the stream nearby. But you have plenty of vegetables, and lots of grain, which you make into "gruel" (like runny oatmeal) and heavy, dark loaves of bread. And in the summer there is honey from your beehives, and apples, blackberries, and walnuts from the trees and bushes that grow around your village.

Now imagine that you live in a lord's family. You live in a huge stone house—a castle! Bright embroidered hangings called tapestries cover the stone walls of your rooms, and rugs make the cold floor warm. Lavender, rosemary, and other sweet herbs lie on the floor; when you step on them, good smells rise up. You spend most of your time in the largest room of the castle, the Great Hall, where logs burn on a huge fireplace, and oil lamps line the walls. Your meals start with turnip and parsnip soup, chicken broth, or onion and leek soup. For a main course, you might eat beef, pork, eels, or pigeons, along with vegetables, salads of flower petals, fruit, cheese, bread, and plenty of wine and beer! Your cook spends hours making the food look as good as it tastes. He

makes cakes shaped like castles with little flags flying
from the towers, bread carved into warships floating on
gravy seas, pies with top crusts that open up so that
songbirds can fly out, and "boar intestines"—dried fruit
carved into long strips with raspberry sauce, piled under
the stomach of a tiny pastry boar! Your feasts last for
hours, with musicians, jugglers, acrobats, and jesters
performing for you while you eat. On special occasions,
you eat off silver plates, but usually you eat your food off
a huge slice of hard bread that soaks up all the extra
grease. And you use your knife and your fingers to eat,
because forks haven't been invented yet! You have a
good life. But you hope that no foreign armies ever
invade England. Because if they do, you'll have to leave
your comfortable castle, strap on your armor, and head
off to war.

Stone Castles

When William first gave parts of England away
to his knights, the English peasants were furious! They
had always lived on their own land, grown their own
food, and taken care of themselves. But now these
foreign soldiers were all over the place, claiming England
for themselves and telling the English farmers what to
do. So the English peasants rioted! They disobeyed their
Norman overlords, threw rocks at their horses, and tried
to burn their wooden houses. So the Normans began to
build heavy stone castles instead. These castles were
often on the tops of hills, surrounded by moats and thick
stone walls. They were the first English buildings made
of stone.

William and Anne live in one of these stone
castles. It was built by their grandfather, who fought for

William the Conqueror himself. Now their father is away, fighting in a war for the king, and their mother is supervising the servants, who are preserving fruit in honey for the winter. Their nurse has decided to have a little nap. "Run off and play for a bit," she tells them, "and leave me in peace."

So William and Anne decide to play hide-and-seek. They go up to their room, a small stone chamber on the second floor of the castle, to start their game. Anne is *it*. She leans against the thick windowsill, covers her eyes, and starts to count to fifty. She hears William's feet run away down the hallway. Anne opens her eyes and looks out the window. From the high hill where the castle sits, she can see a whole patchwork of fields and trees: little strips of gold wheat, with tiny peasants harvesting it; strips of lighter green, where miniature cows and sheep are grazing; and thick dark strips of forest.

Anne goes to the door of their room and looks down the hall both ways. Where has William gone? She runs down the hallway, towards the arched doorway at the far end. This doorway leads into the keep—the square tower that stands at the center of the castle. The keep has its own bedrooms, weapon rooms, and cellars with food stored in them. If the castle is ever attacked, everyone can go into the keep and bar themselves in.

Inside the tower, a spiral staircase leads both up and down. Anne hears feet running overhead. She climbs up and up. The stairs turn so sharply that she can only see two or three steps ahead of her in the light that comes through the narrow windows. The windows are as tall as she is, but barely as wide as her hand, just wide enough to shoot arrows through. Anne comes out onto the top of the tower. But William has already disappeared. He has run back down the stairs on the other side of the tower! Anne skips across the top of the tower, which is like a huge flat courtyard with a wall all around it. The wall is too tall for Anne to see over, but it has notches in it so that an archer can lean through the wall and shoot at anyone attacking below. Anne stops at one of the notches and leans forward to look far, far down. A strong wind whirls past her. Below her is the castle's outer  wall—eight feet wide, thicker than her father is tall—and the castle's front gate. The gate has a wide wooden gate, a *portcullis,* suspended overtop of it. If enemies come to the castle, the portcullis can be dropped down to close the gate. Anne can see the guard who keeps the portcullis, leaning against the top of the wall, drowsing in the warm sunshine.

She sees someone standing next to the guard, waving up at her. It's William! He has run down the keep, through the courtyard of the castle, and up onto the top of the castle walls! Anne darts for the stair and runs back down the cool stone spiral as fast as she can. She rushes out of the bottom door of the tower, into the castle courtyard. The castle walls tower high over her. All around her are the smaller buildings of the castle: the kitchen tower, the prison tower, the outdoor laundry, and the *garderobe* (the outhouse). She looks up towards the portcullis, but William is gone.

She darts across to the kitchen tower and pulls its heavy door open, straining her shoulders against it. A wave of heat hits her face. A huge fire is burning in the fireplace, and two hindquarters of beef are roasting over it on a spit. A little boy, not much older than she is, is turning the spit by its wooden handle. He is sweating and hot, but he's turning the spit with his right hand and eating a piece of candied fruit with his left. Her mother must have given him some fruit! At the huge wooden table in the center of the kitchen, the cook is making pastry for a pie. One of her helpers is plucking the feathers from a pheasant, and another is rubbing the dirty dishes with sand to clean them. But William isn't there.

She lets the door close and looks around the courtyard. Where is William? She crosses over to the outdoor laundry. On the flat stone platform, the laundresses are pouring liquid soap over the dirty clothes and pounding them with a bat in a huge barrel. Anne wrinkles her nose. The soap is made out of animal fat and wood ash; it smells bad! The sheets will smell better after they've been laid out in the sun to dry, and then folded up with lavender and dried chamomile. She peers behind the platform. No William! Anne goes over the little stone building behind the laundresses—the garderobe. She pulls the garderobe door open. A rat scuttles out of sight, underneath the stone toilets. She wrinkles her nose. The toilets have holes that lead down into a cesspit far beneath the castle, but in warm weather, they smell bad!

She pushes the door shut again and looks around. A movement on the other side of the kitchen garden catches her eye. Something is sticking up from behind the low wooden fence. It is the back of William's robe! He must think that he's invisible. She sneaks around the back of the garden. There he is, lying flat on his stomach. She jumps on him, and he shrieks. The game of hide-and-seek is over!

Knights and Samurai

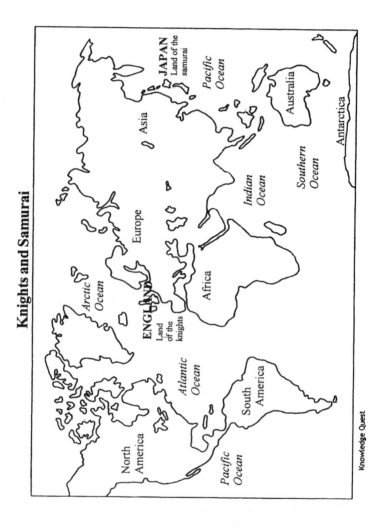

Knowledge Quest

Chapter Seventeen
Knights and Samurai

The English Code of Chivalry

The knights who lived in England's castles got their land from the king because they were good fighters. They were better at fighting than at anything else! So when there were no wars to fight in, these knights wandered around the countryside fighting. They threatened peasants, rode over the crops, killed animals, raided monasteries, and stole from churches.

So the leaders of the Christian church began to teach that knights owed loyalty to God, not just to the king. A knight had a sacred duty to defend the church and to take care of the weak: women, monks and priests, widows, and orphans. Knights were supposed to be more than just good fighters. They were like policemen, responsible for protecting others and making sure that laws were obeyed. This new way of being a knight was called "chivalry." Chivalry meant that a knight had to be brave, loyal, honest, generous, and good at fighting. He had to fight for the church whenever it was threatened. He had to love his country, honor his lord, and fight his country's enemies. Most of all, he had to protect women! And if a knight fell in love with a lady, he had to promise to serve her—and to do any task she gave him, no matter how difficult it was!

Becoming a knight was a long, complicated process. When you were seven, you would begin to learn how to ride and how to fight with a sword and spear. Your family might send you to stay with another family so that you could train with other boys. In this training camp, you become a *page*. You learn how to put on heavy armor and how to carry your shield properly. You learn how to take care of a horse and how to clean your saddle and bridle. You might even practice charging with a spear. But your spear is a broom handle, and your horse is a wooden horse with wheels, pulled by other pages!

When you are fourteen or so, you become a servant to one particular knight. Now you are called a *squire*. You look after the knight's horse and armor, help him to put his armor on and take it off, clean his armor and weapons after a fight, and take care of all his needs. In the meantime, you go on learning how to fight. And you also learn how to be polite: how to speak courteously and eat neatly, how to carve meat and serve it, and how to behave at a great feast.

Finally you go through a ceremony in which you become a knight. You go to the lord's castle and spend an entire night praying in the castle chapel. The next morning, you take a cold bath and dress in three colors: a white shirt to remind you of purity; a red cloak to remind you of the blood you will spill as a knight; and brown pants to remind of the earth where your body will be buried. You go to the Great Hall of the castle, where you swear always to be faithful to the church and to your lord. The lord taps you with a sword and announces, "Now you are a knight!" He gives you a sword of your own, and a priest blesses you.

Now you have a squire of your own, and you can take part in the first big tournament of the year! Hundreds of knights will be fighting in this tournament. You have your own colorful tent on the tournament grounds, where your squire helps you get dressed in your armor. Knights used to wear "chain mail," made out of thousands of tiny steel rings linked together. But this chain mail won't stop the blade of an axe or the point of a lance. So instead, you wear armor made out of plates of steel, hinged together. First, your squire helps you put on a thick padded jacket to cushion your armor. Then he helps you step into the plate armor legs of your suit. He fastens a chain-mail skirt around your waist and then straps on your back plate, your breast plate, and your arm and shoulder guards. You're starting to feel hot, but you're not done yet. You put on leather gloves and pull on plate mail gloves, or gauntlets, over top of them. Your squire straps your sword onto your belt and puts your helmet on. It covers your whole face, except for narrow eye slits where you can see out. Your friends only recognize you because of the special symbol painted on your shield. This symbol, or coat of arms, tells everyone

A knight's horse in tournament armor

who you are. It is painted with gold and scarlet paint, so that other knights can see it far away.

You walk stiffly out of the tent and over to your horse. You are so heavy that your squire has to hoist you onto your horse with a rope thrown over a tree branch! You join a parade of other knights, riding in front of the ladies of the court. The ladies look carefully at all the coats of arms. If they recognize a knight who has broken the rules of chivalry and been rude to a lady, they can point at him and the heralds will order him out of the tournament!

But no one points at you, and finally it's time for you to joust. Your squire gives you a blunt-ended lance, and you trot down to the end of the ring and turn around. Another knight is waiting to charge at you! The herald gives the signal, and you kick your horse into a gallop. The other knight looks enormous, thundering towards you on a huge black charger. You grit your teeth and close your eyes—and feel an enormous jolt on your lance arm. For a minute, you think you are going to fall backwards off your horse, but you manage to catch onto the high front of your saddle and pull yourself upright as your horse gallops on towards the end of the ring. You hear the crowd shouting your name! As soon as you can pull your horse up, you wheel around to look for your opponent. His horse is galloping off into the distance, and he's sitting on the ground, with his shattered lance in his hand. You've won the joust!

The Samurai: Japanese Knights

Knights and lords were part of English life during the Middle Ages. But England wasn't the only country that had a *feudal system,* where knights swore to obey lords in exchange for land. Far, far to the east, a very different country also had knights and lords. Only in this country, the knights were called *samurai.*

We've already read about Japan, which lies right off the coast of the giant country of China. If you were to go from England, across the sea to France, where the Normans live, and then travel east, you would go through wild, mountainous country, inhabited by nomadic tribes that no one in England knows much about. If you kept traveling east, you would reach the Black Sea and then the Caspian Sea. Down to the south is the Arabian peninsula, where Muhammad was born. Keep going east and you'll pass through Central Asia; if you look down to the south now, you'll see India. But you're not in China yet! Travel east a little more, until you see the shores of the Yellow River in front of you. *Now* you're in China. Follow the Yellow River all the way to the coast of China, cross over the Yellow Sea, and you'll see the southern tip of Japan.

Japan and England are both islands. But the two islands could not be more different. England is one large island; Japan is made up of four long, thin islands, surrounded by almost four thousand smaller ones! And while England is a peaceful island covered with forests and calm fields, Japan's islands have sixty-five active volcanoes! The Japanese islands were formed by the collision of two parts of the earth's crust, which pushed up against each other and formed a ridge with molten lava beneath it. This lava still boils up through the crust and erupts through Japan's volcanoes. And throughout Japan, hot springs, called *onsen,* bubble and steam up from the earth, heated by the molten rock beneath the surface. Japanese samurai used to bathe in these hot springs.

We've already read about the Yamato emperors of Japan, who wanted Japan to develop its own way of life rather than borrowing the Chinese ways of living. At the same time that William the Conqueror became king of England, a Yamato emperor was still ruling in Japan. But this emperor, who lived in a huge elaborate palace, was treated more like a god than like an emperor. He was almost never seen, and he certainly didn't run his country. He left all of that to his noblemen, who were called daimyos. But the daimyos quarreled with each other and didn't take care of the country either. Laws began to break down. Robbers roamed from place to place, taking whatever they liked. And these noblemen found that they needed protection for themselves and for their land!

So the daimyos hired warriors to protect them. They promised these warriors land and money—and these warriors, called samurai, promised in return to protect the daimyos and their land from bandits. Just like English knights, samurai took land from a lord (the daimyo) and gave service in return. And just like English knights, the samurai gave pieces of land to peasants who worked on the land and grew food for the samurai. Japan, like England, had a feudal system. Peasants worked for the samurai, the samurai served the daimyos, and the daimyos served the Emperor.

The samurai also wore armor, but their armor was made out of iron plates, lacquered with bright colors and tied together with silk and leather strips. The lacquer paint kept the iron from rusting in Japan's damp air. And their helmets were shaped into faces, often with elaborate iron mustaches, and painted to look snarling and fierce. They spent years learning how to fight with special curved swords, calls *katanas*. Young samurai were taught to perform different sword-strokes, named after animals like the cat, the monkey, and the bird. Many samurai thought that their katanas had magical powers! They hired skilled sword smiths to make the swords and to decorate them with gold, jewels, and figures of dragons.

A samurai

Just like English knights, samurai lived in castles. But Japan had more wood than stone, and although the castles had stone foundations, their walls and towers were often made of timber. Knights in England followed the code of *chivalry,* but samurai had their own code, called "the way of the warrior." A samurai always had to defend his daimyo, or lord, no matter what. And if he had to fight for his lord, he was required to win—or die. To be taken prisoner was a terrible humiliation for a samurai. If he showed cowardice or fear of death, he was expected to kill himself with a special sword in a complicated ceremony called *seppuku.*

But these fierce warriors also wrote poetry and made beautiful gardens. Many samurai wrote short poems called *haiku* in praise of nature. Here is a medieval Japanese haiku, written by the great samurai Mtsua Basho:

This ancient pond here:
A frog jumps into the pond:
Sound of the water.

The gardens of these fierce warriors were full of quiet ponds, lovely flowing streams, moss-covered banks, and peaceful patterns raked into expanses of white sand.

Samurai even learned how to dance gracefully! As a matter of fact, one of the greatest samurai warriors ever, General Oda Nobunaga, did a beautiful dance with a fan in front of his soldiers before leading them into war! Nobunaga became the most powerful soldier in Japan, but he still knew how to dance. Samurai used to say, "Practice the arts of peace on the left hand, and the arts of war on the right." That meant that they didn't fight all the time—only when they needed to. And in times of peace, they spent their time gardening, writing, and painting instead.

The World of the Crusades

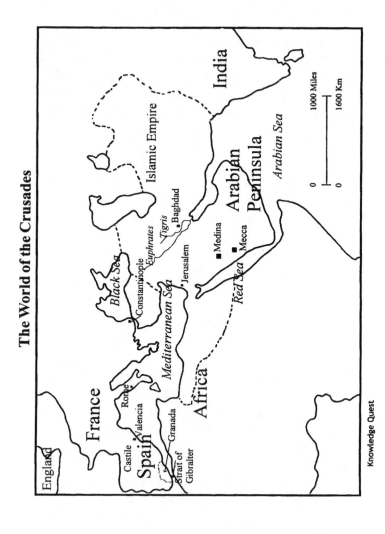

1000 Miles

1600 Km

England

France

Spain

Castile

Rome

Valencia

Granada

Strait of
Gibralter

Mediterranean Sea

Black Sea

Constantinople

Euphrates

Tigris

Baghdad

Islamic Empire

India

Jerusalem

Medina

Mecca

Red Sea

Arabian
Peninsula

Arabian Sea

Africa

Knowledge Quest

Chapter Eighteen
The Age of Crusades

A Command from the Pope

In the last chapter, we traveled from England all the way east to Japan. Now let's call your flying carpet to take you back. Do you remember flying all around the Roman Empire, back when we first started to read about the Middle Ages? Your flying carpet took you far, far up above the Mediterranean Sea, and hovered there so that you could look down. You could see the land all around the Mediterranean Sea, and the land all the way down into Egypt and up into Britain, glowing yellow. All through this Roman territory, people spoke Latin and followed the Roman laws.

Now hop back on your flying carpet and soar up, up above China. If you glance down now, you might see the Great Wall snaking across China's mountains! Your carpet whisks you across Asia, then turns south so that you fly down over India and across the Indian Ocean, and then turns north again. You peer over the edge of the carpet. Below you, you can see the Arabian peninsula, with the Red Sea on one side of it and the Persian Gulf on the other. The Mediterranean Sea is just ahead.

But something has happened to the land around the Mediterranean. It isn't glowing yellow any more. Instead, it shines with a deep, clear scarlet. The entire Arabian peninsula is scarlet. So is the whole northern coast of Africa. Spain is scarlet, although the scarlet line stops at Tours, where Charles the Hammer stopped the Muslim army and turned it back. But the scarlet stretches up from Arabia all the way over to Jerusalem, on the coast of the Mediterranean. It stretches up to the Caspian Sea and over into India. This is the land that belongs to the Islamic empire—now bigger than Rome's empire ever was.

The Muslim warriors who fought to spread the Islamic empire had one great desire: to spread Islam across the civilized world. And this frightened the other nations in the medieval world! Their kings were afraid that Muslim rulers would take control of their cities. And the leaders of medieval Christianity were worried as well. If Islam spread all across the world, what would happen to Christianity?

Christians were particularly upset when the rulers of the Islamic empire made it hard for them to visit the city of Jerusalem. Jerusalem was a holy city for Muslims, because they believed that Muhammad had ascended to heaven from a great rock inside the city. But Jerusalem was also a holy city for Jews, because it was the city of David, the great Hebrew king, and because the ruins of the Temple destroyed by the Romans were there. And it was holy for Christians, because Jesus was crucified there. Many Jewish and Christian believers made special journeys to Jerusalem. These travelers were called *pilgrims* (people who made trips to show their devotion to God, and sometimes to ask forgiveness for their sins).

When the Islamic empire first took control of Jerusalem, Jews and Christians were allowed to visit the city. But then the Muslims in Jerusalem began to turn against Jewish and Christian pilgrims. Muslims started to attack and rob Christian and Jewish pilgrims. Some were even killed! Eventually the roads to Jerusalem were blocked to Christians and Jews, so that pilgrims couldn't go to the holy city any more. And the Islamic empire itself was creeping closer and closer to Constantinople and the Christian churches there.

Finally, the Byzantine emperor, who lived in Constantinople, sent a message to the pope. "We need help here in Constantinople!" he begged. "Surely knights from the other Christian kingdoms can help to protect the city of Constantinople from Muslim conquest? If we are conquered, no Christian will be able to worship at the great cathedral, the Hagia Sophia, again!"

The pope thought about this request. He decided that knights from Christian kingdoms *did* need to fight against the spread of Islam. But instead of sending them to Constantinople, he sent them to Jerusalem. He promised knights that they would get rewards in heaven for driving back the Islamic invasion. And he even promised them that anyone who joined the army would have their sins forgiven!

Knights responded to the Pope's command.

"Arm for the rescue of Jerusalem, under your captain Christ!" he exhorted the knights. "Wear His cross as your badge."

So knights from England, France, Italy, and other countries with Christian kings set off for Jerusalem. They sewed crosses on their clothing to show that they belonged to the armies fighting for the Holy City. The Latin word for cross is *crux*, so these warriors attacking Jerusalem became known as crusaders. And their attempts to recapture Jerusalem from the Islamic empire became known as the *Crusades*.

The crusaders who went out to fight the Islamic empire were determined to defeat the warriors of Islam. But the Crusades went on for years and years, and the crusaders spent a long time living in Arab countries. And although they thought of Arab warriors as their enemies, they still learned some of the Arab customs. For one thing, they started to take baths more frequently! The Muslim warriors washed often, because they had to bathe before their daily prayers. But in England and France, people only took baths once or twice a *year*. So when the crusaders came home clean, they were suspected of having become Muslims. Have you ever heard the saying, "Cleanliness is next to godliness?" Well, during the Crusades, dirtiness could prove that you were still a good Christian!

Recapturing Jerusalem

When the pope called all Christian knights to recapture Jerusalem, nobles and knights from many different countries started to organize themselves into an army. But the first crusaders to set out on a crusade didn't even own swords. They were farmers and peasants who went on the *People's Crusade*.

The People's Crusade began when a wandering preacher named Peter the Hermit decided that common people should join in the effort to recapture Jerusalem. He went through the countryside, making loud excited speeches to all of the peasants and farmers he met. "Come with me to Jerusalem!" he would shout. "God will forgive your sins and give you the strength to fight! You too can be a warrior for God!"

Peter the Hermit wasn't very well liked by other churchmen. A priest called Abbot Cuibert remarked, "With his long face framed in a dirty old hood, he looked remarkably like the donkey he rode!" But Peter the Hermit was a very persuasive speaker. The people he spoke to believed he had been appointed by God. And he became so popular that people would crowd around him wherever he went, pulling hairs out of his donkey's mane and tail to keep for souvenirs.

When Peter the Hermit set out for Constantinople—his first stop on the journey to Jerusalem—forty thousand common people followed him! None of them knew how to fight. A few had axes, but many had no weapons at all. And they didn't know exactly who they were fighting. On their long journey, they attacked Christian villages, stole food, and mistreated the people of the countries they went through. Most of them never even reached Constantinople. And the ones who did were quickly captured and made into slaves. This crusade, the People's Crusade, was a disaster!

Meanwhile, real knights had collected a fleet of ships so that they could sail to Constantinople. Once they arrived in Constantinople, they set off on the long march to Jerusalem. We call this first attack on Jerusalem the First Crusade.

It took two years for the crusaders to march from Constantinople to Jerusalem! The entire way, the crusaders were trailed by Muslim fighters. They called these enemies *Saracens*. The Saracens set up ambushes for the crusaders. They went ahead of the crusaders, burning fruit trees, and putting poison in the wells. The crusaders had a hard time fighting off these sneak attacks, and many of the knights were killed on the journey.

But finally, the crusaders arrived at Jerusalem. A medieval historian tells us that the army wept for joy when the knights finally saw Jerusalem's walls. But those walls were thick and lined with Saracen warriors, and a deep moat surrounded the city. How could the crusaders break into the Jerusalem? The best way would be to build tall wooden towers called *siege engines,* which they could roll over to the walls and use to climb over into the city. But the sandy, rocky hills around Jerusalem had few tall trees—certainly not enough to provide lumber for siege towers. The crusaders tried to use battering rams against the walls, but the Saracens threw bales of straw over to keep the rams from hitting the stone. The crusaders set fire to the straw, but this didn't even scorch the walls. And soon the crusader army began to suffer from hunger and thirst. The Saracens had prepared for their arrival by bringing all the food inside the city—and poisoning all the water outside the city walls.

Without siege engines, the crusaders would never be able to take the city. Finally, merchants who were bringing goods to the ports of Italy broke up their ships and carried the wood across land to the crusaders. The knights used this wood to build two enormous wooden towers on wooden wheels. They covered these siege engines with animal skins soaked in water, so that Saracen defenders wouldn't be able to shoot flaming arrows into the towers and set them on fire.

Then the crusaders brought stones, one by one, and threw them into the moat around Jerusalem. Finally, the moat was filled. The knights rolled the siege towers across the stones, climbed up them, and fought their way across the walls. Several of them climbed down the inside of the walls and ran to open the city's gates. As soon as the gates were open, the whole crusader army poured into the city. They were hungry, thirsty, exhausted, and angry. And once they were inside Jerusalem, they killed everyone they could find. Thousands of Muslims and Jews died. Many of them weren't soldiers and didn't even have swords.

It had taken three years for the First Crusade to recapture Jerusalem. Once the Holy City was in the hands of the crusaders, they went on to capture the land around Jerusalem too. They divided this land into little kingdoms. Crusader knights became princes of these new little kingdoms. They tried to live in peace with the Saracens. Saracens who swore allegiance to the crusader princes were given land and wealth. The crusaders learned to dress and act more like Muslims. Some crusaders even married Saracen women!

But even though Saracens and crusaders lived without fighting for a little while, they were never truly at peace. Most crusaders never forgot that the pope had called the Muslims "enemies of the True Faith." And the Muslims were never able to forget the cruelty that the crusaders had shown at the capture of Jerusalem.

Saladin of Jerusalem

Now Jerusalem was in the hands of the crusaders. The land all around the Holy City was ruled by crusader princes. But the Saracens wanted Jerusalem back! They organized themselves into an army, attacked one of the little kingdoms near Jerusalem, and defeated its crusader prince.

When news of this revolt reached England, France, and the other Christian countries, a new army of knights set out to fight the Saracens. We call this the Second Crusade. But the Second Crusade failed! The crusader army couldn't retake that rebellious little kingdom. It remained in Muslim hands. The crusader army fell apart, and the knights crept back home, ashamed of their failure. And the Saracens, under the great warrior Saladin, began to prepare for an even greater attack: on Jerusalem itself.

When Saladin was born, Jerusalem had been in the hands of the crusaders for almost forty years. And Saladin was just as anxious to win the city back for Islam as the crusaders had been to conquer it for Christianity! From childhood on, he prepared himself to be a warrior. He spent years learning how to follow the Koran, and training himself to fight. As a young man, he fought in the army commanded by his uncle. More and more Muslims noticed Saladin and praised his bravery.

Finally Saladin became the second-in-command, or *vizier,* over all the Muslims in Egypt. Now he had his own army. And he was determined to bring all the Muslims together into one powerful army with one goal—to retake the city of Jerusalem.

But before he could do this, Saladin had to convince the Muslim warriors to follow *him,* rather than any other Muslim leader. So he was careful to be a model Muslim. He never broke his word. He always prayed five times a day, even when he was traveling or fighting. He gave so many alms to the poor that his treasury was almost empty! He gained a reputation for justice and fairness.

Saladin became more and more popular. At last, he had gathered a huge and faithful army around him. He was ready to march towards Jerusalem.

When the crusader ruler of Jerusalem, King Guy, heard that Saladin's army was approaching, he called all of his knights together to ask them for advice. "Saladin is marching towards us with a huge force of Saracens behind him!" he said. "What should we do? Stay here in the city, or go out to meet him?"

The oldest and strongest knight said, "We should stay here and defend the city. It's too hot to march out across the plains. If we stay here, Saladin's armies will have to tire themselves out coming to us. And do you remember how hard it was for us to conquer the city as long as the Saracens stayed inside it?"

But another knight disagreed. "We should go out and meet this army!" he shouted. "Staying here is cowardice! Let's be courageous and attack Saladin first!"

King Guy didn't know what to do. But he was afraid that the oldest and strongest knight was out to take the throne of Jerusalem away from him. So he decided to follow the second knight's advice instead. He collected all of his men together and marched out to meet Saladin and his army.

That was a terrible mistake.

The summer day was the hottest of the year. The sun poured down on the crusaders. Their heavy steel armor heated up like frying pans on a stove. The rocks were too hot to touch. Dust choked the horses and made the men cough. They grew so weary and thirsty that King Guy ordered them to stop in the middle of the afternoon and set up camp near a well. So the crusaders unloaded their horses, set up their tents and hurried to draw water from the well.

The well was dry.

By now, the crusaders were sick from thirst. And even worse, they were down in a valley between two mountain peaks called "The Horns of Hattin." An enemy army could hide behind the trees and rocks above the valley and shoot arrows down on them.

But King Guy's army was too exhausted to move. They lay in their tents in the heat, barely able to reach for their weapons. Sure enough, Saladin's army surrounded the valley. The Saracens set fire to the brush and trees around the valley's edge, so that the crusader army couldn't escape. But the crusaders were so weak that they didn't put up much of a fight. They were defeated, and King Guy surrendered.

Now Jerusalem was undefended! So Saladin led his army into the city in a triumphant parade.

Saladin told his men not to kill the Christians in Jerusalem. Instead, he took them captive and sold them as slaves. But he allowed the weak and the elderly to go free. And after he declared himself the ruler of Jerusalem, he announced that Jewish and Christian pilgrims would be allowed to enter the city in peace. For ninety years, Jerusalem had been under Christian rule. Now it was in Muslim hands once again.

A Third Crusade was launched to get Jerusalem back, but Saladin could not be defeated. After this, there were five more crusades. Each of the crusades tried to take part of the Islamic empire away from the Muslims. But none of the crusades were very successful. Crusades weren't a very good way to win land back from the Islamic empire!

El Cid and the "Reconquest of Spain"

The most successful attack against the Islamic empire wasn't a crusade, and didn't take place in Jerusalem. Muslim armies kept control of Jerusalem. But over in Spain, Christian kingdoms pushed the Muslim rulers out. We call this time the *Reconquest* of Spain.

Do you remember reading about the Muslim invasion of Spain? Four hundred years before the Crusades, the Visigoths who lived in Spain had invited the Muslim warrior Tariq bin Ziyad to come in and help them settle a fight over the Spanish throne. Tariq came—with an army! And he took Spain for Islam. The Arabs lived in Spain for centuries. They became known as *Moors*, and their kingdom was called *Al-Andalus*. The Spanish language became full of Arabic words. Beautiful mosques were built in Spain. Moorish artists, musicians, poets, and philosophers became famous all through the world. Only a few small kingdoms in the north of Spain remained under the rule of Christian kings.

For many years, the Muslim rulers of Al-Andalus were *tolerant*. They allowed Jews and Christians to live in Spain in peace. But a hundred years before the Crusades began, a new Muslim king came to the throne of Al-Andalus—a king who was only twelve. This young king didn't really know how to rule a country. So he left most of his decisions to his tutor. This tutor, Al-Mansur, became the king's vizier (his second-in-command).[1]

Al-Mansur didn't want Christians or Jews in Spain. He made new laws that kept Christians from meeting and worshipping together. And he declared that Christians and Jews would have to pay higher taxes than Muslims. So many Christians left Al-Andalus and traveled up to the north of Spain, to the Christian kingdoms where they would not have to worry about persecution.

Now, all the Christians in Spain were gathered together in one place. And they began to think about fighting back against the Muslim kingdom of Al-Andalus.

---

[1] Al-Mansur acquired his nickname (which means "the victor") after his campaigns; his full name is Ibn-Abi Amir.

They started to venture out from the north and attack Muslim cities. One by one, these cities began to fall to the Christian armies.

One Christian fighter, Rodrigo Díaz de Vivar, became the greatest hero of the Reconquest. So many stories are told about him that we cannot be sure which are true and which are legends! But here is one account of Rodrigo's life.

During the Reconquest, the Christian kingdom of Castile, in the north of Spain, hired the young warrior Rodrigo to lead its armies. Rodrigo fought so bravely that the king of Castile, Alfonso, grew jealous of him and banished him from Castile. Rodrigo knew that he had done nothing wrong. He swore that he would not shave or trim his beard until he was pardoned. And so his beard grew for years and years! It became so long that Rodrigo braided it and tied it into a knot so that no one could grab it and pull him down in battle.

When Rodrigo left Castile, he traveled around Spain, fighting for whoever would hire him. He led Christian armies into battle against the Moors, and the Moors into battle against the Christians! Both sides grew to respect his strength. They called him, simply, *El Cid.* This means "the lord," or "the boss"!

El Cid eventually settled down in a small castle in the east of Spain. But he wouldn't be allowed to rest for long. Alfonso's kingdom, Castile, was growing more and more powerful, capturing more and more Muslim cities. And the Islamic rulers of Spain were afraid that they would not be able to fight the Christians off. So they sent a message to the Muslims of North Africa, asking for help. A huge army of Muslim warriors poured across the Strait of Gibraltar into Spain. They defeated the Castilian army and began to drive the Christians back into the north. The Christian attempt to reconquer Spain seemed doomed!

King Alfonso realized that he needed his strongest general to come help him. So he sent messengers to El Cid, begging the great warrior to fight against these invading armies. "Help us to fight against the Islamic forces!" the king pleaded. "They have driven the Christians out of the city of Valencia, and have filled it with Muslim warriors. If we cannot retake these cities, we are doomed!"

The city of Valencia was near El Cid's castle. So he chose four thousand fighters and led them out to attack the city. He rode ahead them, his braided beard tucked carefully into his helmet, his armor gilded with gold and silver, and a scarlet dragon on his shield. The Muslim army in Valencia was much larger than El Cid's small force. But El Cid chose his battlefield carefully. It was a small field, surrounded by trees and rocks, with a narrow entrance, and only a small part of the Muslim army could get into it at a time. Little by little, El Cid and his army defeated the forces of Valencia. El Cid claimed the city for his own and turned its mosque into a Christian church.

El Cid's triumph was not the last Christian victory. The tide of the war had turned against the Moorish forces. The Christian armies called the crusaders to come and help them drive the Moors from Spain. Eventually, five Christian kingdoms covered most of Spain. Only a small kingdom far to the south, Granada, remained in Muslim hands. Spain had been "reconquered."

Richard I's Route to Jerusalem

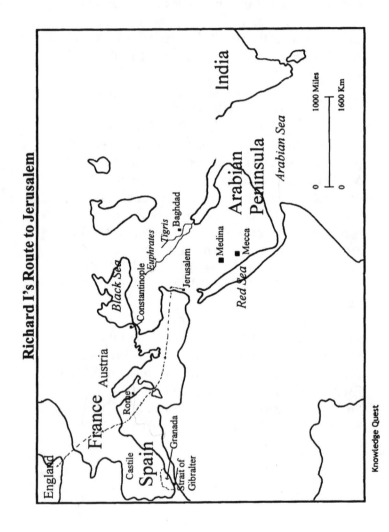

Knowledge Quest

Chapter Nineteen
A New Kind of King

Richard the Lionhearted

Many knights and noblemen of England went off to fight in the Crusades. And so did one of England's most famous kings: Richard I. For his courage in battle, Richard became known as Richard the Lionhearted.

Richard was tall, golden-haired, strong, and broad-shouldered. He looked exactly like a king. But Richard the Lionhearted spent very little of his reign *being* a king. When he was still a prince, he heard that Jerusalem had been recaptured by Saladin. And from that moment on, Richard's only desire was to go and fight in the Crusades.

Two years later, Richard's father died and Richard was crowned king of England. As soon as he became king, he started to sell off his possessions so that he could raise an army to take on a crusade. He declared, "I would sell London itself if only I could find the man to buy it!" And as soon as he had enough money, Richard left England and stayed away for years and years. "Almost everyone was angry," one medieval historian tells us, "that the king would leave his own kingdom with so much speed, as though he didn't care anything about it!"

When Richard arrived in the Holy Land, he joined forces with the king of France and the Duke of Austria. But soon he quarreled with the king of France, who decided that it would be easier to go back to France than to keep on dealing with Richard. And then Richard announced that the Duke of Austria shouldn't be flying his banner right next to Richard's. After all, Richard was a king, and the Duke was just a duke. When the Duke refused to move his banner, Richard told his men to go steal the banner and throw it in the mud. At this, the Duke took his soldiers and went home. Richard had lost all of his allies!

Richard marched on towards Jerusalem with his English crusaders. But Saladin's army came out to meet him and kept him from ever reaching the city. Once Richard fought his way into sight of Jerusalem. But although his armies gazed at it longingly, Richard himself would not turn his gaze towards it. "I will not even look," he announced, "at the walls of the City which God Himself will not allow me to deliver."

Meanwhile, Richard started hearing rumors from home. His younger brother John was trying to steal his throne! So Richard started back to England to protect his crown. He decided to take a short-cut across Austria—and ran into none other than the Duke of Austria. The Duke hadn't forgotten Richard's insults. So he took Richard and shut him up in a tall prison tower. No one knew where Richard was. All of England mourned over his death (except, of course, for John). And Richard himself lay on a heap of dirty straw, staring through his tiny barred window at the blue of the sky.

But one person did not believe that Richard was dead. According to legend, Richard's faithful friend Blondel crisscrossed Europe on foot, peering into every dungeon and pausing outside every fortress. He would sing an English song, and pause to see whether anyone answered. But usually French or German or Italian faces would peer over the battlements, not understanding the English words.

Blondel made his way down the winding green shores of the Danube, pausing and singing at each castle.

It was almost dark one night when he halted at one tall, grim tower, wondering whether the inhabitants might give him a bed for the night. He sat down at the base of the tower, leaning his back against the cool stone. And as he pondered, he idly hummed the first lines of an old, old tune...*Greensleeves*. As his voice trailed off into silence, he heard the second line, hummed waveringly from far above him.

Blondel leaped to his feet. He sang the third line, and a voice sang out the fourth line in English. He looked up and saw Richard's blond head, dirty and matted, his beard grown long and ragged, in the window far above.

Blondel went back to England and announced, "Richard is alive!" Most of England rejoiced to hear it! They sent ambassadors to the Duke of Austria, begging him to release Richard. The Duke agreed to set Richard free in exchange for 150,000 marks.

This was a huge amount of money, almost three million dollars in today's money! John suggested that it would be easier just to leave Richard in jail. But the people of England disagreed. They paid the ransom, and Richard returned home to England.

But he didn't stay long. Soon he was off again, this time to fight the king of France over French cities which Richard claimed belonged to him. And fighting over a tiny French castle, Richard was killed by a stray arrow. He had survived Saladin's fierce armies, only to fall in a meaningless battle close to home. Now his brother John would finally inherit the throne of England.

John Lackland and the Magna Carta

Richard's nickname was "The Lionhearted."
But John's nickname wasn't nearly as pretty. John's
people called him "John Lackland."

Why? John was the youngest son of the king of
England. Remember, England was a *feudal system.*
The king "owned" all of the land that he ruled. So when
John's father died, Richard inherited the whole land of
England. John didn't inherit any of it. He "lacked land."

But when Richard died, John became the king.
Now he wasn't John Lackland. He was the king and
owner of all England.

John's older brother Richard had always treated
him like a little boy who couldn't possibly rule a country.
While Richard was away at war, John tried his best to
claim the throne. But when Richard came home and
took the throne back, he *laughed* at his brother. "What
a child you are!" Richard said, and ordered the cook to
fix John his favorite supper to cheer him up. And John
was twenty-seven years old!

So when John became king, he was determined
to show that he was a strong, grown-up ruler. But he
had all sorts of troubles. For one thing, he wasn't tall and
golden-haired like Richard. He was short, plump, and
losing his hair. The noblemen of England didn't respect
him. And the king of France was trying to take away the
castles that England owned over in France.

John knew that if he could defeat the French
king, he could prove that he was a great warrior like his
older brother. So he fought battle after battle in France.
These battles cost money! He had to pay his soldiers,
feed them, and buy horses for them. So to raise money,

John came up with ideas to get more money from his noblemen. He declared that in emergencies (like wars with France) his noblemen owed him extra money. He announced that whenever a nobleman died and left his land to his son, the son would have to pay extra money to the king—an "inheritance tax." And furthermore, if the son was still a child, John could take control of the nobleman's land and make money from it.

Now, all of these were ways that kings had raised extra money before John came to the throne. But John used them to raise *lots* of money. Soon his noblemen started to feel poor. John became more and more unpopular. And then John did something that was even more tyrannical. He ordered his nephew, the only other possible heir to the English throne, murdered.

Finally, the noblemen revolted. They gathered together into an army, marched into London (England's capital city), and captured it! We call this a civil war (when soldiers are fighting in their own country, against their own people).

John realized that he wouldn't be able to recapture London. So he dressed himself in his royal robes, gathered his court together, and went out to meet the rebels at a field called Runnymede.

At Runnymede, the noblemen presented John with a paper and told him to sign it. The paper described new laws that the king had to follow. According to these laws, the king could only take extra money from his noblemen if the payment was fair, and if he got the noblemen's permission to ask for it. The laws also said that the king couldn't throw his noblemen in jail unless they had actually committed a crime. This paper was called the "Magna Carta," or "Great Charter."

John didn't want to sign this paper. After all, he was the most powerful man in England. He could do whatever he wanted, as long as his soldiers were strong enough to force the people to obey him. He didn't have to follow the law. He was the king, so he *was* the law! Whatever he said had to be done.

But he knew that unless he signed the Magna Carta, he would lose his crown. So he signed. Now the king of England had to obey the law, like everyone else in his kingdom. This was a new idea! For the first time, the *law* was the most powerful force in a country— instead of the king.

Today, we still follow the ideas of the Magna Carta. If you live in Canada or in the United States, your leaders don't "own" your country. Instead, they have to follow the law like everyone else. The President or the Prime Minister can't suddenly decide, "Today I want everyone in my country to pay me fifty dollars so that I can start a war." They have to ask the people's permission to raise taxes and start wars.

But instead of traveling to Washington, D.C. (where the President of the United States lives) or to Ottawa, Ontario (where the Prime Minister of Canada has his office) and giving them permission ourselves, we choose *representatives*—people who go to Washington or Ottawa and speak to our leaders for us. If the President or Prime Minister wants to start a war or raise taxes, these *representatives* have to give permission. In the United States, these elected people are called "Representatives" and "Senators." They meet together in "Congress." In Canada, these representatives are elected to the "House of Commons." They are called "Members of Parliament." This system got started eight hundred years ago when John signed the Magna Carta!

Robin Hood

When John was ruling England, before the Magna Carta was signed, the people of England were poor and miserable. When John took money from his noblemen, his noblemen took money from their peasants and serfs. And there was no one to help them resist this tyranny.

Except for Robin Hood!

The people of England told stories about a mysterious man who lived in the royal forests with a band of outlaws. He wore a green jacket and a green hood so that he would blend in with the forest. When King John's noblemen took money from the people of England unjustly, this outlaw stole the money and gave it back to the poor. He was loyal to King Richard, not to King John, and he hoped that Richard would return soon from the Crusades. In some tales, this mysterious outlaw was called Robin of Lockesley; he was said to be a nobleman whose lands had been seized by King John. But in other tales, he is simply called Robin Hood. Here is one of the tales of Robin Hood.

Robin Hood and the Butcher

Long ago, in the days when Richard the Lion-hearted was away fighting in the Crusades, his younger brother John ruled over England. Now John was a greedy man, and he appointed other greedy men to run the villages of his country. The worst of all his men was the Sheriff of Nottingham, who stole from his people and gave money to King John. The people of Nottingham could barely survive on the scraps and pennies left to them by the Sheriff and his men. And although they lived on the edge of a forest filled with fat deer, plentiful enough to feed the whole village through the cold winter, they were forbidden to kill a single buck. For the forest belonged to King John. And although he never walked in it, he threatened to hang any man who shot one of his deer.

One day, Robin Hood was out walking with his companion Little John. Little John was a stout man, who

Robin Hood

could fight even the strongest warrior with nothing but his quarterstaff and come out the victor! The two friends were strolling through the deep forest, along the road that led to Nottingham, when they heard the clop of horse's hooves. So Robin and Little John stepped off the road and hid behind a tree. As they watched, a butcher's cart came into sight, loaded with fresh meat.

"Aha!" said Robin to Little John. "This man is headed for the house of the Sheriff. No one else buys such rich food! Let's step out and have a word with him."

So Robin and Little John came out from behind their tree. As soon as the butcher saw them, he wheeled his cart around, for he knew (as did everyone) that outlaws haunted the forest. But Little John seized the horse's bridle, and Robin said, "Good butcher, I'll change clothes and places with you for ten pieces of gold. Let me take your cart into town, while you rest here in the forest with my men."

The butcher didn't want to rest in the forest—but Little John was holding his horse's bridle with one hand, and a thick quarterstaff with the other. So he climbed down, quaking with fright, and gave his clothes to Robin Hood. Robin fixed a black patch over one eye to conceal his face, climbed onto the cart and drove into Nottingham, to the house of the Sheriff. When he arrived there, he gave the Sheriff's wife such a good price on his tenderest, choicest pieces, that she invited him to stay for dinner.

So Robin the outlaw tied his horse to the Sheriff's fence and went in to eat with the Sheriff! He sat at the table, chuckling to himself as the Sheriff complained about that pestilential nuisance Robin Hood. But he pricked up his ears when he heard the Sheriff say, "And worst of all, this fellow Blondel who once knew Richard insists that Richard is not dead at all, and that our gracious King John is no more than a usurper!"

"Indeed?" Robin said, politely. "Does he think Richard will return?"

"He swears he'll find him," the Sheriff said, taking a good swig of ale. "He has gone to wander through the world, looking for Richard. If he should find Richard, our days of ease will be over! But maybe he'll die of plague first. More meat?"

"I thank you," Robin said, "no. I must be getting back to my herds and flocks."

"By our Lady," the Sheriff swore, "if your herds are as fine and fat as these, I would buy them myself."

"I'll sell them to you!" Robin said. "Ride on my cart with me, and I'll give you as good a price on the whole lot as I gave you on this day's meat. But be sure to bring all your money with you."

Now, the Sheriff was too greedy to resist such an offer. So he filled a bag with gold and went with Robin at once. The two drove the butcher's cart deep into the thick forest of Nottingham. And the farther they went, the more uneasy the Sheriff became. "Butcher!" he whispered, "where are your herds?"

"Close by!" Robin promised him.

"That fellow Robin Hood might be near," muttered the Sheriff.

"Robin Hood is no worry to me!" Robin answered, with truth. "But we need go no further. Just let me call my herdsmen." And with that he put his horn to his lips and blew three clear notes. At once a huge herd of fat deer poured across the road in front of him. And just after came a crowd of men in green, with bows on their backs and quarterstaffs in their hands. At the sight of them, the Sheriff turned white and begin to shake with fear.

"These are my men," said Robin, pulling off his eye patch, "and those deer are my herds. They roam the forest, protected by John's unjust laws, while the people of Nottingham starve. But you've brought them money to buy meat! Hand over your bag, Sir Sheriff."

The Sheriff, his hands trembling with dread, handed over his money. Little John spread his cloak on the road and poured out a river of gold onto it, while Robin's men shouted their approval.

"Take him to the edge of the forest, blindfold him, and leave him there," Robin ordered. "Let him go back and tell John that the people of Nottingham serve King Richard, not the cruel prince who starves and beggars them. Long live Richard, King of England!"

"Long live Richard, King of England!" all the men cheered. But the Sheriff snarled, "One day I'll hang you, Robin Hood, and all your men too!"

"But first," Robin said, "you'll have to learn the difference between a butcher, and an outlaw."

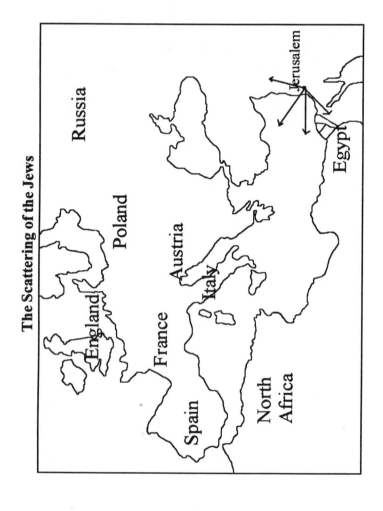

The Scattering of the Jews

202

Chapter Twenty
The Diaspora

The Scattering of the Jews

We've been reading about the time of the Crusades—the years when knights from all over the world fought over the city of Jerusalem. But Jerusalem was built by the Jews. Why weren't the Jewish people in charge of their own city?

Long ago, back before the beginning of this book, the Roman Empire was still strong and powerful. The land of the Jews, called Judea, was ruled by Rome. And some of the governors appointed by Rome taxed the Jewish people heavily, arrested and executed Jews for no reason, and refused to let the Jewish people worship God in their own way.

Finally, the Jews of Jerusalem revolted. They rose up against the Roman army that occupied Jerusalem. The Roman soldiers in Jerusalem weren't ready for a rebellion, and they had to retreat. But soon Rome heard of this rebellion at Jerusalem, and sent a huge army of sixty thousand men into Judea. This army marched through the countryside, destroying the villages where Jewish freedom fighters, called *Zealots,* were hiding. Finally they arrived at Jerusalem and put the city under siege. The siege lasted for months, until the Roman soldiers broke down the walls of Jerusalem and poured into the city. They burned the Temple, where the Jews worshipped, and took the Jewish people captive.

Now Judea was under Roman rule again. But the Romans were tired of putting down Jewish rebellions. They thought, "As long as we leave the Jews in their own city, they'll keep trying to take it back from us." So the Romans scattered the Jews all through their empire. And they refused to rebuild the Temple.

This was a problem for the Jews. After all, they were Jews because of their worship of God! An Englishman was someone born in England, and a Frenchman was someone born in France. But a Jew was someone who worshipped God in the Temple. Without the Temple, how could the Jews be Jews?

One Jewish scholar, Yohanan ben Zakkai, believed that the Jews could still remain Jews, even though they could not worship in the Temple. He thought that the *Torah*, the sacred writings of the Jews, could be the "glue" that held the Jewish people together. If they could all remember and follow the Torah, they would still be Jews, even if they were scattered all over the world.

But Yohanan had a problem. He was in Jerusalem, and the Romans were knocking down the walls. He knew that Jerusalem was doomed. So he bought a coffin and lay down in it, pretending to be dead. He had his students carry him out of Jerusalem, weeping and wailing the whole way, telling everyone who stopped them that they were going to bury their leader.

Once they were safely away, Yohanan ben Zakkai climbed out of the coffin. He went to a little town near the sea with his pupils, and there set up a school for the study of the Torah. He trained other teachers, or *rabbis*. These rabbis went out to other towns where the scattered Jews were living, and taught them how to worship God in little local "temples" called *synagogues*. For hundreds of years, the Jews went right on living all over the world, worshipping God in their synagogues and reading the Torah. Throughout the Middle Ages, Jewish people lived in many different countries: England, Spain, France, Russia, Italy, Egypt, and more. But even though they were English, Spanish, French, Russian, Italian, Egyptian, and all other nationalities, the Jews also remained *Jews*.

Jews were often viewed with suspicion by the kings of the countries where they lived. In England and France, they weren't considered "good Englishmen" or "good Frenchmen" because their worship of God was more important than their loyalty to England or France. So the Jews were often mistreated. During the Middle Ages, England and France both declared that Jews were not welcome in their countries! But many Jews settled in Spain, because the Muslim rulers were friendlier towards Judaism than were the Christian kings. The Islamic kingdom of Spain was so friendly to Jews that the Jews talk about their time in Spain as the "Golden Age of the Jews."

The Jews would not have a land of their own again until the twentieth century. But because of the rabbis and the Torah, they remained Jews, even without a country to call their own. We call this scattering of the Jews the *Diaspora*.

A Tale of the Diaspora

After the Jewish people were scattered, they lived in many different countries. In each country, they learned the language and customs of the people who lived around them. Jewish children in France learned to speak French, and they heard French fairy tales. The Jews in England listened to English bedtime stories. And those who lived in Spain began to speak like the Moors, and told stories they had heard from the Moors.

But although the Jews borrowed stories from many other lands, they also changed them, so that the

205

stories became very much their own. In many of these stories, cleverness and faith triumph over wickedness and hatred. Here is one of these stories: "The Clever Rabbi of Cordova," a story told by the Jews who lived in Spain.

The Clever Rabbi of Cordova

Long ago, a clever Rabbi lived in the city of Cordova, in the days when the Emir of Cordova was willing for the Jewish people to live in his city. But the Emir grew older, and listened to evil advisors, and allowed his mind to be changed. One day the Emir decided that the Jews must leave Cordova, never to return.

But he did not wish the other inhabitants of the city to think him a cruel and heartless ruler, so he decided to make his command look like a test. He announced, "The Jews must prove their worthiness to live in our beautiful city. They must choose one from among their number to come to my palace and pass three tests. Only if that man can pass all three of my tests may the Jews stay."

Now, the people in the *aljama* (the Jewish part of the city of Cordova) were terrified to hear this edict. They didn't want to leave their homes and gardens, cows and donkeys, shops and farms. So they gathered together and elected their clever Rabbi to go to the palace of the Emir.

The Rabbi went to the palace with a heavy heart. "For how can I save my people, if the ruler is determined to throw us out?" he sighed to himself. "Our fate must be in the hands of God." He walked under the cool arches into the presence of the Emir.

Now, the Emir had determined to set three tests which no man could pass. So he said to the Rabbi, "Your first test will determine how learned your people are. Tell me this: How many stars shine in the sky?"

"Five million, four hundred thousand, three hundred and two," answered the Rabbi promptly.

The Emir stared at the Rabbi in disbelief, for he had been certain that no man could answer this question. "How—how do you know such a thing?" he stammered.

"I counted them," the Rabbi said. "If you don't believe me, count them yourself and tell me whether I'm right."

The Emir realized that he had been outwitted. And so he said, "Very well. My second test will determine how wise your people are. Tell me this: What is the distance between the truth and a lie?"

Now this was more difficult, and the Rabbi had to think. Just as the Emir was opening his mouth to say, "The Jews must leave my city!" the Rabbi announced, "I have it! The width of one hand."

"What?" the Emir said, puzzled.

"The truth is what you see with your own eyes," the Rabbi explained. "A lie is what another tells you to be true, but which you cannot see. The distance between your eyes and your ears is the width of one hand. So this, too, is the distance between the truth and a lie."

The Emir did not know what to say to this. So he cleared his throat and said, "You have one test left to pass. Now we will see how fortunate your people are." He gestured to his servant and the man brought forward a bowl. In this bowl were two pieces of paper. "On one piece of paper," the Emir said, "I have written the word 'Stay.' On the other, I have written, 'Go.' Choose one piece of paper. Whichever piece you choose, you and your people must do as it says."

Now indeed the clever Rabbi was distressed, for he knew that, as sure as the sun rises, the Emir had written the word "Go" upon both pieces of paper. Whichever he chose, the Jews would be forced to leave Cordova. So he thrust his hand into the bowl, chose a piece of paper—and put it his mouth!

"What are you doing?" shouted the Emir. "Why are you chewing up the paper? It has the fate of your people on it!"

The Rabbi chewed and swallowed. When the paper was safely in his stomach, he smiled at the Emir.

"Oh, mighty Emir," he said, "Now I will abide by your judgment. The paper I chose, I have destroyed. But its opposite is still in the bowl. Whatever the paper in the bowl says, I chose the other one."

The Emir, speechless with amazement, unfolded the remaining paper. Sure enough, it read "Go."

"So you see," the clever Rabbi said, "the paper which I chose must have said 'Stay.' As you have decreed, then, we will stay in Cordova."

So the Rabbi bowed and left the palace of the Emir, having passed all three tests. And the Emir, caught in his own trap, honored his word and let the Jews of Cordova remain in their homes, as long as he reigned in that beautiful city.

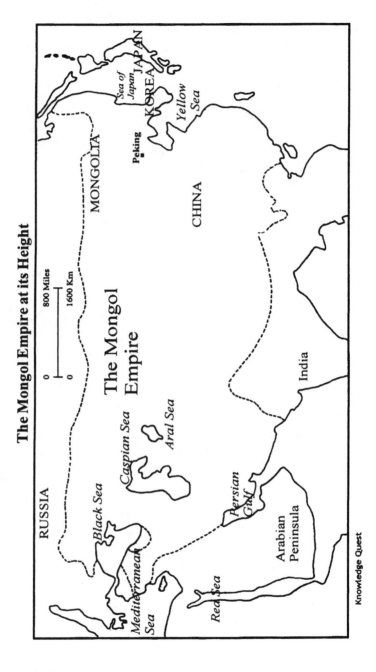

The Mongol Empire at its Height

Knowledge Quest

Chapter Twenty-One
The Mongols Devastate the East

Genghis Khan, Emperor of All Men

While Christian and Islamic armies were fighting with each other in the West, a different kind of battle was going on in the East. The eastern kingdoms of China and Japan didn't have to worry about invading Muslim armies. But they did have to worry about the Mongols.

The Mongols came from the wild, cold mountains north of China. They lived in felt tents which they

A medieval drawing of a Mongol warrior

took down each morning, leaving nothing but ashes behind. They were nomads who swept over the countryside, conquering and killing. The bone-chilling cold of the north didn't stop them; they wore furs and leather and rubbed their skin with grease to keep the wind away. They never settled down and grew crops; instead they ate foxes, rabbits, and other small wild creatures. But they could go without food for days at a time. If they were in danger of starving, they would open the veins of their horses, drink some blood, and then close the vein and ride on.

The Mongol tribes raided Chinese villages on the northern edge of China. They killed merchants and stole their goods. But they never tried to invade China itself—until Genghis Khan became their leader.

Genghis Khan belonged to a small Mongol tribe called the Yakka. His father was the Yakka chieftain, or *khan*. But the Yakka was only one of many Mongol clans. And the Mongols fought with each other as often as they fought with the Chinese.

Genghis Khan had a better idea. He thought that the Mongols should all join together and attack China. Just on the other side of the Great Wall lay the rich Chinese city of Peking, where people lived in warm houses, heated by fires, with soft beds, plenty of food, and bags of gold. Genghis Khan wanted to conquer this rich city.

But first he had to convince all the Mongol tribes to follow him. When his father died, Genghis became leader of the Yakka. He set out at once to conquer the other Mongol clans as well. He fought savagely against them, forcing their leaders to swear allegiance to him. He promised, "Anyone who doesn't follow me will be killed. I will flatten his tent far into the ground, so that a horse galloping across it at midnight won't even stumble. The greatest joy in my life is to kill my rivals and steal their possessions!"

Would *you* surrender to a man who talked like that? Most of the Mongols did. And those who didn't were killed. After Genghis Khan killed one rival leader, he moved his tent to cover the body. Then he ordered his servants to remove the body through the tent's smoke hole, late at night, while everyone was watching the front of the tent. In the morning, he announced that the gods had killed his rival and spirited the body away as punishment for defying Genghis Khan. After that, *everyone* followed Genghis!

Now it was time for Khan to lead the unified Mongols against China. They swarmed down out of the north, destroying every city they came across, leveling every building to the ground. They broke through the Great Wall, into China. And while King John was signing the Magna Charta over in England, Genghis Khan was conquering the city of Peking.

But then Genghis Khan decided to turn his armies to the West. He told his followers that the sky-god Tengri had chosen them to conquer the earth. And then he led them against the frontiers of the Islamic empire.

No one could stop this horrific invasion! Genghis Khan and his Mongol horde seemed like the punishment of God. Muslims called him "The Scourge." He terror-ized the western part of the Islamic empire for five years and conquered cities almost as far as the Caspian Sea. Villagers were so frightened of him that when the Mongol warriors came into sight, they would lie down on their faces and surrender without even trying to fight. One Muslim historian, Ibn Athir, tells this story about eighteen men who were riding along when a single Mongol horseman thundered up. "The Mongol told them to tie each other up," Ibn Athir writes, "and so terrified were they that they began to do so. Then one of them said, 'There's only one of him and eighteen of us. Why don't we just kill him and go on our way?' But the other seventeen were too frightened. 'He will kill us if we defy him!' they wailed, and went on tying each other up. So the eighteenth man rode up and knocked the Mongol off his horse. Then the other seventeen galloped away, crying, 'Allah preserve us! A Mongol is here!'" No wonder Genghis Khan conquered such a huge empire! His enemies were too scared to fight back

Genghis Khan was still fighting when he grew ill and died. His people took him back to China to bury him. But they killed everyone who saw the funeral procession pass by, so that no one would know where his grave was. Even today, no one has ever discovered the burial place of Genghis Khan.

The Mongol Conquest of China

When Genghis Khan died, the Mongols ruled an enormous empire—and their kingdom soon expanded even more. The Mongols took land away from the Islamic empire. They conquered part of the Byzantine Empire. Their kingdom stretched from the Yellow Sea to the west as far as the Mediterranean. And when Genghis Khan's grandson Kublai Khan came to the throne, he completed what Genghis Khan had begun. He became the emperor of China.

Kublai Khan already had control of the city of Peking, which his grandfather Genghis had conquered. Now he began to fight his way to the south. It wasn't an easy fight! The Mongols were ferocious warriors, but the Chinese were shrewd and well-educated. Their scientists had developed new weapons to defend against invasion. They knew how to make poisonous fogs which could be blown across a battlefield: the "soul-hunting fog," which had arsenic in it; the "five-league fog," made out of gunpowder, wolf dung, and other strange ingredients; and the "magic smoke," powdered lime shot into the air to make a choking cloud.

But in the end, the Mongol fierceness defeated the Chinese wisdom. Kublai Khan marched into China

214

and removed the emperor from the throne. Now he was emperor of China! And he founded a new dynasty—a Mongol dynasty to sit on the Chinese throne.

Kublai Khan lived in great luxury. He built a huge palace in the city of Peking and hired ten thousand bodyguards to protect him. Everyone who came into his palace had to take off his shoes to show humility in the presence of the Khan. And whenever his officials called out "Bow down and worship!" all of his visitors would bow down until their foreheads touched the floor.

A medieval portrait of Kublai Khan

Now that he was the emperor, Kublai Khan wanted to conquer the countries on China's coast. Korea, the small nation on China's east coast, was defeated at once. But when Kublai Khan attacked Japan, he met with his only big defeat.

At first, Kublai Khan sent the Japanese a message. "Surrender and your lives will be spared!" he announced. But the Japanese refused to surrender. So the Mongols built a fleet of warships and tried to sail across the water to the coast of Japan. The Mongols didn't know much about fighting at sea—but they never even got close to Japan. A huge wind blew up and forced the ships back towards the Chinese coast. Many of the Mongol warriors drowned. And the weakened Mongol army retreated back into China to gather its strength.

Seven years later, the Mongols returned with even more warships and a larger army. They sailed towards Japan and met the Japanese ships for a battle at sea. The battle raged on and on. But just when the Mongol army seemed to be winning, another great wind howled down on the Sea of Japan. The Mongol ships were driven back towards China once more. Many sank. A storm had saved Japan for the second time! The Japanese believed that the gods had sent these two storms. They called these storms "kamikaze," or "divine winds." A thousand years later, Japanese fighter pilots would remember these battles when they called themselves "kamikaze pilots" because they descended from the air to destroy their enemies.

Even though he never conquered Japan, Kublai Khan ruled over the largest empire in the world. For twenty-three years, he was the emperor of China *and* the Great Khan of the Mongols. His name was feared throughout the entire world.

But the Mongol empire didn't last. After Kublai Khan died, his relatives divided his empire into small kingdoms, each one ruled by a minor chieftain. And in China, the dynasty Kublai Khan had founded grew weaker and weaker. Soon, Kublai Khan's descendents lost the Chinese throne. The huge Mongol empire had been like a mushroom that springs up and grows to an enormous size overnight – and then fades away just as quickly. In all, the Mongol domination of the world lasted for less than a hundred years.

The Ming Dynasty of China

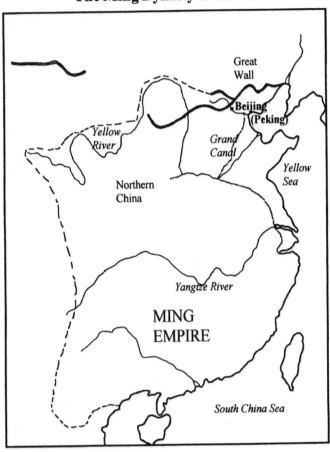

Great
Wall

**Beijing
(Peking)**

Yellow
River

Grand
Canal

Yellow
Sea

Northern
China

Yangtze River

MING
EMPIRE

South China Sea

Knowledge Quest

Chapter Twenty-Two
Exploring the Mysterious East

Marco Polo Goes to China

For people who lived in Europe, China was on the other side of the world. The long road that led to China, the Silk Road, led through mountains and along the edges of steep rocky cliffs. It wound through dry deserts where the only water was found in small pools under the scattered oases. Merchants who set off down the Silk Road to buy spices and jewels in China might be lost in a sandstorm in summer, or a snowstorm in winter. And China was so far away that it could take five years to travel down the Silk Road and return!

But the merchants who *did* manage to travel the Silk Road found wonderful things at its end: gold, cloves and ginger, jade and lacquer, rare and beautiful flowers, wine, sweet-smelling wood, rugs with rich complicated patterns, and the mysterious shining silk cloth that only the Chinese knew how to make. Europeans marveled over these treasures and hurried to buy them as soon as the caravans from China arrived.

Kublai Khan knew that trade with Europe would make China even more prosperous. So he did his best to encourage traders and merchants to come to his cities. He turned his Mongol soldiers into road-keepers and policemen and sent them out to guard the roads and protect travelers against bandits. As the journey grew safer, more and more merchants and adventurers traveled along the Silk Road to see the marvels of China's cities.

One of these adventurers was named Marco Polo. Marco Polo was the son of an Italian merchant named Niccolo. Before Marco was born, Niccolo left on a journey to China. He didn't come back until Marco was fifteen years old! When he did return, he told his son, "It took me three years to travel to the palace of the Great Khan. When I arrived, the Khan made me welcome and gave me a position as his messenger. All this time, I have been working for the emperor of China! He sent me back home to ask the pope for a hundred wise men who could explain Christianity. And he wants me to bring him back some holy oil from Rome. You're a strong boy, and growing to be a man. You can travel with me to China."

So Marco and his father started back down the Silk Road, carrying holy oil for the emperor of China. The journey took four years! Marco and his father were attacked by bandits. They had to take a detour to avoid a war in one of the countries they passed through. Marco became ill and had to rest for a whole year.

But finally Marco and his father arrived in the city of Peking. There, they met the emperor, Kublai Khan. We know what Marco Polo thought about this meeting, because he wrote a book about his journey to China. This book, which he named *The Book of Marco,* was read all over the world. For many years, Marco Polo's book was the only way for people in the west to find out what China was like.

In his book, Marco Polo described the marble palace of the Khan. The palace stood in a huge walled garden where wild animals roamed the grounds. A man-made mountain rose up in the garden's center, with beautiful trees from every part of the world planted all over it. A lake filled with fish lay at the foot of the mountain, and a small palace for the Khan to relax in was built at its top.

Inside the palace, carvings of dragons and colorful paintings of battle scenes covered the walls. Marco Polo was led to a dining hall where six thousand people could eat at once. In his book, he wrote, "It is all painted in gold, with many histories and representations of beasts and birds, of knights and dames, and many marvelous things. Over all the walls and all the ceiling you see nothing but paintings in gold." Here the great feasts of the Khan were held—and Marco Polo tasted his first ice cream.

Marco Polo was amazed by the beautiful clothes that the Chinese people wore, by the abundance of fresh

meat and vegetables in the Chinese markets, and by the size of the fruit. "Certain pears of enormous size," he wrote, "weigh as much as ten pounds each." And he was astounded to see fires made out of black rocks that burned. Marco Polo had never seen coal before!

Marco and his father stayed in China for almost twenty years. Marco traveled all around

A medieval Chinese gentleman

China, seeing its great cities with their beautiful buildings and its tiny villages filled with peasants and farmers. When Marco Polo grew older, Kublai Khan put him in charge of governing different cities in his empire. He sometimes asked Marco to judge between Chinese officials who were arguing with each other. And once he even asked Marco to find out whether his soldiers were plotting against him.

When Marco and his father finally returned home, their relatives refused to let them in. Marco was now a man of forty, and Niccolo had a white beard. And they were wearing ragged, dirty clothes. "You aren't Marco and Niccolo!" their relatives scoffed. "They've been dead for years! You're just beggars."

So Marco and Niccolo ripped open the seams of their coats. Jewels tumbled out: emeralds, rubies, and sapphires! The two men had worn their oldest clothes and had sewn their jewels into the seams so that robbers would not attack them. Finally, their relatives let them in. Marco and Niccolo had returned from China.

The Forbidden City of the Ming

Marco Polo was lucky to make his journey to China during the reign of Kublai Khan. The Great Khan wanted Europeans to come to his country, so he tried to make the Silk Road safe. But after the Great Khan's death, traveling to China became more and more difficult. The land between Europe and China itself had once been controlled by Kublai Khan and protected by his soldiers. But now other Mongol leaders divided this in-between land among themselves. They fought with each other over the borders of their new little kingdoms. Now there were wars all along the Silk Road! Merchants traveled to China less and less often—and then hardly at all.

The new rulers of China, the emperors of the Ming dynasty, didn't *want* Europeans to come to their country. Kublai Khan had been anxious to learn all about the religions, the science, and the people of the west. But the Ming emperors believed that China was already the best country in the world. They thought that Chinese art and science was already perfect, and that the Chinese way of living couldn't possibly be improved. So instead of trading with the outside world, or sending Chinese people to start new settlements in different countries, the Ming emperors made the Great Wall even stronger, to protect against invaders—and stayed home. One of the emperors even made it illegal to build ocean-going ships. He told sailors that anyone who tried to sail to other countries and trade with them would be executed.

That same Ming emperor decided that, instead of traveling to other countries, he would put his time into building a palace right at the center of China's capital city, Peking (today, we call this city Beijing). This palace would show the beauty of Chinese architecture and the skill of Chinese builders. The royal family would live in it. The emperor's home and all of his official buildings would be part of the palace. And no foreigner would ever be allowed to enter it. We call this palace the *Forbidden City* because it was as large as a small city, and because foreign visitors were forbidden to see it.

The Forbidden City took fourteen years to build. Its walls were made from enormous stones that were cut from stone quarries outside of Beijing. The stones were too heavy for oxen to pull into the city—especially during the winter, when the roads were covered with frozen ruts. So the Chinese laborers dug a well every three or four hundred feet along the road. They poured water on the road and waited for it to freeze into ice, and then slid the stones along on the ice, right into Beijing!

The stone walls that surrounded the palace were thirty feet high. Inside these walls, the Chinese built 9,999 smaller buildings. These buildings are made not only out of stone, but out of hard red bricks made from rice and lime. The bricks are attached together with a cement made out of mashed rice and egg whites. These bricks have remained strong for centuries!

Yellow is the color of royalty in China, so the buildings were decorated with gold dragons and yellow paintings, and the roofs were covered with yellow tiles. Each building inside the Forbidden City had a special name. The largest buildings, where the emperor worked on the business of ruling his country, were called the Hall of Supreme Harmony, the Hall of Military Might, the Hall of Peace, and the Hall of Terrestrial Tranquility. The emperor's throne room was in the Hall of Celestial Purity, which had walls lacquered red, a marble floor, and golden carved dragons all around the walls.

Bridge of the Summer Palace in the Forbidden City

The emperor himself lived in great luxury. He had entire buildings all to himself! He ate alone, waited on by dozens of servants. A food-taster stood beside him and took a bit of each dish before the emperor ate it, to

224

make sure that none of the food was poisoned. The cooks of the Forbidden City would make roast chickens, roast deer, glazed duck, raised sweet buns, iced cakes, rice, several kinds of soup, a dozen vegetables and wine for every meal, just for this one man! There was so much food at each one of the emperor's meals that his leftovers were served to the others who lived in the palace.

The emperor's family and other relations also lived inside the Forbidden City. A royal child could grow up inside the Forbidden City and never need to leave! Children could spend their time doing lessons, but also painting, flying kites, ice skating, and playing with pet birds. They could go see plays and concerts, performed for them in a special theatre called the Pavilion of Cheerful Melodies. But they probably had the most fun raising crickets! Special pet crickets were kept in cricket cages and taken for walks on narrow leashes made of thread. Cricket-fights were held to find out whose cricket was the strongest. In a museum in China, you can still see the cricket-cages owned by the last emperors of China when they were children!

The emperors lived in the Forbidden City for centuries. About ninety years ago, the last Chinese emperors were driven out of the Forbidden City. Some of the buildings were destroyed. But today, the Forbidden City has been restored and rebuilt. Tourists can go see the palace that no medieval traveler ever saw.

The Territory of the Rus

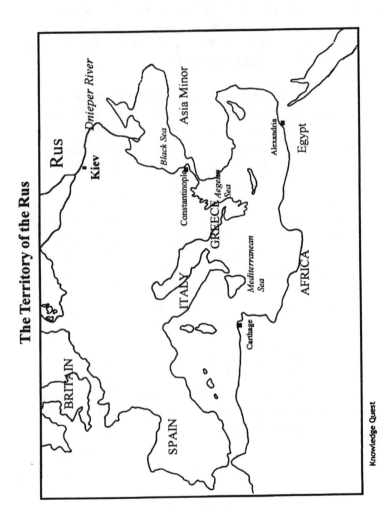

226

Chapter Twenty-Three
The First Russians

The Rus Come to Constantinople

Let's leave the Forbidden City now, and travel back west, to the great city of Constantinople. Constantinople was the capital of the Byzantine Empire. (Remember, the Byzantine Empire was the eastern half of the old Roman Empire.) The emperor of Byzantium lived in Constantinople. And whoever conquered Constantinople could rule the whole Byzantine Empire! So Muslim warriors tried to conquer Constantinople—and failed. Mongol warriors tried to conquer Constantinople—and failed. But now Constantinople would face yet another attack from yet another band of warriors: the *Rus*.

The Rus lived to the north of Constantinople, in the middle of the continent of Europe. They were tall, blond, blue-eyed warriors, descendants of Viking explorers. Back when the Vikings were invading France and England, a Viking warrior named Rurik wandered into central Europe and decided to stay. He and his men settled down to rule over their own little kingdom. The people who already lived there, the Slavs, had to obey them. They called these Viking invaders the Rus, because "Rus" sounded like Rurik's name.

The Vikings hadn't brought very many women with them, so they married Slavs. The children and grandchildren of the Vikings and Slavs formed their own tribes, built their own cities, and traded with the other countries around them. Soon the tribes of the Rus were becoming a powerful people.

The Rus were good sailors, like their Viking forefathers, and often sailed south down into the Black Sea to trade with the city of Constantinople. The Rus had ivory tusks from walruses, honey and beeswax from their own hives, nuts from their trees, and slaves that they had taken captive in their battles with other countries. They exchanged these for silk, glass, and silver in Constantinople, which they called the "Great City."

But sailing to Constantinople was hard work, even for the grandchildren of Vikings. The rivers leading to the Black Sea were full of rapids (shallow water, running over sharp rocks). Sometimes, the rivers were so shallow that the Rus would have to pull their ships out of the water on giant log rollers, roll the ships past the shallows, and then roll them back down into the river. Each trip to Constantinople took weeks—or months.

"You know," the Rus chieftains said to each other, "it would be a lot easier to just conquer Constantinople than to keep sailing down these shallow rivers." So they armed themselves with swords, shields, and spears, launched their ships in one huge war fleet, and set off to attack the Great City.

Conquering Constantinople wouldn't be easy! The city was built on a little peninsula, so that water surrounded it on three sides. Three thick walls circled the city, and between the walls and the edge of the sea was a moat sixty feet wide (as long as six or seven cars parked end to end). On one side of the city, towers rose up the wall, so that archers could fire out to sea. On the other side an enormous chain was stretched across the water, between two towers, so that enemy ships couldn't approach the city's shore.

But the Rus were sure that they could conquer Constantinople. After all, they were Vikings! Sailing into battle was what they did best.

Meanwhile, the Byzantine army was preparing their secret weapon: Sea fire! Sea fire was an oil that kept on burning even when it was spread out on water. When the Rus ships appeared on the horizon, the defenders of Constantinople threw this oil into the water and set it on fire—and the water itself burned. The wooden ships of the Rus couldn't break through the sea fire. And so they had to leave Constantinople and sail back home. "The Greeks possess something like the lightning in heaven!" they wrote in their histories. "They released it and burned us. For this reason we did not conquer them."

One of the strongest of the Rus princes decided that it would be better to make friends with Constantinople, rather than attacking the city again. This prince, named Vladimir, sent the Byzantine emperor a peace present: Six thousand fierce Rus warriors, who would fight for the Byzantine Empire. The Byzantine emperor was delighted with his new army! He made them into his own personal bodyguard. From now on, the Rus would be the official guardians of the Emperor. They were called the *Varangian Guard*. And soon they were known all over Byzantium for their ferocity and their strength! The emperor was so grateful that he promised the Rus free food, beds, and baths whenever they came to Constantinople to trade. Eventually Vladimir himself married a Byzantine princess—and was baptized as an Eastern Orthodox Christian. Many of his people followed him and became Eastern Orthodox Christians as well.

Soon the country of the Rus became known by their name. Today, we call this kingdom *Russia*, after the Rus.

Ivan the Great and Ivan the Terrible

In its early days, Russia (the land of the Rus) wasn't one country with one ruler. Instead, warrior princes ruled over several different Rus tribes. Vladimir was the prince of Kiev, but other strong Russian cities—like Moscow—often fought with him. Before Russia could be a great country, the Russian cities would have to be joined together.

The prince who finally brought the Russian cities together was named Ivan. He was a descendent of Rurik, the Viking invader who first settled in Russia. Because he made Russia into one country, he is remembered as *Ivan the Great*. But Ivan's grandson wasn't so great. As a matter of fact, he was such a dreadful ruler that he was called *Ivan the Terrible*.

Ivan the Great was the prince of the Russian city of Moscow. [1] When Ivan began to rule in Moscow, his first task was to get Moscow free from the local Mongol kingdom. Remember: after Kublai Khan died, the enormous Mongol Empire broke up into smaller kingdoms ruled by the warlords called khans. One of these Mongol kingdoms claimed part of the land of Russia. And the local Mongol khan demanded that Ivan pay him *tribute*—money to show that Ivan recognized the Mongols as the true rulers of Russian land.

Ivan refused to pay the tribute The Mongol khan sent a message saying, "Pay up, or I'll attack you!" "Go ahead!" Ivan retorted. So the khan assembled his army

---

[1] Ivan the Great became tsar after the final fall of Constantinople to the Turks, described in the next chapter. His story is told here to connect it with the earlier history of Russia.

and marched up to Moscow's walls. Ivan gathered *his* soldiers and got ready to fight back. And then the khan turned his men around and marched home. His army wasn't really strong enough to defeat Ivan's Russians. He had been bluffing, hoping that Ivan would pay tribute to avoid a fight. But the truth was that Ivan was more powerful than the Mongols. Now Moscow was free from Mongol rule.

Ivan's next job was to conquer the other Russian cities and make them loyal to him. He captured Kiev and the other large Russian cities, took their princes off their thrones, and replaced them with governors who would be loyal to Ivan. He made Moscow the capital city of this new unified Russia. An ancient fortress called the *Kremlin* lay at the center of Moscow; Ivan the Great built strong walls around the Kremlin and hired a famous architect to build beautiful cathedrals inside it. He ran the country of Russia from his palace inside the Kremlin. Today, Moscow is still the capital of Russia, and the Kremlin is still the center of the Russian government.

Ivan the Great was a good Russian king. But his grandson, Ivan the Terrible, became legendary for his wickedness. By the time Ivan the Terrible became king, the people of Moscow liked to call their city the *Third Rome*—the most important city in the world after Rome itself and after Constantinople. [2] And the ruler of this Third Rome was a powerful man! As a matter of fact,

---

[2] Moscow was also called the "Third Rome" because of its importance to Eastern Orthodoxy; Rome was the center of the Catholic faith, and Constantinople was the center (or "Rome") of the Eastern Orthodox faith. But after the fall of Constantinople to the Turks, Moscow became the world center of Eastern Orthodoxy.

during the reign of Ivan the Terrible's father, the leaders of Moscow announced, "By nature, the king is like any other man. But in power, he is like the highest God!"

Ivan the Terrible took this power seriously. He called himself *tsar,* which means "Caesar," to show that he was as powerful as the ancient Roman emperors had been. And at first, he used his power to make Russia stronger.

Based on a famous painting by Repin, "Ivan the Terrible and His Son Ivan: November 16, 1581"

But then Ivan's beloved wife died. And after her death, Ivan began to go mad. His hair and his beard began to fall out. He accused his advisors of treachery and ordered them executed. And he formed a special, secret band of police who were supposed to look out for anyone who might be plotting against the tsar. These secret police rode black horses, with black saddles and bridles. Each carried a flag with a picture of a broom and a dog's head on it, to show that they were pledged to sniff out evildoers and sweep them away.

But the secret police were the worst evildoers of all! They killed innocent people, took land and houses from anyone they pleased, stole from stores, and burned down the homes of anyone who tried to oppose them. Ivan himself sometimes joined in their crimes! If the secret police told him that a village contained traitors, Ivan would order the entire village executed. And when the Eastern Orthodox Archbishop scolded Ivan for his cruelty, Ivan had his cathedral looted, stripped off the Archbishop's clothes, and sent him away in the snow.

The noblemen of Russia wanted Ivan's son, now a grown man, to become tsar in his father's place. But Ivan refused to give up his throne. One day, he and his son began to argue over the future of Russia. Ivan grew so angry that he struck out at his son with his staff, a heavy oak stick tipped with iron. The blow landed on the younger man's head—and killed him.

When Ivan realized what he had done, he tried to throw himself from the tallest tower in the Kremlin. But his courtiers held him back. For the rest of his life, Ivan the Terrible dressed in black. He paced the halls of his palace at night, weeping and groaning. When he saw a comet in the evening sky, he announced, "My death is near!" Shortly afterwards he collapsed and died. The grandson of Ivan the Great was dead—and Rurik's dynasty was at an end.

The Greatest Extent of the Ottoman Empire

Caspian Sea

Baghdad

Trebizond

Black Sea

Jerusalem

Istanbul (Constantinople)

Hungary

Albania

EGYPT

Italy

Mediterranean Sea

NORTH AFRICA

500 Miles

800 Km

0

0

©2001 Knowledge Quest

Chapter Twenty-Four
The Ottoman Empire

The Ottoman Turks Attack

The Byzantine Empire resisted Muslims and Mongols. It stood strong against Russians and a dozen other invaders. But when the Ottoman Turks attacked, the great city of Constantinople was finally forced to open its gates.

At first, the Ottoman Turks were just a ragged band of nomads who wandered through the center of Asia, hunting for their food and fighting with their neighbors. [1] When the Mongol armies began to sweep across Asia, the Turks fled to the west. They wandered through mountains and across deserts, looking for a new place to live. On their journeys, they attacked villages and stole food. But they also traded with Muslim merchants, heard the Koran read—and became Muslims.

Soon these nomads settled down on the edge of the Byzantine Empire. They began to build houses and plant farms, gardens, and orchards. They got up with the sunrise and worked hard to grow crops in the hard, stony ground of their new home. Some Turks became shepherds and wandered with their sheep from pasture to pasture, looking for fresh grass and selling butter, cheese, and wool as they went. Other Turks traveled through their little kingdom, entertaining each village with stories, songs, and dancing bears who shuffled in time to music.

---

[1] The Turks are not known as "Ottoman" until slightly later in their history, but this name will be used throughout this chapter to avoid confusion.

One of the stories told by these traveling entertainers describes the rough, rocky ground of the land where the Muslim Turks now lived. This Turkish legend is called "The Sheep-Rocks."

The Sheep-Rocks

One hot, dry day in summer, a shepherd decided to take his flock to the cool slopes of the mountain above him. So he herded the sheep along the winding, dusty road, climbing up farther and farther. Sweat rolled down his face, and his throat grew drier and drier. Slowly, the air grew cooler. Finally, the shepherd halted at a green, breezy field high on the mountainside. The sheep put their heads down and started to tear up the juicy grass, and the shepherd threw himself down to rest. But he was so thirsty that he soon got up and started to search for water. He looked and looked—but there was no water, not even a single drop.

"Allah!" the shepherd cried out. "Send me water and I promise that I'll sacrifice seven of my best sheep to you! Only keep me from dying of thirst!"

At once a clear fountain of water gushed out of the earth at his feet. He bent down and drank, and the sheep crowded around him and drank their fill as well. But once his thirst was quenched, the shepherd couldn't bring himself to fulfill his vow. He said to himself, "Well, instead of killing seven of my sheep, I'll kill seven of the insects that live in their wool. That's just as good a sacrifice."

So he searched through the thick wool of the fattest sheep and found seven lice. He lined them up and squashed each once, and dropped them into the water. "Here is my sacrifice!" he announced to Allah.

At once the shepherd and all of his sheep turned

236

into stone. When he didn't return home, the men of his village came out to search for him. But all they found was a green pasture filled with rocks, and a stream bubbling quietly up from the ground.

Not all of the Turks were farmers and shepherds, though. Many were fierce, disciplined warriors who were determined to make the Turkish kingdom larger. Devout Muslim families often raised their young men to become *ghazi,* Muslim soldiers who were dedicated to conquering unbelievers and spreading Islam. These warriors set out to increase the size of the Ottoman Turk kingdom and spread Islam at the same time.

The kingdom of the Turks became larger and larger. Under the leadership of their king, called the *Sultan,* the Ottoman Turks attacked the borders of the Byzantine Empire again and again. City after city fell to their armies. The Byzantine Empire shrank—while the empire of the Ottoman Turks grew.

Soon only Constantinople was left to the Byzantine emperor. The people of the Byzantium retreated behind its walls as the Turks attacked. But the three thick walls defeated the Turkish warriors. They could not get through! So they retreated, leaving the emperor in charge of his city. The people of Constantinople began to believe that their city could not be captured. "The city will only fall when the moon turns dark," they told each other.

But the Turks had not retreated for good. They were making plans for a new assault on Constantinople's walls.

The Capture of Constantinople

After years of fighting and conquering, the Turkish armies had expanded the borders of the Ottoman Empire to an enormous size. And as the Ottoman Empire expanded, the Byzantine Empire shrank. Now, the Byzantine emperor only had one city to call his own: Constantinople. The Turks had attacked it again and again, but could not break through its walls.

But then a new sultan came to the Ottoman throne: Mehmed the Conqueror.

From the moment he became sultan, Mehmed was determined to take Constantinople for his own. But he was a crafty warrior. He spent months pretending to be on good terms with the Byzantine emperor, sending friendly messages to the court. But all the time, he was planning to attack. He was building cannon so huge that each cannon had to be pulled by a hundred oxen. He was preparing to fight with gunpowder, which the Byzantine army didn't know how to use. He was hiring *mercenaries* (paid soldiers from other countries). And he was quietly assembling his army, ready to send his warriors against Constantinople in a final attempt to take the city.

When the Byzantine emperor realized that Mehmed was preparing for war, he sent messengers to protest. Mehmed cut off their heads. The war had begun!

Mehmed marched his armies up to the western wall of the city—the only wall that could be reached by land. (Remember, Constantinople was surrounded by water on three sides.) He sent a message to the emperor, inviting him to surrender. The Byzantine soldiers

238

inside Constantinople were outnumbered by Mehmed's Turkish army twelve to one! But the emperor refused to give up without fighting. So Mehmed began to fire his cannon against the wall. The defending soldiers didn't know how to guard their city against these loud, destructive new weapons! The cannonballs cracked the walls and crumbled the tops of the towers.

The walls stood firm, though. Cannonballs alone wouldn't bring Constantinople down.

Mehmed knew that the only way to conquer the city was to surround it with his warships and attack it from all sides. But although he had his troops lined up along the western wall and his warships attacking the southern wall from the water, he couldn't reach the northern wall of Constantinople. The only way to get to this northern wall was to sail his ships up into the Golden Horn, the *harbor* (a deep, quiet body of water where ships can anchor) on the city's north side. But the entrance to the Golden Horn was guarded by Byzantine ships, and the Ottoman warships couldn't break through.

One morning, the Byzantine armies were gazing over the western walls when they saw an extraordinary sight: Ships sailing on the land! Mehmed had ordered his armies to attach hundreds of ropes to the warships anchored on the southern side of the city. Thousands of men and cattle hauled on these ropes to pull the warships up onto the land, right past the western wall of the city, down into the northern waters! Seventy ships traveled past the horrified onlookers and slid right down into the Golden Horn—far away from the Byzantine ships guarding the other end of the harbor. Now the Turks could attack the city from all sides.

As the fighting continued, the city began to run out of food. Water became scarce. Some of Constantinople's people tried to escape from the city late at night, when the Turkish camp was asleep. But others said, "Constantinople won't fall. Remember: the city is safe until the moon turns dark!"

Almost two months after the siege began, the Turkish army lay outside Constantinople, waiting for morning. The moon shone brightly down, casting long clear shadows next to the tents. Suddenly, the moon began to disappear, a little at a time, as though some enormous creature were slowly eating it away! The Turkish soldiers began to murmur and point, and then to shout with joy. And inside the city, the Byzantine defenders were struck with horror. Was this a sign of disaster?

Actually, it was an eclipse. The earth had moved between the sun and the moon, blocking the sun's light so that it could not reflect from the moon's surface. But no one knew this! The Muslim Turks and the Byzantine Christians both thought that the eclipse predicted the end of the war. The Turks began to prepare for a final attack. The priests in Constantinople held a final Christian service in the Hagia Sophia, the great Christian cathedral built by Justinian hundreds of years before. The last Byzantine emperor attended this service and then went out to join his soldiers in their fight against the invaders.

The Turks threw themselves against the walls. Finally, one of the gates to the city was forced open. Mehmed, seeing the defenders fall, shouted to his men, "Friends, we have the city!" The Ottoman Turks poured into the city. The emperor was killed in the fighting. And the Turks flooded through Constantinople, stealing and killing. "Some of the troops turned to the houses of the rich," writes the Greek historian Kritovoulos, who lived during this time. "They robbed the wealthy. Others looted the churches. They threw crosses and holy cups into the street and broke them into fragments, and burned holy books. And still more went to the houses of the people. They stole, plundered, murdered, and took slaves—men and women, children and old people, priests and monks. Ten thousand terrible deeds were done!"

Mehmed went straight to the Hagia Sophia and set his throne right in the middle of it. His men began to make the cathedral into a Muslim mosque. Four days after the last Christian service in the Hagia Sophia, the first Muslim service was held there. And the city of Constantinople was renamed *Istanbul,* a name it still bears today.

The fall of Constantinople is one of the great events of medieval history. From this moment on, the way of life begun by the Romans centuries ago was truly over. The last remnants of the old Roman Empire had disappeared. Sometimes the conquest of Constantinople is called the End of the Middle Ages.

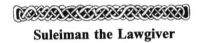

Suleiman the Lawgiver

Now the Ottoman Turks had the largest empire in the world! It covered the Middle East and spread into North Africa. Constantinople, now called Istanbul, was their capital city. The Ottoman Turks repaired the broken walls, laid new stones down over the streets, and dug new wells. They re-opened the harbors for trade. Soon the countries around them were recognizing the Sultan of the Turks as one of the most powerful rulers in the world. "No one doubts that you are now the Emperor of Rome," wrote one scholar to the Sultan. "Constantinople is the center of the Roman Empire, and whoever rules Constantinople is Emperor!"

The greatest Emperor and Sultan of all was Suleiman. Suleiman was named after the Hebrew king

Solomon, the wisest ruler of ancient times. Just like his namesake, he became known all over his kingdom for his fairness. Suleiman wanted to make sure that all the people of his country were treated fairly, and that the laws he passed were followed. This was a big task—in an empire as large as the Ottoman Empire, there were many different courts, in many different villages and cities! And different parts of the empire sometimes followed different laws.

So Suleiman took all the different laws that the Ottoman people followed and put them together into one set of laws that his whole empire would follow. Justinian, the great Byzantine emperor, had done the same thing when he came to the throne of Byzantium. Both of these great rulers knew that they could only hold their large empires together if everyone had the same set of laws to obey!

Suleiman went one step further than Justinian. He chose governors who would supervise the different parts of his empire and make sure that his new laws were followed. But he wanted to make sure that these governors were being just. So he would dress in disguise, so that no one knew who he was, and travel around his empire, watching all of his governors to make sure that they were behaving properly.

And that's not all. Suleiman also had the largest spy network in the world! His spies lived all through the empire, keeping an eye on all of the empire's officials. They told him whenever a official was acting unjustly.

The spies also told Suleiman whether or not he was popular. The Sultan knew that he could only be a good ruler if his people liked him. So he told his spies to go listen to Friday prayers all over the empire. Muslim worshippers pray every day, but on Fridays, they are supposed to pray that their Sultan will live a long time and be healthy. The spies were supposed to tell Suleiman whether or not his people prayed for him on Fridays. If everyone prayed that the Sultan would live a long time and be healthy, Suleiman knew that his people liked him and wanted him to go on ruling. But if they decided not to pray for him, Suleiman knew that he was in trouble.

Suleiman wasn't just the head of his empire. He also declared that he was Caliph—the head of all the Muslims in the entire world. Not all of the world's Muslims agreed that Suleiman should be their spiritual leader! But Suleiman had an advantage: His empire had spread to include Mecca, Medina, and Jerusalem, the three holiest cities in Islam. Any Muslim pilgrim who wanted to travel to a holy city had to enter Suleiman's empire. So when Suleiman announced, "I am the Caliph!" no one argued with him too loudly.

Suleiman was just as careful to be a good spiritual leader as he was to be a good emperor. Old stories tell us that although Suleiman had guaranteed all pilgrims a safe journey to the holy cities in his empire, he hadn't bothered to rebuild the walls around Jerusalem, which had been destroyed during the Crusades. One night, Suleiman was sleeping when he had a dreadful dream. He was standing on the plain in front of Jerusalem, watching pilgrims go into the city, when two huge golden lions appeared from behind the city's walls, snarling at him. He tried to run, but the lions pounced on him and started to tear him apart! And a voice said sternly to him, "This has happened because you have not protected the holy city of Jerusalem."

When Suleiman woke up, he thought, "That dream came from God! It is a command to rebuild the wall around Jerusalem." He ordered his craftsmen and masons to start to work at once on a thick, strong wall to protect the holy parts of Jerusalem from any invasion.

And he also commanded them to build a gate in this wall with a carved lion on either side, as a reminder of his dream. Today, the Lion Gate still stands in Jerusalem.

By the time Suleiman died, he ruled over so much land that he called himself "Slave of God, Master of the World, Shah of Baghdad and Iraq, Caesar of all the lands of Rome, and the Sultan of Egypt." Actually, Suleiman's empire never spread over to Italy, where Rome stood. But he did rule the largest empire in the world. And the rest of the world called him Suleiman the Magnificent.

After Suleiman's death, his son inherited his throne. But this new Sultan was a weak ruler; his people called him The Drunkard because he spent more time at parties than he did running his country. The Ottoman Empire began to shrink. It lasted for more than three hundred years before it disappeared completely—but never again was it as powerful as it had been under Suleiman the Magnificent.

The Spread of the Black Death

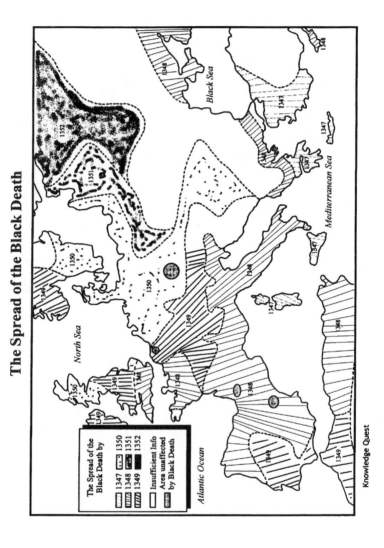

The Spread of the
Black Death by

1347　1350
1348　1351
1349　1352

Insufficient Info

Area unaffected
by Black Death

North Sea

Atlantic Ocean

Black Sea

Mediterranean Sea

Knowledge Quest

Chapter Twenty-Five
The End of the World

The Plague

The people who lived in the Middle Ages had to face one invading army after another: Muslims, Vikings, crusaders, Mongols, Russians, and Turks! But the most dangerous enemy of all wasn't an army. It was a sickness that spread across the world—and killed more people than all these armies put together.

At first, strange stories began to come out of the distant parts of China. Travelers told about a mysterious illness that killed almost everyone who caught it. It began with terrible headaches and high fevers. The sick coughed, sneezed, and suffered from terrible pains in their arms and legs. Swollen lumps as large as baseballs appeared under their arms. Rumors said that thirty-five million people had died from this sickness.

Soon the rumors became reality! People who lived near the Black Sea began to grow sick. In the villages and plains nearby, hundreds died. An old story tells us that the villagers blamed foreign merchants from Italy for bringing the sickness. They gathered into an army and drove the Italian merchants into the city of Caffa, at the edge of the Black Sea.

The people of Caffa (and the Italian merchants) barred the gates and fought back. So the attackers put the dead bodies of those who had died from the sickness into catapults and hurled them over the walls. Soon illness broke out in Caffa as well. The Italian merchants panicked! They ran from Caffa, boarded their ships, and sailed back home to Italy. But by the time they got there, almost everyone on board the ships was sick—or dead. The people of Italy refused to let them come ashore. But despite this, the sickness soon appeared on land. It spread through Italy, up into Europe, across the sea to England, and down into North Africa. Millions of people died. No one could stop this sickness, which people called the *Black Death*.

An Italian writer named Giovanni Boccaccio, who lived during the Black Death, describes it in his book the *Decameron*. Here is a retelling of part of his story:

Doctors were helpless. Most people who got sick died within three days. Anyone who came near the sick or touched their clothing became sick also. With my own eyes, I saw the clothes of a beggar who died of plague thrown out into the road. Two pigs came along and nosed at the clothes. Not an hour later, both pigs began to turn round and round, and then, just as if they had been poisoned, dropped dead in the road.

Thousands of people grew sick every day, and there was no one left to take care of them. Many fell down in the streets and died where they lay. Bodies were everywhere. There were so many dead that there were not enough priests to bury them all. Many times a priest would begin to lead a funeral procession, and then would look behind him and find that three or four other coffins had fallen in behind him to join the burial service. And when the bodies arrived at the churchyards, they were thrown into huge trenches with hundreds of others, covered only with a thin layer of dirt.

When the sickness came to the cities, many people shut themselves up in their houses and refused to come out. Others pretended that nothing was wrong, and went about singing and eating and drinking and having parties at all hours. They wandered into any house they pleased and used it as their own—and no one cared, because so many houses were left empty by the dead.

Some carried with them, no matter where they went, flowers and scented herbs that they held to their noses. Others left the city and fled into the country. But many of these people fell sick as well. Farmers died; their crops lay ungathered in the fields, and their oxen and donkeys wandered free into the fields, glutting themselves with grain.

Oh, how many lords and ladies died, leaving their rich houses empty; how many families perished, leaving not a single heir; how many brave men, beautiful women, and strong youths ate breakfast in the morning with their families and friends, and then that same evening ate supper with their ancestors in the world which is to come! And there were no tears, or candles, or mourners. So many died that soon no one paid any more attention to dead bodies of people than they did to the dead bodies of goats.

Today, scientists know that the Black Death was an illness we call *bubonic plague*. The plague was an infection carried by fleas that lived on rats. When traders moved along the Silk Road from China, back towards the Black Sea, the rats came with them, eating the grain they carried and hiding in their bales of cloth. The rats (and the fleas) ran through the countryside and into the city of Caffa. When the Italian traders left Caffa, the rats went with them in the cargo holds of their ships. And when the Italian ships arrived back in Italy, the rats ran down the anchor ropes onto shore—even though the sick sailors stayed on board.

From there, the fleas that carried the disease went from rat to rat, all over Europe. Rats were everywhere in the Middle Ages! Cities threw their garbage and leftover food into the streets, so there was always plenty of food for them. And wherever the rats went, the Black Death went with them.

But people of the Middle Ages didn't know that rats were spreading the disease. Some thought that the plague was the judgment of God. Others thought that it had been caused by earthquakes, evil spirits, or bad food. No one knew how to prevent it. They carried flowers and herbs with them, ate onions and garlic to keep sickness away, and slept on their

During the plague, doctors wore bird outfits to avoid catching the illness.

stomachs instead of their backs so that sickness wouldn't settle down into their noses at night.

But nothing helped. One medieval history tells us, "So many died that all believed it was the end of the world."

A New Way of Living

The Black Death raged for years. When the plague finally ended, a very different world was left. One out of every three people had died! Whole villages and towns were wiped out. Fields grew up full of tangles and weeds; grain rotted before it could be harvested.

Cows, sheep, and pigs wandered loose and turned wild—or died because there was no one to look after them.

Noblemen who owned huge estates wanted their fields to be farmed again. But so many peasants had died that they couldn't find anyone to work on their land. One priest wrote, "So few servants and laborers were left that nobody knew where to turn for help. The following autumn it was not possible to get a harvester….Because of this, many crops were left to rot in the field." [1]

The peasants and farmers who *were* left alive found themselves in very high demand. Everyone wanted them! They no longer had to work for nothing on the land of rich farmers. Instead, they could demand to be paid higher wages. The noblemen who had to pay them grew poorer; because they couldn't afford to pay workers to farm all their land, their huge estates grew smaller and smaller. The peasants and farmers grew a little bit richer, and were able to buy land of their own. The feudal system, in which peasants worked for noblemen in exchange for land, began to fall apart.

Many of the villages wiped out by the plague were never rebuilt. The survivors went to the cities instead. As more and more people left the countryside, the cities began to grow larger. So craftsmen (workers who could make wagon wheels, barrels, iron tools, cloth, and other goods) went to the cities as well, where they could sell their crafts to more people. Priests, left with empty churches, moved into the city also. We call this move out of the country and into the city *urbanization*. "Urban" is the Latin word for "town" or "city," so urbanization means "becoming citified."

---

[1] This comes from the account kept by Henry Knighton of Leicester Abbey.

Back out in the country, hundreds of farms and houses were left empty. Some of the peasants who remained moved into these unclaimed houses and farmed the deserted land as their own. They took over their masters' beds, clothes, tools, and flocks. And there was no one to chase them out! They became the new owners of this land. In one city in Scandinavia, everyone died except for one little girl. She lived with the animals for years, until rescuers came along and discovered her. By then, she had forgotten what other people were like. She was afraid of them and preferred the animals! But the rescuers took her in and taught her to be human again. When she grew up, they gave her all the land in the whole town, since she was the only survivor. She and her family became the new noblemen of that city.

Becoming a craftsman was easier too. Before the Black Death, anyone who wanted to follow a special trade such as weaving, wagon-building, carpentry, or ironwork had to be an *apprentice,* or student, for many years. But after the plague, few craftsmen were left. Wagon wheels, iron tools, and blankets were soon in short supply! So the length of time that an apprentice had to study before setting up his shop became much shorter.

The Black Death even changed the land itself. Before the plague, forests all over Europe had been cut down and the land turned into fields. But now, with so few farmers left, the trees began to grow back. Forests sprang up all over Europe. Seventy years after the Black Death ended, the woods had grown up so close to the borders of the huge city of Paris that wolves skulked along the city's edge! And a hundred and fifty years after the plague, huge, dense woods covered mile after mile where farmland and villages had once stood.

The Black Death is long past, but it left its traces all over the people and the land of the Middle Ages. And today, we still have at least one reminder of the plague with us. Have you ever heard this nursery rhyme?

Ring around a rosy,
A pocket full of posies.
Ashes, ashes,
We all fall down!

Many historians think that this nursery rhyme got its start in the days of the Black Death. "Ring around a rosy" describes the red rash that broke out on sick people. A "pocket full of posies" is the bouquet of flowers and herbs that many people carried to keep sickness away. Today, we say, "Ashes, ashes," but in the oldest version of this rhyme, the third line goes "A-tishoo! A-tishoo!"— the sound of an ill person sneezing. And "All fall down" reminds us that most people who caught the plague died.

France and England

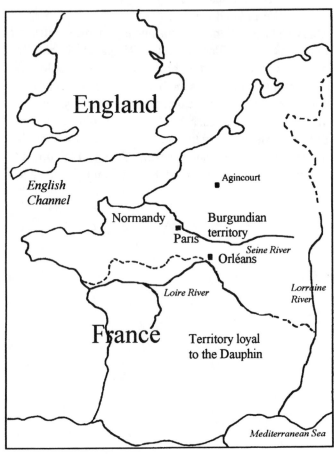

England

English
Channel

Normandy

Paris

Agincourt

Burgundian
territory

Seine River

Orléans

Lorraine
River

Loire River

France

Territory loyal
to the Dauphin

Mediterranean Sea

Knowledge Quest

Chapter Twenty-Six
France and England at War

Henry V and the Battle of Agincourt

When the Black Death swept across Europe, it interrupted a war between England and France. For ten years, the kings of England and France had been fighting over French land that the English claimed should belong to England. (Do you remember that Richard the Lionhearted was killed in France while he was trying to capture a French castle for England? The English and French had been fighting over land for a very long time!)

When soldiers on both sides began dying of plague, the two countries gave up fighting—for a little while. But as soon as the Black Death passed, the war started up again. In all, France and England would fight each for almost a hundred years. We call this long quarrel the *Hundred Years' War*.

The English king who came closest to winning the Hundred Years' War was named Henry V. He is one of the most famous of all English kings, because a poet named William Shakespeare wrote a play about his attack on France.

When Henry V became king, he was determined to bring an end to the war between England and France once and for all. And he had a plan for getting that "English" land back from the French. You see, Henry's great-great-grandmother Isabella was a French princess who married an Englishman. So Henry sent a message to the French king saying, "The land I want actually belongs to me, because I should have inherited it from my great-great-grandmother, the French princess

Isabella. Give it to me, and also give me your daughter Katherine to be my wife. Or else I'll invade France with my army!"

The French king, who was named Charles VI, knew perfectly well that he couldn't give Henry the land *and* his daughter. If he gave Henry the land, he would be admitting that land belonging to a French princess should actually go to the princess's children—even if those children were English. Then, if Henry married Katherine and had children, Henry could claim that Katherine's children should inherit all the land belonging to Katherine. And since Katherine was the daughter of the king of France, Henry could claim that she had a right to own all of France. Henry's demands were a sneaky way of getting France for himself!

So Charles VI sent back a message rejecting Henry's claims. And his son, the heir to the French throne, sent Henry a rude insult along with his father's message. He packaged up several tennis balls and told Henry, "You're just acting like a child. Stop running around threatening France, and go play some tennis instead to burn off all that extra energy."

That was the last straw! Henry V prepared to invade France. In Shakespeare's play, Henry V sends the French prince back this message after he opens the tennis balls: "Tell the prince that I am glad he can make jokes with me. Tell him that when I have hit these balls with my racket, I will hit his father's crown right out of bounds. Tell that joking Prince that this joke of his has turned his tennis balls into cannonballs. And although a few people may have laughed at his joke, thousands more will weep because of it." Here are Shakespeare's actual words (remember that "Dauphin" is the French word for "prince"):

We are glad the Dauphin is so pleasant with us....
When we have match'd our rackets to these balls
We will in France, by God's grace, play a set
Shall strike his father's crown into the hazard....
And tell the pleasant prince this mock of his
Hath turn'd his balls to gun-stones....
....And tell the Dauphin
His jest will savour but of shallow wit
When thousands weep more than did laugh at it.

(Henry V, Act I, scene ii)*

When Henry's army first landed in France,
everything went wrong. He was defeated in several
small battles with the French. His soldiers got sick.
Their shoes began to wear out. And then winter started
to come down on them. Henry knew that his army might
not survive a long, cold winter camped out in the open.
So he decided that he should go back to England and try
again the following year.

But the French didn't intend to let Henry try
again. The French army cut off Henry's retreat and met
his ragged band of soldiers at a field called Agincourt.
Henry was outnumbered, but he had no choice. He had
to fight, even though his soldiers were tired, cold, hungry,
afraid, and outnumbered.

In Shakespeare's play, Henry inspires his men to
fight with a famous speech in which he tells them that
they are lucky to be at Agincourt, because men will
always remember them. And he tells them that the battle
will make them all equal. Even those who are peasants,
or "vile" (the word "vile" used to mean "from a lower
part of society") will be like nobility (they will be
"gentled," or "made like gentlemen"). Here is part of
Henry's speech before the battle:

We few, we happy few, we band of brothers—
For he today that sheds his blood with me
Shall be my brother; be he ne'er so vile
This day shall gentle his condition—
And gentlemen in England, now abed,
Shall think themselves accurs'd they were not here,
And hold their manhoods cheap while any speaks
That fought with us upon Saint Crispin's Day.

(*Henry V,* Act IV, scene iii)

(St. Crispin's Day was the day when the French and English fought at Agincourt.)

Of course, we don't know exactly what Henry V said to his men before the battle of Agincourt. His speech probably wasn't as stirring as the one that Shakespeare imagines for him! And we don't know whether he convinced his men that they were lucky to be fighting the French. But we do know that the English won the battle—even though the French army was so much bigger.

The Battle of Agincourt was a turning point in the Hundred Years' War. Henry went on to take control of a large part of France. And the French king, Charles VI, gave Henry his daughter, Katherine, as his wife. Charles also agreed that when he died, Henry V would become the king of France as well as England.

But even though Henry V had conquered France, he never got to be its king. He died only seven years after the Battle of Agincourt, two months before Charles VI also died. With both men dead, Henry and Katherine's son, Henry VI, became the king of England and France—even though he was only a year old!

Joan of Arc

The baby Henry VI became the king of England and France while he was still in diapers—but many of the French didn't want an English king to rule them. Instead, they wanted the Dauphin to be crowned king of France. Do you remember the Dauphin—the prince of France? He sent Henry V tennis balls, back when Henry first threatened to attack France. If it hadn't been for Henry, the Dauphin would have inherited the French throne from his father, the king of France. And now that Henry was dead, he wanted his crown back.

But not all of the French wanted the Dauphin to be king. Some of the French thought that the baby Henry VI would grow up to be a better king than the Dauphin—and they also hoped that the English would give them money and land. These French followed a powerful nobleman called the Duke of Burgundy. They were called *Burgundians*.

Now France was divided in a *civil war* (a war where the people of a country fight against each other). The French who wanted the Dauphin to rule were on one side. On the other side were the Burgundians (the French who wanted the English Henry VI to be king). And English soldiers fought on the side of the Burgundians as well.

The Dauphin and his army needed to keep control of one of the most important cities in France—the city of Orléans. But the Burgundians and the English surrounded it and started a siege. Unless the Dauphin and the rest of his army could drive the attackers away, Orléans would have to surrender. One day, the Dauphin and his generals were planning out their next move in their headquarters when a messenger arrived. "Sire," he announced, "a girl is demanding to see you."

"Who is it?" the Dauphin snapped.

"It is Joan, the Maid," the messenger said. "She says that God told her to save the city of Orléans from the siege."

Now, the Dauphin knew who Joan was. For several years, he had been hearing rumors about this peasant girl. Joan of Arc claimed that saints and angels appeared to her in visions and told her to lead the French into battle against the Dauphin's enemies. Many people believed her. A French knight had even given her a horse, armor, and soldiers to follow her. Now Joan was here at the Dauphin's headquarters. But how could this girl help him get his throne back?

"Send her away!" he ordered. But his advisors convinced him to see Joan. "The people love her!" they whispered to him. "They believe that she has been sent by God to deliver France from the English. And Sire— one of your guards has already insulted her. She told him, 'Do not mock God, so near your death.' And not more than an hour later, he fell into the moat and drowned!"

Finally the Dauphin sighed. "Very well," he said. "Send her in. If God has sent her, she'll recognize me, even though she's never seen me before." He gave his crown and royal robe to one of his friends to wear, and he hid in the crowd that filled the room.

When Joan came into the throne room, she ignored the man wearing the crown. She pushed through the crowd until she found the Dauphin, and knelt down in front of him. "Dauphin," she said, "I have come to see you crowned king of France!"

At this, the Dauphin was almost convinced that Joan was sent by God. But he ordered his priests and scholars to ask her questions about the Christian faith, to make sure that she was a true Christian and not a sorceress. When the priests told him that Joan was a follower of God, the Dauphin agreed to let her attack the army of Burgundians and English that surrounded Orléans.

When Joan arrived at Orléans at the head of her army, she called out to the English to surrender. But they

The Dauphin's soldiers fought under this battle flag.

shouted back, "We'll burn you if we ever get our hands on you! You're nothing but a cowgirl. Go back and tend your animals at home!"

So Joan ordered her generals, "Attack!" The French soldiers, sure that Joan was blessed by God, fought ferociously against the enemy. At last, the Burgundians and English were forced to retreat from Orléans. Joan had her first great victory! From now on, she was often called "Joan, the Maid of Orléans."

Now Joan was determined to take the Dauphin to the great cathedral at Rheims, the center of the Christian faith in France, so that he could be crowned king. She marched to Rheims with the Dauphin and her army, defeating enemies as she went. Finally, the Dauphin reached Rheims and was crowned king. Now, he was called Charles VII of France. All he had to do was defeat the last remaining Burgundians and drive the rest of the English out of his country. Joan was ready to help him.

But the Dauphin hesitated. Instead of fighting, he tried to make deals with some of the Burgundian leaders. He told his army to wait while he sent messengers back and forth. As time went on, his soldiers began to desert him. And then all of his deals fell through. The Burgundians attacked him, his army was defeated, and Joan was captured.

Charles VII didn't even try to get Joan back. He let the English and the Burgundians put Joan on trial for witchcraft. During the trial, no one who liked Joan was allowed to testify for her. Witnesses who hated her made up false stories about her. She was found guilty and was taken out to be burned alive. But still, Charles VII did nothing! And so Joan was put to death. Many of the people who saw her executed wept. Even some of the English cried out, "We have burned a saint!"

After Joan's death, Charles VII and his generals finally managed to drive the English out of France. The Burgundians swore allegiance to the French king, and Henry VI lost his claim to the throne of France. France was free of England once more.

It took fifteen more years for Charles VII to remember Joan. Perhaps, as he grew older, he began to feel guilty about abandoning her to his enemies. Whatever the cause, he finally asked the church to re-examine the case against Joan. Twenty-five years after Joan died, she was announced to be innocent of all charges against her—twenty-five years too late.

Chapter Twenty-Seven
War for the English Throne

The Wars of the Roses

The French weren't the only people to fight with each other over who should be king. England had its own civil war over the throne! Cousins from one side of the royal family, called *Lancastrians*, fought against cousins from the other side of the family, called *Yorks*. The Yorks had a white rose on their banners, and the Lancastrians had a red rose on theirs. So today we call these wars over the English throne the *Wars of the Roses*.

The Wars of the Roses began during the reign of Henry VI, the baby son of Henry V. When Henry VI grew up, he began ruling England for himself. He was a very good man. He spent hours and hours in prayer, he refused to have his enemies put to death, and once he even left a dance given in his honor because he thought that the dresses worn by the young ladies weren't decent enough! But Henry VI preferred reading and praying to ruling. Once, he was reading in his room when his dukes came to ask him about a problem in his country. King Henry VI sighed and said to the priest who was with him, "They do so interrupt me by day and night. I can hardly find a moment to read holy teachings without disturbance!"

After he had been king for years and years, Henry VI had a fit of madness. Suddenly he stopped speaking to anyone. He sat in one place, staring in front of him, for hours. He didn't seem to hear his friends when they spoke to him—even when they told him that his wife had just given birth to a son.

Henry VI's madness was probably inherited. His grandfather, the king of France, had struggled with fits of insanity all his life. He even believed that he was made of glass, and that he would break if he fell over! Now this madness had passed down to the English royal family.

England needed someone to run the country until Henry VI recovered. So Henry's family asked Henry's distant cousin, the duke of York, to become *Protector,* or substitute king. The duke of York agreed. But when Henry VI began to get better, the York family didn't want to give up the throne. Henry and his queen had to gather an army and march against the duke of York's army. After a huge battle, the York supporters were defeated, and the duke himself was killed. The queen ordered his head put up on the city walls, with a paper crown on it!

Now Henry VI could rule again. But the York attempt to get the throne wasn't over. The duke of York's son, Edward, raised another army and attacked the royal forces again. And this time, the Yorks were victorious. They put Henry VI in jail, and Edward took over the throne, proclaiming himself to be Edward IV, the rightful king of England.

Edward was a handsome youth of nineteen, six feet tall, a good dancer and a good fighter. He was also a capable king. He learned the names of every important man in his kingdom, so that he could greet every one like a friend. But Edward fell in love with a woman his family didn't like. Elizabeth Woodville was older than he was. And she had been married before—to a knight who died fighting on Henry VI's side! Edward knew that his mother and his advisors would never approve of Elizabeth. So he married her in secret. Months later, when his advisors tried to arrange a marriage between Edward and a foreign princess, Edward had to admit that he was already married. He ordered London decorated with colored paper and tinfoil, and brought Elizabeth Woodville into the city in a great parade. He also gave her five brothers important jobs in his government.

Many of the English nobles didn't like that! They thought the Woodvilles were gaining too much power. So several of the nobles joined together with Henry VI's supporters and let Henry VI out of jail. They marched towards Edward's palace in the middle of the night to arrest him. But he heard they were coming, jumped out of bed, and fled from the country!

Now Henry VI was king again—but not for long. Edward was busy raising another army. He marched back into England and took Henry VI prisoner. "My good cousin," Henry VI said, when he was taken captive, "I know that in your hands my life will not be in danger." But he was wrong. While he was in prison, someone killed him. We don't know who the murderer was, but Edward probably gave the order for Henry VI's death.

Now that his rival was gone, Edward IV was able to reign for twelve uninterrupted years. When he died, his twelve-year-old son became king in his place. But this young king, Edward V, was too little to rule all alone. So his uncle Richard, Edward IV's brother, offered to help.

That was the end of the twelve-year-old king's reign! Richard took over the throne and announced that he was now King Richard III of England. Young Edward V and his little brother mysteriously disappeared. The people of England murmured about Richard's cruelty. They whispered that he had ordered his brother's two sons murdered so that he could take the throne. They told stories about his wickedness. According to one story, Richard was born with a full set of teeth and ate live frogs for fun! According to another, he had a withered arm because Elizabeth Woodville, the young king's mother, had put a curse on him.

Richard may have gotten his crown by wickedness, but he didn't keep it for long. Two years after he became king, another royal cousin, Henry Tudor, gathered yet *another* army and challenged Richard's claim to the throne. Richard marched his own soldiers out to meet Henry at a battleground called Bosworth Field. Richard should have won the "Battle of Bosworth Field," because his army was twice as large as Henry's. But his soldiers didn't fight very hard. As a matter of fact, only a few hundred men were killed in the battle. The rest surrendered!

When Richard's advisors saw that Henry was winning, they told Richard to run. But Richard refused. "I will not budge a foot!" he yelled. "I will die king of England!" And he did. He was killed in the battle, and the royal plume on his helmet was lopped off and given to Henry Tudor. Henry put it on and announced that he was now the new king of England. The Wars of the Roses were finally over!

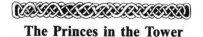

The Princes in the Tower

When Richard III died at the Battle of Bosworth Field, he left a mystery behind him. Remember, at first Richard wasn't king. He was the *regent* for his nephew, Edward V. But then Edward V and his little brother disappeared. What happened to these two boys?

No one knew.

Here is the story of the two princes in the Tower. When Edward IV married Elizabeth Woodville (the woman his family didn't like), they had two sons. The elder boy was named Edward after his father. The younger boy was named Richard, after his uncle. The younger boy lived with his mother, the queen, in London, but little Edward lived in a quiet castle out in the country, with servants and tutors to look after him. One of the queen's brothers lived with him as his governor. He made sure that Edward finished all his schoolwork and did as he was told.

When Edward IV died, his elder son was only twelve. Someone needed to help him rule England until he was old enough to be king on his own. Edward had left papers making his brother Richard the Protector, or "substitute king," for the little boy. But young Edward's mother and her brothers wanted to be the ones who helped the new king rule. So they didn't tell Richard, who was far away in the north of England, that Edward IV was dead. Instead, they planned to bring the little boy to London and have him crowned right away. Once young Edward was crowned king, he could choose his own helpers.

But one of Richard's friends saw what was happening and sent Richard a frantic message. "Hasten to the capital with a strong force!" he wrote. "Avenge the insult done by your enemies! You should take the young king immediately under your protection!"

As soon as Richard got this message, he set off for London himself with a band of soldiers. He met Edward, his servants, and his governor on their way to London for the young king's crowning. When Richard saw Edward, he knelt down and bowed his head. But he also told his nephew, "Your mother and her brothers are trying to take over your kingdom. And if you allow them to rule for you, they might try to get rid of you. I fear for your life!"

Edward insisted, "My mother and her brothers are innocent of any wrongdoing!" but Richard and his soldiers disagreed. They locked Edward's governor in a nearby inn and arrested Edward's servants and soldiers. Then Richard put all his *own* soldiers in their place. And Richard sent a message to Edward's mother and her brothers, saying, "I haven't kidnapped the king, my nephew. I have rescued him. I am more worried about his welfare than any of you. I will bring him to London very shortly so that he can be crowned."

The queen and her brothers didn't believe Richard. They were sure that Richard would kill Edward and take the crown. But most people in London trusted Richard and refused to join the queen in fighting against him. So the queen took her younger son, Edward's little brother, and hid in a church where she would be safe.

Meanwhile, Richard did just what he said he would do. He brought young Edward, now King Edward V, to

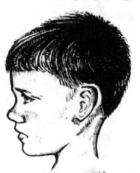

London and rode with him through the streets while people cheered, "Long live the King!" He made all the important people of London swear allegiance to Edward V.

But he still wouldn't allow the queen or her brothers to see Edward. And soon he suggested that Edward would be safer if he moved to the Tower of London. The

Edward V, boy king of England

Tower had been built hundreds of years before by William the Conqueror—as a jail! Since then, other kings had added walls and buildings to the Tower, so that it was a palace as well as a jail. Edward had his own apartment in the Tower, with his own servants and his own soldiers. But all of his servants and soldiers were chosen by Richard.

Next, Richard sent a whole band of armed men to the church where the queen was staying. He ordered the queen to send Edward's little brother to the Tower of London to live with Edward. "Edward is lonely," the message said. "He has no one to play with."

The queen didn't want to send her youngest son to stay at the Tower. Then, Richard would have control over both of the heirs to the throne. But with all of those armed men surrounding her, she had no choice. So she sent the little boy out to his uncle. And Richard took his nephew to live in the Tower with his brother Edward.

The next day, Richard announced that Edward's *coronation* (the ceremony in which he would be crowned king) would be put off until later. A few days later, a famous priest preached a sermon saying that Richard, not Edward, should be king. And a few days after that, a group of noblemen gathered together and asked Richard to take the crown away from Edward for the good of England. Many people suspected that Richard had ordered the priest and the noblemen to say these things. "The people who had loved him as Protector," one London man wrote in his journal, "started to complain about him when he made himself King." But most people didn't complain very loudly, especially after Richard ordered Edward's governor beheaded. No one wanted to be next!

Just a few weeks later, Richard rode to the Tower of London himself—for his own coronation! His supporters crowned him king. Now Richard, the king's uncle, was Richard III, king of England.

But what about Edward and his younger brother?

They were still living in the Tower. But fewer and fewer people were allowed to see them. Soon the people of London began to mutter that the princes had been killed. The rumors spread through England and even over to France. But for the next two years, no one knew for sure where the princes were or what had happened to them.

Then Henry Tudor invaded England, killed Richard at the Battle of Bosworth, and became king. When Henry arrived in London, he had the Tower searched—but there was no sign of the boys.

No one ever discovered what happened to the princes. Twenty-five years later, one of Richard's knights claimed that he had murdered the two boys—but he confessed to avoid being tortured, so he might have made this story up. Two important historians then wrote that Richard had ordered the boys killed. But both of those historians wanted to please Henry VII, who had replaced Richard on the throne, so they were anxious to make Richard look as bad as possible. Other historians later suggested that Henry VII did away with the boys when he had the Tower searched, so that he would have no trouble keeping his throne.

Almost two hundred years later, workers were clearing away a clutter of old buildings in the Tower of London when they found an old chest, buried in the ground. When they opened the chest, they found two skeletons. Almost everyone agreed that these two skeletons were those of the Princes. But who killed them?

We'll never know for sure, but one thing is certain: In the late Middle Ages, being the heir to the throne was dangerous!

Spain and Portugal

FRANCE

Aragon

Castile

SPAIN

The Balearic Islands

Portugal

Granada

Route of Portuguese explorers

AFRICA

| 0 | 90 Miles |
| 0 | 150 Km |

Knowledge Quest

272

Chapter Twenty-Eight
The Kingdoms of Spain and Portugal

Ferdinand and Isabella Unite Spain

Now let's leave England and travel back over into Europe. Go across the English Channel, the water on England's southern side (remember that south is *down* on your map). You'll find yourself in France, the country that fought with England in the Hundred Years' War. Now go southwest (*down* and to the left) and you'll cross over into another powerful country: Spain.

We've already read about the Reconquest of Spain, when the Christian kingdoms of Spain conquered the land that had been ruled by Muslims for hundreds of years. The Reconquest was carried out by small, divided Christian kingdoms all over Spain. But as time went on, these small kingdoms joined together. Two large and powerful kingdoms called Aragon and Castile grew to cover most of Spain. A third, smaller kingdom, Portugal, lay on the western coast of Spain.

The king of Castile, Enrique, was a young man with big ambitions. He wanted to make Castile into the greatest kingdom of Spain. But to do this, he needed more soldiers for his army. So he promised one of his noblemen, a famous fighter named Pedro Giron, his sister Isabella in marriage—in exchange for plenty of soldiers who would make Enrique's army stronger.

Pedro Giron was delighted by this offer. He could become the king's brother-in-law by marrying the Castilian princess! But Isabella was horrified. She was only thirteen years old; Pedro Giron was over forty. And he was a scoundrel with a reputation for drinking, quarrelling, and killing. She begged her brother to call off the marriage, but he refused. A great wedding feast was planned. Soon the castle was full of cooking, sewing, and baking. But Isabella went weeping in her room, praying that something would prevent this horrible marriage.

Pedro Giron set out for his wedding in a fine mood, boasting about his great match. But on the journey, he began to feel sick. Before he could reach Isabella's castle, he died of stomach pains. Isabella was filled with joy—and relief!

But her relief didn't last long. Four years later, her brother decided that she should marry the king of Portugal, so that Portugal and Castile could be united into one stronger kingdom. The king of Portugal was a fat, wheezing man, old enough to be Isabella's father.

Once again, Isabella begged her brother to change his mind. But once again he refused. "You'll marry the king of Portugal whether you like it or not!" he told her.

So Isabella sent a secret message to Ferdinand, the young prince of the kingdom of Aragon. She had never met Ferdinand, but he was just her own age, and she had heard that he was handsome, courteous, and gentlemanlike. "My brother is determined to make a great match for me," she wrote to him. "I won't marry the king of Portugal, but you are as good a match as that old man. Meet me at a secret place in Castile, and decide whether you will marry me instead."

Ferdinand agreed! But he didn't want Enrique to know that he was coming to Castile. So he collected six of his knights together and told them to dress up like merchants in a trading caravan. Ferdinand put on rags and pretended to be their servant and donkey-tender. Meanwhile, Isabella crept out of her room in the middle of the night, stole a horse from her brother's stables, and galloped away on horseback. When the two met at the secret rendezvous, they talked for two hours—and decided to get married right away. Four days later, they were husband and wife.

Isabella's brother Enrique was furious! But when he died, six years later, Isabella became the queen of Castile. And when Ferdinand inherited the throne of Aragon, Isabella and Ferdinand combined their two kingdoms together into one large kingdom of Spain.

Ferdinand and Isabella decided that they would finish the job of unifying Spain by conquering the very last bit of Spain still under Muslim rule. This last Muslim stronghold was a small, mountainous southern kingdom named Granada, where a Muslim king ruled over his subjects from a castle called Alhambra. For ten years, Ferdinand and Isabella battered away at Granada. Ferdinand himself led the army into battle. Isabella traveled all around Castile on horseback, begging the men of Spain to join the army and fight.

Finally, the Spanish armies were victorious. The Muslim king of Granada surrendered the castle of Alhambra and fled. According to legend, he turned around, as he trudged out of Granada, and sighed over the last view of his lost kingdom. But his mother, who was walking along behind him (and who was very angry over losing her home) snapped, "Don't weep like a woman over what you couldn't defend like a man!" The place where the king stopped to sigh is still called The Last Sigh of the Moor.

Now that Granada was theirs, Ferdinand and Isabella declared all of Spain to be a Christian kingdom. And they made it illegal to practice any other religion in Spain. The Jews who lived in Spain were forced to leave! And almost every Spanish village had Jewish families in it. They sold their homes, often for mere pennies, and set out from Spain in overcrowded ships. Many died in the long, dangerous journey out of Spain.

Although Ferdinand and Isabella were good rulers, they are also remembered for this unjust act. They brought all of Spain together into one country—but they also forced the Jews in Spain to leave their homes forever. [1]

Henry the Navigator, Prince of Portugal

Ferdinand and Isabella drew Castile, Aragon, and Granada together into one Spanish kingdom. But Portugal, the kingdom on Spain's western coast, kept its independence from the rest of Spain.

Portugal was a small kingdom, not much wider than the state of Florida. It had a long coast with many beaches and harbors. Wildcats and wild pigs roamed the countryside. Eagles and falcons soared overhead; flamingos stood in the marshes at the water's edge. The Portuguese were known for their grapes, their olives—and their tripe. Tripe was a medieval dish made of the lining of cows' stomachs, cooked together with calves' feet, onions, cow fat, and fermented apple cider. The Portuguese thought tripe was one of the greatest delicacies in the world!

Because Portugal had such a long coastline, it was easy for the Portuguese people to build boats and sail them. One prince of Portugal, Henry, wanted to use

---

[1] Ferdinand and Isabella also presided over the Spanish Inquisition, one of the most important events of their reign. I have chosen not to discuss it here because it is a complicated and disturbing topic for elementary school children.

276

these boats for more than short trips. He wanted the Portuguese to learn how to sail farther than anyone else in the world.

Prince Henry was the fourth son of the king of Portugal. That meant that he would never inherit the throne, so he didn't need to worry about learning to rule Portugal. He could use his money and his time in another way—to make the Portuguese into great sailors and explorers. Because of his love of the sea, Prince Henry became known as *Henry the Navigator*.

Henry first began to think about building a fleet of sea-going ships when he was a young man helping his brothers fight in North Africa. Henry's father had sent them down to North Africa to capture an important Muslim trading city. Merchants from Africa came to this city with ivory, gold, silver, and salt. Merchants from India came with spices: pepper, cloves, and nutmeg. In the Middle Ages, there were no refrigerators, so people put a lot of spices in their meat. That way, they could eat the meat even when it started to spoil. The spices covered up any bad tastes! Spices were so important that pepper was almost worth its weight in gold.

But Muslim traders knew that the Portuguese were Christians who had driven the Muslims out of their country. And as soon as the Portuguese took control of the city, Muslim traders began to avoid it!

Henry realized that if the Portuguese wanted gold and ivory from West Africa, they would do better to sail down the African coast and trade with the West African tribes face to face. So he hired shipbuilders to build new ships that were fast and light, perfect for exploring strange waters. He paid mapmakers to draw new maps of the coastlines, so that sailors would know exactly where they were when they came ashore. And he built a school for *navigation*. *Navigating* (following a map to a certain destination) is hard to do at sea, because there aren't any roads, trees, or landmarks! So Henry's sailors had to learn how to read star maps so that they could find the North Star and other important stars at different times during the year. They had to learn to use an *astrolabe* (a special measuring tool) to measure how far the sun or the North Star lay above the horizon, and then they had to be able to calculate a ship's position from this information. They had to know how to use a *compass* (an instrument with a magnetic needle that always pointed north). And they had to

An astrolabe, used to measure the position of the stars.

be able to calculate a ship's speed. In the Middle Ages, sailors measured how fast a ship was moving by tying knots at regular intervals on a long rope. Then they would put a piece of wood weighted with metal on one end of the rope and wind the other end up onto a reel. As the ship sailed, the sailors would toss the wooden float off the back of the ship and turn over a glass which had just enough sand in it to run out in exactly one minute. They would let the rope unwind while the sand trickled out of the glass. Then they would stop the reel and count the number of knots along the length of rope that had unwound. This would tell them the speed of the ship. Today, a boat is still said to be traveling at "so many *knots* per hour."

Once Henry's sailors learned how to navigate through unfamiliar waters, they were ready to head south to Africa. But they were frightened. No one had ever sailed down the coast of Africa before. They called the mysterious waters that lay down south the *Sea of Darkness*. They were sure that sea monsters and whirlpools lay in this Sea of Darkness. They were afraid that the ocean became so shallow that ships would wreck on the sea's bottom. They were certain that strong currents would pull them off into nowhere, so that they could never return. And they thought that the sun down south was so hot that the seawater boiled and roasted men alive!

Henry tried to convince his men to sail further south. He paid for expedition after expedition. But all of his sailors were too frightened to go very far! Finally, after fourteen expeditions, a brave explorer named Gil Eannes dared to venture down into the Sea of Darkness. And he discovered that the water there was the same as the water closer to home! Slowly the Portuguese began to follow the example set by Gil Eannes. They sailed further and further down the coast of West Africa to trade for ivory, salt, gold, jewels, ostrich eggs, seal skins—and slaves.

But although Henry the Navigator had hoped that his ships would find their way to India, he died before this could happen. You see, maps in the Middle Ages didn't show how huge Africa was. No one had ever sailed all the way around the continent, so mapmakers couldn't draw an accurate picture of Africa. And no one knew exactly how far they would have to sail to get around the tip of Africa. Some sailors thought that Africa might stretch all the way down to the bottom of the world!

West African Kingdoms

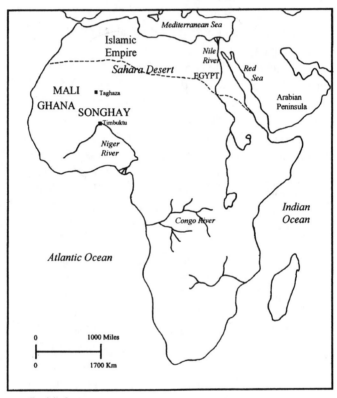

Knowledge Quest

Chapter Twenty-Nine
African Kingdoms

Gold, Salt, and Ghana

Africa was a strange and mysterious place to most Europeans. Beneath the North African coast was the Sahara Desert, a wide, barren, oven-hot stretch of earth where a traveler could be lost in a sandstorm or die of thirst in the trackless, dry wilderness. Few people crossed the Sahara Desert to find out what lay south of it! So hardly anyone knew what lay south of the desert. Because they had never seen the rest of Africa, Europeans called Africa the *Dark Continent*.

But if you look at your map, you'll see that the northern coast of Africa and the Sahara Desert are only two small parts of Africa. The center of Africa lies between two mountain ranges, so high that their tops are always covered with snow and ice. Between these mountains, tropical rain forests grew—hot, damp, tangled green jungle, for hundreds of miles. And further south, Africa has not only jungle, but open grasslands, wide rivers, and rolling hills.

In the Middle Ages, much of this land was home to nomadic tribes who roamed through the jungles and the fields, hunting and fishing, moving from place to place. These tribes did not write down their history in books, or build huge cities. But in West Africa, many Africans lived in kingdoms with houses, roads, palaces, and schools. Archaeologists can see the remains of these buildings today. And these kingdoms welcomed European visitors, who wrote descriptions of what they saw. So we know much more about these West African kingdoms than we do about the tribes who lived in the center and south of Africa.

In the Middle Ages, the three largest West African kingdoms were Ghana, Mali, and Songhay. Ghana lay in the "bulge" on Africa's western coast. The people of Ghana lived in houses made of red clay, dried as hard as cement and covered with roofs made out of reeds or straw. Most were farmers who grew rice, cotton, okra, pumpkins, watermelons, and sesame seeds. They kept chickens and hunted buffalo, antelope, and wild birds for meat. Each man had to serve in the army for one month out of every year, so they spent part of every workday making swords, shields, bows, and arrows. Craftsmen made pots, cloth, copper jewelry, and iron tools. Ghanian iron-workers were treated like magicians. They kept their iron-working skills secret, so that no one knew exactly how the iron tools were made, and blacksmiths had religious rites and rituals of their own!

But Ghana didn't become rich and powerful because of its iron and its pumpkins. It became rich by taxing the gold and salt that traveled *through* it.

Europeans called Ghana the *Land of Gold*, but Ghana itself didn't have very much gold. Gold was found in the earth south of Ghana. The tribes who lived there washed grains of gold out of the soil of riverbeds and banks. They dug it out of the ground by chipping thousands of short *shafts,* or mine tunnels, into the hard earth. Each shaft might yield enough gold to make one small coin. But all together, the shafts produced tons of gold. The West Africans made jewelry, daggers, royal ornaments, and even masks from gold. And they sold gold to the Arab merchants who lived in the north of Africa.

In exchange for the gold, the Arab traders offered salt. In a hot country like Africa, the people needed to eat salt in order to stay healthy. But south of Ghana, there was very little salt in the ground. Most of Africa's salt was found in the Sahara Desert, up in the north. Slaves dug it out of the ground, working in hot, dry salt mines. These salt mines were terrible places to be! Everything was salty—the water, the food, and the ground. In the city of Taghaza, where the largest mines were located, even the houses and mosques were built out of blocks of salt, covered with camel skins. All the trees and plants had died, and there was nothing but sand and salt as far as the eye could see. Today, we still say that unpleasant work is like "working in the salt mines."

The Arab traders brought their salt south to trade for gold. And the West African gold miners brought their gold north to trade for salt. Both the salt and the gold had to go through Ghana. So the king of Ghana charged a toll for every pound of gold and salt that went through his kingdom. Soon Ghana became very rich indeed!

Eventually Ghana grew into an empire that spread all the way out to the West African coast. It boasted an army of two hundred thousand archers and a huge capital city. The king lived in his own private section of the city, with the houses of his priests and wise men surrounding him. A Muslim historian named Al-Bakri visited the king of Ghana and wrote down what he saw for others to read. This is how he described the royal court:

> When the king invites his people to come before him and tell him about their complaints, he sits beneath a tent with his horses tethered all around it, each horse draped in gold cloth. He wears necklaces of gold, bracelets of gold, and a cloth

cap woven with gold. Ten pages stand behind him, each holding a shield and a sword with a golden hilt. His noblemen sit on his right. They wear gorgeous clothes and have gold braided into their hair! The governors and city officials sit on the ground at his feet. The entrance to the tent is guarded by dogs with collars of gold and silver, and they never leave their master's presence.

The kingdom of Ghana flourished for many years. But when its kings refused to convert to Islam, other African Muslims attacked its cities again and again. Ghana began to grow weaker. And the Islamic kingdom just north of Ghana, Mali, was growing stronger.

Mansa Musa of Mali

When Ghana began to crumble, the kingdom of Mali (just above Ghana) took over the gold and salt trade. Like Ghana, Mali lay between the gold mines of the south and the salt mines of the north. Like Ghana, Mali made money on the gold and salt that moved along its roads. But unlike Ghana, Mali was an Islamic kingdom.

Islam spread to the kingdoms of West Africa from the Muslim traders who brought salt down from the north. And although the kings of Ghana had refused to become Muslims, many other West Africans accepted the Islamic faith. The kings of Mali built schools so that their people could learn to read the Koran. They built universities so that students could discuss the important ideas of their religion—along with ideas in mathematics, history, philosophy, and science. As Mali grew, it became famous for its schools, universities, and libraries.

The people of Mali had great respect for their kings. An Islamic adventurer named Ibn Battuta traveled to Mali in the Middle Ages. He described the attitude of the king's subjects like this:

> They submit to their king and grovel in front of him! Anyone who is summoned to see the king takes off his good clothes, puts on rags and a dirty old hat, rolls his trousers up to his knees to show his humility, and then goes in and puts his elbows on the ground. Whenever the king speaks, they all take off their turbans and hats and put them on the ground to show their respect. And if anyone asks the king a question, if the king answers him, he scoops up dust from the ground and throws it all over himself the whole time the king is speaking—just to show how unworthy he is of any answer!

All Mali kings were treated with this kind of reverence! But the most famous of all Mali kings was respected, not just by his own people, but by the rest of the world. His name was Mansa Musa.

When Mansa Musa came to the throne of Mali, he gathered the largest army in all of West Africa. He commanded over a hundred thousand archers, cavalry-men, and foot soldiers. He conquered neighboring kingdoms and expanded the kingdom of Mali until (as he boasted) a traveler would need a year to travel from one end of Mali to the other!

Mansa Musa was famous in West Africa. But he attracted the attention of the world when he decided to make a pilgrimage, or *hajj,* to Mecca, the holy city of the Muslim faith. Every good Muslim was supposed to visit Mecca at least once during his life. But the journey all the way from West Africa to Mecca and back again would take over a year. And for all that time, Mansa Musa would have to leave his country in the hands of his advisors.

But he was determined to show his devotion to Allah by making the pilgrimage. And he was equally determined to show the rest of the world that he, Mansa Musa, was one of the greatest monarchs of the Middle Ages. He decided to take his wife with him—and not

just his wife, but his children, sisters, brothers, cousins, nieces, and uncles. And also his cooks, servants, body-guards, palace advisors, soldiers, and holy men. One medieval writer claims that sixty thousand people traveled to Mecca with Mansa Musa.

As the caravan wound its way towards Mecca, Mansa

A medieval portrait of Mansa Musa

Musa himself rode in the center of the column. Five hundred slaves walked in front of him, wearing robes of silk and carrying walking sticks of pure, heavy gold. A hundred camels followed behind, hauling three thousand pounds of gold. Whenever Mansa Musa halted the caravan for Friday prayers, he paid to have a mosque built on the place where he stopped. When he passed through Egypt, he gave away so much gold that the price of gold plummeted! There was so much gold in Egypt that it wasn't worth as much any more. Twelve years later, the price of gold in Egypt was *still* low because Mansa Musa had given so much gold away to the Egyptians as he traveled through.

When he arrived in Mecca, Mansa Musa took off his royal robes and his gold. Like every Muslim pilgrim, he washed himself, put on a white robe and prayed in the holy city. He gave away *alms* (gifts of money) to other pilgrims and to the poor. And after he had completed his worship, he turned his caravan around and started home. But he had given away so much of his gold that he had to borrow money to get back to Mali!

Mansa Musa's journey to Mecca made him famous. After his pilgrimage, medieval maps began to show the kingdom of Mali, below the Sahara Desert. One of these maps shows Mansa Musa himself, sitting on the throne in the middle of his kingdom, holding a golden nugget in his hand! For the first time, maps also showed roads leading from the northern African coast down into West Africa. Because of Mansa Musa, Europeans now knew all about the West African country of Mali.

The Songhay Empire

The West African empire of Ghana grew rich and powerful, but then began to fade away. Then Mali, just north of Ghana, became the richest and most powerful West African empire. But Mali too began to shrink after the death of the great Mansa Musa. And soon it too was replaced by a new empire: the Songhay. Ghana was known for salt and gold and Mali was known for its great Islamic kings, but Songhay became known for its size. It grew and grew until it covered the land that had belonged to both Ghana and Mali. Its cities were filled with great mosques, strong-walled palaces and mansions, famous universities, and busy marketplaces where salt, iron, ivory, gold dust, and food were traded. Songhay's best-known city, Timbuktu, had eighty thousand inhabitants—and almost two hundred schools.

The medieval traveler Leo Africanus explored the land of the Songhay and wrote about his adventures. Leo was a Muslim, born in the Spanish kingdom of Granada when it was under Muslim rule. When Leo was seven, Ferdinand and Isabella conquered Granada and added it to their Christian kingdom. Most of Granada's Muslims left the country. Leo's parents took him to North Africa to live.

When he grew up, Leo decided to travel from North Africa, down through the Sahara Desert, into the kingdom of the Songhay. The trip through the desert was a harsh one! Leo wrote:

> Many who travel through this desert die because they cannot find water. Their carcasses lie around on the sand, scorched by the sun's heat. Others become so thirsty that they kill their camels and squeeze water out of the camel intestines and drink it! Sometimes this keeps them alive until they can find a pool or well of water.

Leo Africanus made it through the Sahara Desert without having to drink water from a camel's insides! Once he arrived in the Songhay Empire, he traveled from city to city, finally arriving at Timbuktu. Here is how he described this great West African city in his book *His-*

The houses are made out of clay, with thatched roof. But the temple and the king's palace at the center of the city are built of stone. The city is filled with wells of sweet water, and there is much grain and many animals, so the inhabitants eat milk and butter. There is not much fruit, but there are melons, cucumbers, bread, meat, excellent pumpkins, and a huge quantity of rice. But there is not much salt, because it has to be carried here from a mine five hundred miles away.

All of the women wear veils over their faces—except for the slave women. Many of the men are very rich, and the king himself has tremendous amounts of gold. I saw one gold bar belonging to the king that weighed almost a thousand pounds! The king often leads his armies into war, but only against his enemies and those who refuse to pay him tribute. In battle, he and his soldiers ride on horses that they buy from the Arabs. Their servants ride on camels. Both the horsemen and the foot soldiers shoot poisoned arrows at their enemies.

But the king also honors learning and books greatly. Timbuktu is full of doctors, priests, judges, and scholars! And the king pays salaries to learned men so that they can study and teach. Books are the most valuable possession of all; they sell for more money than any other kind of goods. The people are gentle and cheerful. Every night there is singing and dancing in the streets. The people stroll continuously through the city at night, playing musical instruments.

When Leo Africanus published his book, more Europeans found out about the kingdoms of West Africa. The continent was not quite so "dark" any more! Europeans were startled to find out that great cities and empires existed south of the Sahara.

Eventually, the Songhay Empire was destroyed by invaders who wanted to seize the salt and gold mines of the Songhay for their own. The sultan of Morocco, in northern Africa, sent an army of three thousand men across the desert. These Moroccan soldiers had cannons and guns—and the Songhay warriors had only spears and bows. They couldn't resist the stronger weapons of the Moroccans. The Moroccan army seized the salt mines in the north of the empire, but the Songhay refused to tell them where the gold mines lay! Finally, after more than ten years of fighting, the sultan of Morocco gave up on trying to find the gold mines. But the war had already torn the Songhay kingdom apart. The largest West African empire of the Middle Ages had come to an end.

The Moghul Empire at Its Largest Extent

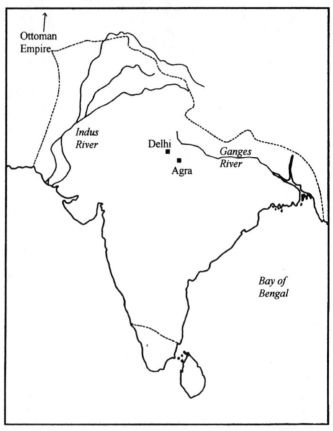

Ottoman Empire

Indus River

Delhi

Agra

Ganges River

Bay of Bengal

Knowledge Quest

Chapter Thirty
India Under the Moghuls

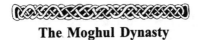

The Moghul Dynasty

When Prince Henry the Navigator first began to send expeditions down the coast of Africa, he hoped that they would find a way across Africa to India. Most Europeans didn't know any more about India than they did about Africa. They simply thought of India as a distant place where valuable spices could be bought. But India, like Africa, had a long and complicated history of its own.

When we first began to read about the Middle Ages, we learned that India was made up of many different small kingdoms until a king named Chandragupta set out to bring these small kingdoms together into one empire. Chandragupta's descendants, the kings of the Gupta dynasty of India, ruled over a strong, united India. For many years, this unified India lived in peace and comfort. Art, science, literature, and music flourished during this Golden Age of India.

But then the Huns, who had already attacked Rome and Byzantium, invaded India. The Indian emperors fought them off, but the effort weakened the Indian empire so much that it crumbled apart again. For hundreds of years after the Hun invasion, India was made up of many small, separate kingdoms that fought constant wars with each other. One of the largest Indian kingdoms, the land surrounding the city of Delhi, was conquered by a Muslim warrior who made himself its Sultan. Other Indian kingdoms were still ruled by Indian noblemen, but their constant battles with each other made India poorer and poorer. And the country also

293

suffered from floods, from famines that wiped out crops, and from diseases that killed thousands. India needed a strong leader to make it peaceful and prosperous once more.

Finally, this leader appeared. But he wasn't from India. He was an Ottoman Turk!

Do you remember how the Ottoman Turks conquered Constantinople? Their greatest emperor was Suleiman the Magnificent. But now the Ottoman Empire, once the largest in the world, had started to divide into small quarrelling kingdoms. One of these small kingdoms, on the edge of the once-great empire, was inherited by a Muslim prince named Babur. Babur was a fierce warrior, a descendent of Genghis Khan himself. His enemies called him *Babur the Tiger* because of his courage. But Babur was driven out of his kingdom by a rival ruler. He wandered through the east, looking for a new home.

When Babur heard that the Sultan of Delhi was having trouble controlling his Indian kingdom, Babur decided to invade India and take Delhi for himself.[1] The Sultan raised a huge army of a hundred thousand men and a thousand war elephants to fight back. But although Babur had only twelve thousand men, he mounted them on quick, strong horses. The elephants ridden by the Sultan's men were huge—but they were also slow and ponderous. Babur's men could dart around these elephants and attack them from behind. And Babur armed his soldiers with muskets, while the Sultan's army had only spears, swords, and bows.

Babur conquered the Indian city of Delhi and named himself its emperor. Then he turned his attention

---

[1] Babur and the other Moghuls called India "Hindustan," not India; Hindustan means "Land of the Hindus" in the Persian language spoken by the Ottomans.

to the other Indian kingdoms around him. These kingdoms were still under Hindu rule, but Babur defeated them, one by one.

These Hindu kingdoms were frightened of Babur's rule. After all, when the Sultan of Delhi had taken over *his* Indian kingdom, he had killed many of his Hindu subjects. He had looted Hindu temples, destroyed Hindu holy places, and smashed holy images.

But Babur wanted to be a good emperor. Although he was a Muslim, he allowed the Hindus of India to keep on practicing their own religion. He set up government offices all over his empire to make sure that laws were followed. He encouraged the Indian people to send their children to school to learn to read and write. Slowly, India began to prosper again.

Even though he ruled India well, Babur wasn't entirely happy in the land he had conquered. "This is a place of little charm!" he wrote, in his own account of his reign. "There are no arts, no poetry, no scholarship, no colleges, no good horses, no meat, grapes, or fruit. And it is hot and dusty! There is no running water, no ice, no baths, no candles, and the country is dry and desolate."

To remind himself of his home, Babur planted a beautiful garden on the banks of the river in his capital city, Agra. In his homeland, good Muslims often planted gardens on the sides of the mountains, where melted snow ran down in streams between the beds of flowers. These gardens were supposed to remind Muslims of the paradise they would enter when they died—a paradise filled with gardens of cool water.

There were no mountain streams in Agra! But Babur filled tanks with water from the river. In these tanks, he built water wheels with jugs tied to each rung of the wheel. Buffalo pulled the wheels around and around. As they turned, the jugs scooped up water and poured it down a carved stone, where it cascaded into streams that ran through Babur's garden. Next to the streams, the homesick emperor planted beds of beautiful flowers. He planted cypress trees, which stay green all year, to represent eternal life. He planted fruit trees, which bloom, bear fruit, and then shed their leaves, to represent life on earth. And he put marble benches in his garden so that he could sit under the trees and pretend that he was back in his homeland again. He called his garden the Garden of Scattered Flowers, but his people called it Ram Bagh. Today, you can still see the remains of the garden of Ram Bagh in the city of Agra, in India.

Babur only ruled his Indian empire for four years before he died. But his descendents ruled India for many years. They became known as the Moghul dynasty. The name *Moghul* comes from Mongol, because Babur was descended from Genghis Khan, the great Mongol.

Akbar of India

After Babur the Tiger died, he left his oldest son Humayan in charge of his empire. But not long after Humayan came to the throne, he was driven out of India by invaders. He spent the next fifteen years trying to get the throne of India back! Finally, Humayan was able to return to his palace in Delhi. But he had lost much of his father's empire.

Just one year after Humayan returned to India, he slipped on the steps of his library, hit his head, and died. His thirteen-year-old son Akbar was crowned emperor in his place. Akbar was young, but he was determined to restore the glory of his grandfather's empire. He launched a furious campaign to reconquer the lands that Humayan had lost. And after he got those lands back under his control, he added even more cities to his empire. By the time he died, after a reign of forty-nine years, Akbar ruled an empire that covered half of India.

Like his grandfather Babur, Akbar was a fair and just ruler. Although he himself was a Muslim, Akbar believed that he would need to be popular with his Hindu subjects if he wanted to stay on the throne. So he married a Hindu princess and allowed Hindu worship to continue in his country.

Akbar became so famous that his people told story after story about him. Most of these stories are probably folk tales that didn't really happen. But they show how well-liked and respected Akbar was! In these stories, Akbar always makes decisions with the help of his state minister, a Hindu named Birbal. Sometimes Birbal corrects the king—but because he is a fair man, willing to do what is right, Akbar always listens. Here is one of those stories from the time of the Moghul dynasty: "The Bad-Luck Servant."

The Bad-Luck Servant

In the days when Akbar ruled in his palace at Agra, there was a servant named Gulshan whom everyone thought to be bad luck. Whenever the eggs were rotten, the cook would yell, "Gulshan, you're bad luck! These eggs turned because of you!" If the bread burned in the oven, the baker would bellow, "Gulshan must have been here! He's bad luck!" And if it rained on a feast day, the whole palace would blame poor Gulshan.

When the emperor Akbar heard about this, he said, "This poor man cannot be the cause of all the bad luck in my palace! Let him be my servant for the day, and when all goes well, my household will see that he doesn't bring bad luck at all."

So he sent his minister Birbal to tell Gulshan that he would bring the emperor his breakfast the following morning. Gulshan was terrified at the thought of serving the great Akbar himself! But when he got up in the morning, he washed his hands, combed his hair, put on a clean tunic and carried the emperor's breakfast into the royal bedchamber. Akbar thanked him, and Gulshan bowed and withdrew.

"There!" Akbar thought to himself. "Nothing bad has happened!" He began to eat his breakfast, but soon discovered a hair in his bread. "Bad luck," he said, out loud, "but surely that could occur on any morning."

He pulled the hair out of his bread and went on eating. But soon his leg began to itch. He peered down and saw that he had been bitten by a sand fly. He slapped the fly and said, "Bad luck. But I've bitten by flies before."

Akbar began to dress. While he was putting on his crown, his captain of the guard rushed in and said, "Your Majesty, the peasants in the north are rioting! They demand lower taxes and better food!"

"Ride north and settle the riot," Akbar ordered. But the captain of the guard had scarcely left when Akbar's steward knocked anxiously on the door. "Your Majesty," he said, "there are maggots in all of the meat that we preserved for the winter. I will have to throw it all out!"

"Throw it out," Akbar ordered. But the steward had barely gone away when the master of the horses called from the door, "Your Majesty! Your favorite horse has gone lame!"

"Saddle me another one," Akbar said, wearily. But the master of the horses had hardly finished speaking when Akbar's queen ran into the room. "Our son has fallen and cut his arm!" she wailed. "Call the doctor at once."

"That's enough!" Akbar shouted. "Gulshan *is* bad luck! Take him out at once and hang him!"

Now, when the minister Birbal heard about the king's order, he went to the prison where Gulshan had been thrown to await his execution. "Come with me at once," he ordered the unfortunate man, "and I will speak to the emperor on your behalf."

Akbar was in his throne room when Birbal arrived with Gulshan behind him. "Why have you brought that man into my presence?" Akbar demanded. "He is bad luck! His was the first face I saw this morning, and nothing has gone right since!"

"Sire," Birbal said, "may I ask this man a question, so that you may hear the answer?"

"What question?" Akbar asked.

Birbal turned to Gulshan. "When you got up this morning, you were a free man, weren't you?" he asked.

"Yes," moaned the unfortunate man. "And now I have been sentenced to hang!"

"What bad luck!" Birbal exclaimed. "And whose face did you see first thing this morning?"

"The—the face of the emperor," Gulshan whispered.

Birbal turned to Akbar. "You saw this man's face this morning and had bad luck," he said. "But you are still alive and master of your country. He saw your face—and now he is sentenced to death. Whose face brought worse luck: his, or yours?"

Akbar was silent for a moment, and then began to laugh.

"Birbal, my old friend," he said, "you have kept me from an unjust act. Gulshan, you may go free. But please…can you find another house in which to serve?"

Journeys of the Great Explorers

Pacific Ocean

Australia

Antarctica

Asia

India

Indian Ocean

Southern Ocean

Europe

Arctic Ocean

Africa

The Journey of Vasco da Gama

Atlantic Ocean

The Journey of Columbus

The Journey of Ferdinand Magellan

North America

South America

Pacific Ocean

Knowledge Quest

300

Chapter Thirty-One
Exploring New Worlds

Christopher Columbus

When the Portuguese began to sail down the West African coast, trade with Africa became much easier. Instead of hauling goods through the hot dry desert, merchants from England, France, Spain, and Portugal could travel by sea down to the West African ports.

But there was still no simple way to get to India. To get spices, merchants had to make the long, rough journey over land. They had to fight off bandits and wandering war-bands. And they had to face hostile Ottoman Turks who guarded the roads to the east. Many adventurers had tried to sail down Africa's coast and find a way to India, but no one had succeeded. [1]

An Italian sailor named Christopher Columbus was determined to find a sea route to India. But Columbus had a new, wild-sounding strategy. Instead of sailing down the coast of Africa, he planned on sailing due west—straight out into the Atlantic Ocean! Columbus had spent years studying maps and scientific reports. He knew that the best scientists believed the earth to be round. And if the earth was round, he should be able to sail right around it and bump into India's eastern coast.

But before he could try out his theory, Columbus had to convince someone to pay for his journey. He

---

[1] Although the Portuguese adventurer Bartolomeu Dias had managed to round the Cape of Good Hope at Africa's southern tip in 1487, he turned back without continuing on to India because his crew was afraid of what might lie ahead.

needed money to buy ships, money to hire sailors, and money to stock the ships with food and water.

At first, Columbus went to the king of Portugal. After all, the Portuguese had been trying harder than anyone else to find a sea route to India. But the king's scientists laughed at Columbus's maps. "The ocean is much larger than you think!" they warned him. "You'll never be able to store enough food and water for such a long journey!"

When the king of Portugal refused to buy ships for Columbus, he tried to interest the kings of France and England in his ideas. Neither king would help him. So finally Columbus went to Ferdinand and Isabella of Spain and told them about his plan.

Ferdinand paid little attention to these wild ideas, but Isabella was fascinated by Columbus's new map of the world. And she also realized that if Columbus could find a way to India, Spain could become richer than England or France or Portugal. Spain could become the richest and most powerful country in the world.

But when Columbus first brought his plan to Isabella, Spain was in the middle of its war to conquer Granada. Isabella was using all of her money to pay soldiers in the Spanish army. Not until the war was over, seven years later, could she buy Columbus his ships.

Finally, Columbus was ready to test his new ideas! Isabella provided him with three ships, named the *Nina,* the *Pinta,* and the *Santa María.* She hired sailors, stocked the ships with enough food and water for several months, and provided Columbus with cloth, gold, and other goods that he could trade for spices when he reached India.

Christopher Columbus set sail in 1492. As the *Nina,* the *Pinta,* and the *Santa María* sailed into the Atlantic Ocean, headed west, the three ships passed other vessels leaving the Spanish shore. Wails and cries rose up from these ships, which were crowded with weeping men, women and children. The Jews were leaving Spain, driven out by the laws Ferdinand and Isabella had passed against them.

Christopher Columbus noted his sighting of these ships in his journal and kept on sailing west, into the huge

trackless waters of the Atlantic Ocean. At first, his ships had good winds, and the journey went well. But as the days passed by, Columbus's men began to murmur. When

The *Santa Maria*, one of Columbus's three ships

would they come into sight of land? Spain was growing further and further away. And they could see nothing but more water ahead of them. Strange birds flew over-head; odd fish arched out of the water. The seaweed grew so thick that the ships could only inch forward. And the men were growing sick with a disease called *scurvy* because they hadn't eaten any fresh fruit or vegetables for so long. Their gums were turning black, and some were even dying.

"We'll never reach land!" the sailors complained. "We'll run out of fresh water and die of thirst out here! The world isn't round—the sea goes on forever, and we'll never reach the end of it!" Others said, "What if the ocean runs off the end of the world? We'll sail over the edge and fall down a never-ending waterfall!"

They plotted to throw Columbus overboard and turn back home. Finally, afraid that his men would mutiny, Columbus agreed to turn around if land wasn't spotted in three more days. All the next day, Columbus paced around his ship, straining his eyes for a glimpse of land. If no land was spotted, he would have to return to Spain—and waste a lifetime of effort!

The sun had barely risen on the morning of the second day when a seaman, high up in the ship's riggings, shouted "Land!" Sure enough, a tiny island lay just above the horizon. As the ships drew closer, Columbus realized that the island was surrounded by dozens of others. He was certain that he had reached the islands off the coast of India!

When Columbus and his men landed, Columbus claimed the islands for the country of Spain. He found that people lived on the islands, brown-skinned people with black hair who were willing to come out and see the goods he had brought with him from Spain. He called these people *Indians*. But as Columbus looked around, he grew more and more puzzled. The language these people spoke sounded nothing like the Indian language he had expected to hear. He saw no gold, no pepper, no nutmeg, no riches. Instead, the people of the islands brought him balls of cotton thread, green and yellow parrots, and strange foods—sweet potatoes and green peppers. Where were the spices—and the treasures of India?

Of course, Columbus hadn't landed in India. He had landed in the islands off the coast of Florida. His maps showed empty water between Spain and India, but two huge, unknown land masses actually lay in his way: North and South America.

After Columbus explored the islands, he headed back to Spain. He brought Ferdinand and Isabella parrots, sweet potatoes, green peppers, pineapples, and even several Indians—but no spices or gold.

Ferdinand and Isabella agreed to pay for several more voyages to this new land. Columbus traveled back across the ocean and began to work on a map of his discovery. He still insisted that he had found the sea route to India. But others soon began to realize that Columbus had found something new—a whole new continent.

Five years after Columbus landed in the Americas, a Portuguese explorer named Vasco da Gama finally managed to sail around Africa and reach India. The journey took him an entire year to make!

Vespucci and Magellan

We often talk about Christopher Columbus and his "discovery of America." But although Columbus laid the way for later Spanish explorers to come to the Americas, he wasn't the first adventurer to land in America. The Viking Leif Ericsson landed in North America long before Columbus was born. And Columbus wasn't the first to recognize America as a new continent. He continued to think that he had discovered a new route to the East. The first explorer to realize that this mysterious shoreline was a brand new land was an Italian merchant named Amerigo Vespucci.

In 1492, when Columbus sailed his three ships from Spain, Amerigo Vespucci was in Spain. He was doing business for his employer, an Italian nobleman. But although Amerigo was a good businessman, he had always wanted to sail to India. He watched with envy as Columbus departed on his great adventure.

When Columbus returned with news that he had reached land by sailing west, Ferdinand and Isabella agreed to pay for more expeditions. Amerigo Vespucci was anxious to apply! He arranged to take three ships of his own out into the Atlantic. Seven years after Columbus's first voyage, Amerigo Vespucci set sail himself.

Over the next ten years, Amerigo made several different journeys to the coast of the Americas. He sailed down South America, almost all the way to the tip of the continent. He sailed up to North America and saw the rivers that flowed into the sea. The more Amerigo saw of this land, the more sure he was that Columbus was wrong. This wasn't India, or Asia. This was something else completely. He wrote a letter to his Italian employer, saying "I am sure that we have found a new land! The coastline and the number of rivers make me certain of it."

So although Columbus discovered America, Amerigo Vespucci was the first to realize that he had found a new continent. And since Amerigo wrote and published many accounts of his travels, more people read about his voyages than about the journeys of Columbus. When a famous geographer made the first maps of the new lands, he decided to name this new part of the world "America," after Amerigo Vespucci. Others suggested that it would be fairer to call it "Columbia," but the name "America" stuck.

Columbus was the first European to land in America, and Amerigo Vespucci was the first to realize that America was a new continent. But another explorer, Ferdinand Magellan, was the first to actually carry out Columbus's original plan, and get to India by sailing west.

Magellan was a Portuguese sailor who set out for the Americas after Columbus and Amerigo Vespucci had both returned. Magellan knew that Vasco da Gama, who had managed to sail around Africa and get to India by going east, had taken a whole year on his voyage. He thought that it would be much quicker to sail west to the Americas, turn south and go down around South America, and then sail on to India.

Of course, Magellan didn't really think he would have to go all the way to the southern tip of South America. He was sure that a river was bound to cut all the way across South America. All he had to do was sail down the coast, find that river, and sail into it.

So Magellan set off. He spent weeks sailing down the coast of South America. Every time he found a river, he would turn and sail into it, hoping that it would lead him all the way across South America. But each river only led him to a dead end.

When Magellan was almost all the way to the southern end of the South America, he found a river that took him all the way across to the other side of the continent. But the journey through this river was a stormy one. The water was so rough that rowboats had to pull his ship along. Gales howled along the narrow passageway. It took more than a month for Magellan to sail down this river! Finally, he came out into the ocean on the other side. The water was so smooth and still, after the choppy water of the passage, that he named this ocean the *Pacific,* which means "calm." Today we call the river that cuts through the southern tip of South America the *Straits of Magellan.*

"Let's go home!" Magellan's sailors begged him. "We've found the way through!" But Magellan refused. He was sure that India must be close by.

But it wasn't! Magellan and his sailors pushed on for more than three months, with nothing but water in sight. They ran out of food. The sailors grew so hungry that they ate sawdust. They were almost out of water.

Finally, they sighted land. The ships anchored, and Magellan's men got busy loading up fresh water and food. But as he looked around him, Magellan realized that he had still not arrived at India. He was on a group of small islands, far off the coast of China! (Today we call these islands the Marianas.)

He ordered his sailors to board the ships and sail on. In a few days, he sighted another group islands ahead of him. Now was he approaching India? No; these islands were the Philippines, south of China. Would Magellan ever reach India?

He never did. In the Philippines, gathering water and food for yet another try at India, Magellan agreed to help a local warrior chief fight a battle with another tribe. In this battle, Magellan was killed. But his lieutenant continued the voyage without him. Magellan had begun with five ships and 280 men. Now there was only one ship left, with thirty-five men aboard. But Magellan's lieutenant sailed this last ship east to India! And then he sailed west around the tip of Africa, back up the African coast, and finally arrived back in Portugal. Magellan had died before reaching India—but his ship was the first one to sail all the way around the whole world.

American Kingdoms

Chapter Thirty-Two
The American Kingdoms

The Mayans of Central America

Christopher Columbus and Amerigo Vespucci called America a *new world* because they had never seen it before. But people had been living in this New World for thousands of years before Columbus or Amerigo ever arrived! These *Native American* peoples are sometimes still called Indians because Columbus gave them this name, thinking that he had reached India.

But of course Columbus had not reached India at all; he had reached the Americas. There are two American continents: North America (the continent on the top of your map) and South America (the continent at the bottom). The bridge of land that links them together is called *Central America*. When Columbus landed in the New World, he landed on islands just across from Central America. He wrote in his journal, "Men and women came out to meet us. Their hair is black and short in front, combed forward. They paint themselves with black and white. Some have scars on their bodies. They tell me that these scars come from battles with other peoples who live nearby, and who try to capture them and make them slaves." Central America had its own empires during the Middle Ages—and those empires fought wars with each other, just like the empires over in Europe and Asia!

The first great empire of Central America was the Mayan Empire. The Mayans lived on the Yucatan Peninsula, which lies between the Gulf of Mexico and the Caribbean Sea. Today, the Yucatan Peninsula is part of Mexico.

The Mayans began to build great cities at the same time that Rome was falling apart. These cities lasted for hundreds of years. But not all the Mayans lived in their cities. Only the most powerful people—kings, noblemen, and governors—lived in the cities. The less important Mayans, such as farmers and craftsmen, lived in the jungles of Central America and came to cities to trade and to worship the gods.

Worshipping the gods was an important part of Mayan life! Stone pyramids with temples on top were built in all of the Mayan cities. The Mayan kings, who sacrificed in these temples, were said to be descended from the sun god! They tried to make themselves *look* "godlike" by filing their front teeth into fangs and painting their faces. When the kings were babies, their mothers would tie pieces of wood tightly around their heads. The wood made their skulls grow up into a peak. So Mayan kings had heads that sloped straight back from their eyebrows and were pointed on top—a sign of divine power! The Mayans also thought that gods were cross-eyed, so a king's mother would often tie a little toy to the front of her baby's hair. The toy hung down between the baby's eyes, so that he had to cross his eyes to look at it.

Because the Mayans believed that their kings were divine, they allowed the kings to have complete power. Over in Europe, other nations (like England) were beginning to put limits on the powers of the king—but in Central America, the king could still declare any law and have it carried out.

Despite his power, a Mayan king did have one unpleasant job to do. The Mayans fought many wars against the other Central American tribes around them. They believed that the gods would come down into the world of men and give them victory—but only if the king opened a door for the gods by shedding some of his own blood. So before a battle, the king had to pierce his ear or his finger or nose and let the blood run out! And often the Mayans would sacrifice their captives from a battle to give more blood to the gods. Even the Mayan games ended in bloodshed. The Mayans liked to play a ball game in which the players tried to knock a ball through a ring twenty feet off the ground. They were allowed to use their elbows, wrists, and hips, but *not* their hands or feet. As soon as one player hit the ball through the ring, he was declared the winner. He was given jade neck-laces, gold bracelets, and sacks full of treasure. The losers were taken up into the temple—and had their heads cut off!

The huge Mayan cities lasted for centuries. But late in the Middle Ages, the Mayan people began to leave their cities. They deserted their temples and their houses. Grass and jungle weeds began to grow over the stones. Eventually the cities crumbled away into the jungle.

What happened? The cities grew so big that the ground around them couldn't grow enough food to support the city's inhabitants. Hurricanes and earth-quakes swept across the Yucatan Peninsula, wrecking houses and temples. The people were growing tired of the cruelty and violence of their kings. And another Central American tribe, the Aztecs, was growing stron-ger—and attacking the Mayan cities with its armies. The Mayan Empire began to crumble.

By the time Columbus arrived, the Mayan people no longer had an empire. They lived in small, separate tribes throughout the land they had once ruled. And the Aztecs had become the greatest nation in Central America.

The Marvelous City of Tenochtitlan

The Aztecs were even more warlike than the Mayans! We don't know where the Aztecs first came

An Aztec warrior

from, but we do know that as they wandered through Central America, they fought battle after battle with the other tribes who lived there. Whenever they won, they forced the conquered tribes to give them food, money, and soldiers for their army. The Aztecs grew richer and stronger. But they still had no homeland.

As they roamed through the highlands of Central America, the Aztecs came to the edge of a wide lake. The edges of the lake were soft and marshy, filled with reeds. Little islands dotted its surface. On one of these islands, a large cactus grew. And on the cactus sat an eagle, holding a snake in its talons.

When the Aztec priests saw the eagle, they cried out, "It is a sign from the sun god! He wishes us to settle here. His divine power will be with us if we build our capital city on the island of the eagle!"

The Aztecs wanted to please the sun god. But when they launched their canoes and paddled over to the island, they found that much of it was soft and muddy. How could they build a city on marshy land?

The Aztecs were determined to find a way. And so they hauled basketfuls of dry earth and stones from the land around the lake and dumped the earth onto the muddy beaches. They pulled basketfuls of mud up from the lake bottom and filled in the pools and swamps. They cut poles from the trees surrounding the lake, drove the poles down into the bottom of the lake, and attached reed mats to the poles. Then they filled the fenced-in areas with more dirt and mud. Slowly, the island became larger and drier. The Aztecs built more and more houses in their new city. They named it Tenochtitlan. Today, the lake where Tenochtitlan stood is called Lake Texcoco.

More and more people came to live in Tenochtitlan. Even though the island was not very big, this floating city had over a hundred thousand Aztecs living in it! More parts of the lake were filled in so that stone buildings could be raised. Canals edged with stone channeled the water away from the foundations of the city. The canals also acted as streets; often, the Aztecs traveled through their capital city by canoe. Smaller cities grew up around the edge of the lake. The people who lived in these cities grew corn, squash, tomatoes, and beans, paddled canoes full of food over to Tenochtitlan, and sold the food to the city dwellers. But the Aztecs of Tenochtitlan didn't rely on the shore for all their food. They learned how to grow crops in the lake! They wove reeds into huge mats and floated these mats in the water. They covered the surface of the mats with dirt and planted seeds in the dirt. When the plants sprang up, their roots grew down through the dirt, through the mats, and into the water. Sometimes the roots reached all the way down into the bottom of the lake. These crops never died from drought or sun; they always had plenty of water. Some Aztecs even built small houses on their floating garden mats.

The Aztecs ate food from the lake as well. They caught fish, but they also cooked and ate water lizards, salamanders, frogs, and fish-eggs. One Aztec delicacy was cakes made out of algae that had been pressed and dried. For meat, they hunted the ducks and birds that swam on the lake's surface, as well as deer and rabbits that roamed on the lake's shores. On special occasions, they drank fermented cactus juice! But getting drunk was against the Aztec laws. Anyone who got drunk could be put to death!

The Aztecs also learned how to make a brand new food: chocolate. The rich dirt around the lake was a perfect place to grow cacao trees—small fruit trees that bear fruit like melons, each almost a foot long. When the purple fruit of the cacao tree turned brown, the Aztecs would pick the fruit and scoop out the insides. But they weren't after the pulp inside the fruit. They wanted the seeds! Each cacao fruit might have thirty or forty seeds in it. The Aztecs pounded these cacao beans into a fine powder, boiled them with corn flour into a soupy paste, strained the paste into a thin brown liquid, and then added vanilla and honey to it. The result: chocolate.

This chocolate was probably bitter and grainy, not smooth and creamy like the chocolate we have today. Today, chocolate makers add milk, sugar, and extra butter to chocolate to make it sweeter and softer. But the Aztecs didn't think their chocolate was bitter. Chocolate was one of their favorite foods. Rich people drank it from golden cups. Cacao beans were as valuable as gold; the Aztecs even used them for money. Chocolate, they thought, was food worthy of the gods.

Tenochtitlan could only be reached by three raised earthen roads that ran through the lake. And between each road and the gates of the city was a moat. Usually, this moat was filled with heavy logs that allowed horses and carts to cross over into Tenochtitlan. But when the Aztecs were at war, they rolled the logs out of the moat. Then no one could cross into the city on foot. And the Aztecs needed to be able to defend their city, because they fought with everyone around them! Even though they had a beautiful capital city and plenty to eat and drink, they raided nearby tribes and kidnapped men, women, and children to sacrifice to their gods. The Aztecs were prosperous—but they were also hated by the other tribes of Central America.

The Incas

When Spanish and Portuguese explorers landed in the New World, they found the Aztecs, flourishing in central America. They met Mayans, living in small scattered tribes throughout Central America. But when they traveled south, down into the continent of South America, they found yet another great civilization: the civilization of the Incas.

The Incas lived in the mountains that run along the western coast of South America. Today, we call this area Peru. Like the Mayans, the Incas believed that their king was descended from the sun god. Here is the story they told about the beginnings of their civilization.

Inti, the god of the sun, presided over the earth. Each day he rose and soared above it, looking dow on it from the clouds; each evening, he sank down beneath it and swam through the waters that lie beneath the earth, back to the earth's far side, so that he could rise and soar over it again.

But when Inti looked down on the earth, he wasn't pleased with what he saw. The people who lived there were like beasts. They lived in the grass and ate what they could catch with their bare hands. Their hair grew in long tangled knots; they wore no clothes, and when they met each other they fought like wild animals.

So Inti said to his great queen, Pachamama, who ruled the earth, "Look at these people! They live like animals in the dirt. We must teach them to build cities and roads, to wear clothes, and to live together in peace!"

Pachamama agreed. So the ruler of the sun and the ruler of the earth summoned their son and daughter into their presence. "My children," the sun god Inti said, "we are going to send you down to earth to teach the people who live there how to be civilized. Take with you this magical golden staff. When it leaps from your hand and sinks into the earth, there you will build a great city."

The son and daughter agreed. Now, the gods can enter the world of men, but they must do so through a door of still water. Inti's son and daughter found the door in Lake Titicaca. They passed through the door, rose from the lake, and begin to walk through the world of men. Everywhere they found hunger, fear, and disease. Wherever they went, they taught men to speak, to build houses, to use herbs and spells to heal their disease, to grow food, to dress and cut their hair. Men began to stand up from the earth and to live as human beings. And Inti's son, Manco Capac, carried the magical golden staff with him everywhere they traveled.

One day, as they walked through a fertile valley, the golden staff leapt from Manco Capac's hand and sank deep into the earth. "Here is where we must build our city!" Manco Capac said to his sister. So they began to build. Soon men came from all around to live in this city, built by the gods themselves. They named this city Cuzco. And the sons and grandsons and great grandsons of Manco Capac, son of the god Inti, sat on the throne in Cuzco until this day.

Cuzco was the capital city of the Incan Empire. This story claims to tell how Cuzco was built, and why the king of the Incas had the right to rule there. Today, archaeologists can see from the ruins of Cuzco that it was a great city where thousands of Incas once lived. It had straight streets, paved with cobblestones. The houses were made of stone, cut so carefully that the blocks fit firmly together without any mortar. They had very small doors and no windows, because the mountain air was so cold! And the city itself is laid out in the shape of a puma, an animal sacred to the Incas.

The Incan people never learned to write, and they kept no histories. So we don't know very much about most of the Incan kings. But we do know that an Incan king named Huayna Capac became king of the Incas in 1493, the year after Columbus first landed in America. Huayna Capac ruled over an empire that stretched along the coast of South America for 2500 hundred miles—almost as long as the United States is wide! He built good, wide roads all throughout his empires. Traders went back and forth on these roads, carrying their goods on llamas. These goods—beautiful cloth, woven from the wool of llamas and sheep and dyed in bright colors; pottery jars, often made in the shape of animals or of men's heads; jewelry of gold and turquoise—traveled from one end of the empire to the other. The governors of the different cities all along the roads sent messages to each other as well, using a complicated code of knots tied into colored rope. Messengers ran along the roads, carrying these ropes from one city to the next.

But when Huayna Capac died, he divided his empire between his two sons. One ruled the north; the other ruled the south. Soon, these two brothers began to fight with each other. Hundreds of Inca warriors died on both sides. The kingdoms of both brothers grew weaker and poorer.

When more Spanish explorers arrived, anxious to settle down in the new continent they had discovered, the two warring kings were too weak to resist. The Spanish marched over those broad, smooth Incan roads, from one end of the empire to the other—and destroyed it.

Empires of Spain and Portugal

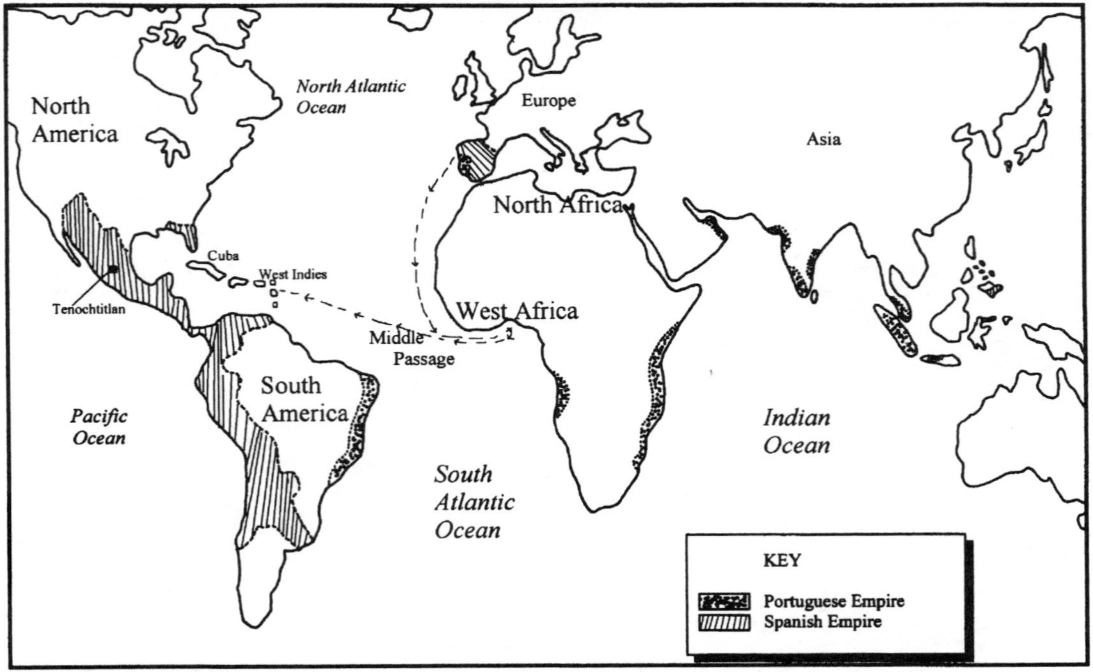
North America
North Atlantic Ocean
Europe
Asia
North Africa
Cuba
West Indies
Tenochtitlan
West Africa
Middle Passage
South America
Pacific Ocean
South Atlantic Ocean
Indian Ocean
KEY
Portuguese Empire
Spanish Empire

Knowledge Quest

Chapter Thirty-Three
Spain, Portugal, and the New World

The Slave Trade

When Ferdinand and Isabella paid for the ships that took Columbus, Amerigo Vespucci, and many other explorers across the Atlantic Ocean, they weren't just being kind. They hoped to make money from this New World! When Columbus landed in America, he claimed the country for Spain. That meant that the king and queen of Spain were saying, "We have the right to send ships to this country, to establish new cities on it, and to take any gold and treasure that we discover here!"

Of course, other countries wanted a part of the New World as well. Portugal also sent explorers to the New World. Soon, the Spanish and the Portuguese were both sending ships across the Atlantic. They hoped to build new cities on the coasts of the American continents and also on the islands just off South America, which they called the *West Indies*.

But the land where they wanted to settle was already occupied by native tribes. Soon Spanish and Portuguese soldiers, called *conquistadores,* were fighting with the Aztecs, the Mayans, and the Incas who lived in Central and South America. They fought with the Native Americans who lived on the islands of the West Indies. And the Spanish and Portuguese also fought with each other!

Finally, Spain and Portugal made a deal. They agreed to divide the land in Central and South America. From now on, Spanish soldiers would claim some of the land, while the Portuguese would settle their colonists in other parts of the new country.

This was the beginning of a very sad time in history. The Spanish and the Portuguese didn't treat the people of Central and South America well. Instead of making treaties with them, they marched into the cities of the Aztecs and Incas, and into the villages of the Mayans, and killed thousands of people. They destroyed temples, houses, and palaces. They built Spanish settlements and claimed the land as their own.

But as the Spanish and Portuguese began to live in their new settlements, they realized that they needed more help. They needed farmers to grow crops to feed the colonists who would come and live in the new cities. They needed miners to help them dig gold out of the ground. And they needed rowers to help pull their heavy ships across the water as they went back and forth between Europe and the New World.

The easiest way to get this help was to buy slaves. After all, you didn't have to pay a slave any money. Once you bought a slave, he had to work for you until he died. So the Spanish and Portuguese began to buy slaves from the Muslim traders who lived in North Africa.

For many years, these Muslim traders had bought slaves from the West African empires of Ghana, Mali, and Songhay. Slavery was a part of life in these empires. Sometimes poor men would sell themselves as slaves so that their families could have more money. More often, the generals and kings of West Africa would capture enemy soldiers in battle and then sell them to Muslim traders. These slaves didn't have a good life, but at least they still lived in Africa. And sometimes they were given a chance to buy their freedom back, or to earn liberty after years of faithful service.

But when the Spanish and Portuguese bought slaves, they took these slaves halfway around the world—far, far away from their African homes! And the slaves taken to the New World had no chance of ever becoming free.

The demand for slaves soon became huge. Muslim traders who bought slaves from the Africans could no longer provide enough slaves. When this happened, the Spanish and Portuguese made slaves out of the Central American tribes. And they also decided to get their own African slaves. Spanish and Portuguese ships sailed down the West African coast and dropped anchor. They sent parties of armed men into West African villages and kidnapped the villagers. These Africans weren't men who had been captured in battle. They were ordinary villagers—men, women, and even small children. They were put into chains, packed onto ships, and taken on the long, rough journey to the West Indies and to the coasts of Central and South America. The journey, which took months, became known as the *Middle Passage*. Slaves on the Middle Passage weren't allowed up on the decks of the ships, so they went for months without any fresh air or sunshine. They weren't given enough to eat or drink. Many died on the long, wretched journey. And when they did arrive in the New World, they were forced to work without any hope of ever escaping this new and horrible life.

The slave trade helped the Europeans to build new, wealthy colonies in the New World. But it also killed hundreds of thousands of West Africans. And it even turned the West African people against each other. Some West African tribes realized that they could make a lot of money by selling other Africans as slaves. So they began to kidnap members of other West African tribes to sell to the white slave traders.

The slave trade continued for over two hundred years. You see, at this time in history, many people in

Europe believed that people with dark skin weren't as human as people with light skins. They thought of dark-skinned people the way you or I would think of a horse or a dog. So Europeans often treated the brown-skinned people of South America and the black-skinned people of West Africa as if they were not really human at all. [1]

Cortés and Montezuma

When the Spanish came to Central America, they discovered that the Aztecs were already ruling an empire there. Before the Spanish *conquistadores* could settle down, they would have to conquer the Aztecs. And the Aztecs were skillful, fierce warriors.

But when the Spanish first arrived, the Aztecs didn't realize they were being invaded. They thought they were being visited by the gods!

The story starts when a Spanish adventurer named Hernán Cortés came to the West Indies (the islands east of Central America). He had hoped to find his fortune in the Spanish colonies there, but he was disappointed. There wasn't very much money in the West Indies! But Cortés heard rumors that over on the mainland of Central America, a fantastically wealthy king ruled over a city with streets made of gold and walls made of jewels.

So Cortés collected a band of soldiers to go with him, loaded Spanish warhorses onto a ship, and sailed to the coast of Central America. When his ship anchored,

---

[1] Although United States history tends to focus on the English slave trade which provided slaves to North America, England did not join the slave trade until the seventeenth century (Volume 3 of this series).

the tribes who lived near the water came out to see who these new visitors were. But when Cortes and his men unloaded their horses from their ships and rode them ashore, the Indians scattered in terror. They had never seen horses before. They thought each horse and rider was a huge monster with six feet, two arms, and two heads.

These Indians spread the word all through the mainland: "Monsters are coming! Perhaps they are the gods!" And Cortés and his men plunged into the Central American jungles, searching for the city of gold. They came closer and closer to the edge of the Aztec Empire.

The Aztecs who lived on the border of the empire weren't entirely sure who these visitors were. So they came out with gifts for Cortés and his men—wheels of gold as high as a man's waist, golden shields, and buckets full of gold dust. When Cortés saw these gifts, he was more convinced than ever that great treasure was just beyond his reach. He ordered his men, "Keep on! The city of gold is still ahead of us!"

Meanwhile, the Aztecs who brought the gifts sent messages back to their capital city, Tenochtitlan. "The visitors are approaching!" they warned. And they described Cortés, his men, and their armor.

The king of the Aztecs, Montezuma, listened to these descriptions carefully. He wondered: Could this be the god Quetzalcoatl, on his way back to Tenochtitlan? Ancient Aztec prophecies said that the god Quetzalcoatl would return five hundred years after leaving his people. And according to the Aztec calendar, the five hundred years was almost up. Also, the description of Cortés sounded like the carved pictures of Quetzalcoatl on the temple walls. (By chance, the helmet Cortés wore was shaped like Quetzalcoatl's hat!) When Montezuma dreamed one night that Quetzalcoatl was approaching to claim his throne, his mind was made up: The god was on his way.

So when Cortés and his men arrived, Montezuma threw open the city gates and welcomed him in. Cortés didn't see streets of gold and jeweled walls, but there was plenty of gold in Tenochtitlan. For eight months, Cortés and his men lolled about in the city, enjoying the luxury and stashing away gold jewelry and treasure for themselves.

But Cortés's men began to get bored. They started quarrelling with the Aztec priests. A fight broke out, and several Aztecs were killed.

When Montezuma and his men saw the bodies of their friends, they shouted, "Quetzalcoatl would never behave in this way!" They armed themselves and began to battle with the intruders. After the fighting raged up and down the city streets, in and out of the palace, Montezuma was killed. Cortés and his men were driven back into Montezuma's royal palace. They locked themselves in—but now they were surrounded by fierce Aztec warriors, waiting for them to emerge!

What would the Spanish do now? They waited, and waited. They waited for days inside the palace! Late one night, one of the lookouts hissed, "The square around the palace is empty!" Cortés peered out. Sure enough, the streets were still. The city seemed to be deserted. Perhaps another war had drawn the Aztec warriors away.

Cortés and his men stuffed their pockets with all the gold they could carry and tiptoed out of the palace. Around them, the city lay quiet beneath a bright moon. They hurried along the stone-paved streets, towards the nearest gate. The gate was open, but the timbers that would fill the moat were missing. Water stretched between their feet and the beginning of the raised road that led to the lakeshore.

"Quick!" Cortés hissed. "Find wood. Anywhere you can! Let's build a bridge."

Their hands shaking with haste, the men ripped wood from nearby buildings and built a makeshift bridge. They lowered it over the gap and began to file across. Suddenly they heard a whoop. The water around them was filled with canoes, and each canoe had an armed Aztec warrior in it. They had walked into the Aztec trap!

The Spaniards tried to fight back, but they were so weighted down with gold that the ones who fell into the water of Lake Texcaco drowned. Only Cortés and a few of his best soldiers escaped. They limped back to the ocean under cover of dark and pushed their ships back out in the water. Cortés had to return to the West Indies, beaten.

But he wasn't finished yet. He collected new men, new horses, and carpenters. With this fresh force, he sailed back over the shore of the mainland and marched back towards Tenochtitlan. On his way, he convinced other tribes to join him in his war against the Aztecs. Many of the villages who lived near Aztec land had been raided by Aztec warriors who kidnapped their young men and women and took them back to Tenochtitlan for human sacrifices. They were very willing to help Cortés fight against the city!

When Cortés arrived at Lake Texcaco, he had his carpenters build twelve small warships, right there on the shore of the lake! He loaded these ships with soldiers and launched them into the water. The Aztec canoes poured out into the lake to meet him. The siege of Tenochtitlan had begun.

The battle went on for three months. But Cortés had collected almost a hundred thousand Spanish soldiers and Indian allies. He cut off all access to the shore, so that the city began to run out of food and water. At last, the city of Tenochtitlan was forced to surrender. Cortés marched into the city and took over. Now he was the governor of the new Spanish colony in Central America.

Chapter Thirty-Four
Martin Luther's New Ideas

Martin Luther's List

When Spain and Portugal started to send their ships to West Africa and the Americas, a new time in history began. You will often hear this time called the *Age of Discovery* or the *Age of Exploration*. For the first time, countries such as Spain, Portugal, France, and England were not just trying to grow bigger by conquering the land next to their borders. Instead, they grew by planting *colonies,* new settlements, in lands far away.

While these European countries were expanding their power into other parts of the world, the Catholic church was trying to *keep* its power in Europe. For most of the Middle Ages, the Catholic church (the Christian church led by the pope in Rome) was as powerful as any country. The Catholic church had its own laws and its own citizens. The pope could even tell kings what to do, and often they obeyed him.

But as the Age of Exploration began, a monk named Martin Luther began to criticize the Catholic church.

Martin Luther grew up in the part of Europe that we now call Germany. His parents wanted him to be a lawyer, but Martin Luther decided to join a monastery instead. As a monk, he had to beg for food and money. He spent long hours praying and studying the Bible. Martin Luther chose this difficult, demanding life because he was afraid that God would punish him for his sins unless he worked day and night to make God happy. He wrote that he was "walled around with the terror and agony" of God's anger.

Martin Luther did everything that the church told him he should do. He went on pilgrimage to Rome. He prayed in front of the relics of saints. He crawled on his hands and knees, reciting the Lord's Prayer, to show how sorry he was for his sins. But he was still afraid that God would be displeased with him.

After he had been a monk for five years, Martin was sent to teach at a university in the German city of Wittenberg. He taught his students about the book of Romans, in the New Testament. He spent hours studying this book. And as he studied, he began to change his mind about what God wanted from him. He thought to himself, "The book of Romans doesn't tell me that I have to earn God's love by working hard to be good. No, no! It says that God gives me the power to believe in him, and the power to be good, because he *already* loves me!" This changed Martin's way of thinking about God! Later, he said, "It seemed to me as if I had been born again, and as if I had entered paradise through newly opened doors."

Think about it this way: Imagine that you have two aunts. Both of them say that they love you. But the first aunt lives in a very clean house with a white rug on the floor. When you come to visit her, she opens the door and looks at you very carefully to see if your hands and shoes and face are clean before she lets you in. She invites you to have hot chocolate and cookies with her, but you have to sit on a white velvet couch while you eat. During your snack, she keeps checking to see whether you are sitting straight and chewing with your mouth closed. When you drip a little bit of hot chocolate on the sofa, she gets rubber gloves, a big bucket of hot soapy water, and a sponge. She makes you scrub at the stain, but it won't come off. So she shouts, "Leave this house at once, and don't come back until you learn how to eat neatly!"

Now imagine that you go to see the second aunt. She throws her door open and says, "I'm so glad to see you! Come in!" And she hugs you even though you've been playing in the dirt. You get a little bit of mud on her apron, but she dusts it off and says, "Why don't you wash your hands before you have a snack?"

The bathroom has good smelling hand soap and big blue towels in it. After you wash your hands, she takes you into the kitchen and sits you down at a big wooden table for your cookies and hot chocolate. When you spill a little, she gives you a napkin and says, "That's not the worst thing that's been spilt on this table!" When your snack is done, she says, "Let's go upstairs and do some finger-painting in the playroom, and then you can have a bubble bath to wash off."

Which aunt would you rather go see? The first aunt is a little bit like the way Martin Luther used to think of God. The second aunt is more like the way he learned to think about God after reading Romans.

When Martin Luther looked around, he saw that many other people also seemed to have the wrong ideas about God. And he thought that the church's teachings made these wrong ideas stronger. The Catholic church had begun to teach that God would only forgive sins if the sinners did *penance,* special deeds (like giving money to the poor or confessing their sins in public) to show how sorry they were. But the Church also taught that sinners could get out of doing penance by paying a certain amount of money to the Church. This practice was called *selling indulgences.*

Martin Luther believed that indulgences were wrong. He preached that God would forgive any sinner who believed in Jesus Christ, not just those who did penance or bought indulgences. "Christ has nowhere commanded indulgences to be preached," he wrote. "Only the Gospel!"

So he made a list of ninety-five reasons why indulgences were wrong. He nailed a copy of this list,

called the Ninety-five Theses, to the church door in Wittenberg. This was his way of inviting other churchmen to argue with him about his ideas.

But Luther found that people all over Germany were interested in his list. Soon, hundreds of people were discussing Martin Luther's Ninety-five Theses. For the first time, people were beginning to say out loud that the Catholic church might not always be right about God.

Martin Luther nails the Ninety-five Theses to the church door in Wittenberg.

Henry VIII's Problem

Over in England, the king of England was delighted to hear about Martin Luther's new ideas!

Before you can understand why the English king was so happy about the Ninety-five Theses, you have to think for a moment about the history we've already read. When the princes in the Tower disappeared, their uncle Richard became the king of England. But then Henry Tudor marched into England, killed Richard, and took the throne away. He became Henry VII, king of England.

Henry VII had already fought a war to get England's throne. He didn't want another war to start after he died! He wanted to make sure that his son and his grandson and his great-grandson would all inherit the crown after him, peacefully and without any arguments. So when his oldest son, Arthur, was only two, Henry VII arranged for him to get married to the three-year-old daughter of the king of Spain. The two even had a wedding ceremony, with grownups standing in for them (since the groom fell asleep and the bride was busy chewing on the hem of her dress). This was called a *proxy* wedding. It meant that the two *had* to get married as soon as they were old enough.

When Arthur was fifteen and Catherine was sixteen, the prince and the princess had a real wedding. The young princess let down her hair, which came all the way to her feet, and danced with the prince. Everyone feasted and sang songs and hoped that the two would have children right away. Arthur and Catherine went away to live in a castle of their own. But only six months later, Arthur came down with a high fever—and died!

Now the heir to the throne was Arthur's little brother, Harry. Henry VII arranged for Catherine to get married again, this time to Harry. Because Catherine had been married to Harry's brother, they had to get special permission from the pope to marry each other. When the pope agreed to give this special permission, Harry and Catherine got engaged.

But before the two could marry, Henry VII died. Harry became King Henry VIII at the age of seventeen. Two months later, he married Catherine. Now the two could have sons. The crown would pass peacefully on to a little boy who could become Henry IX.

The years went by. Catherine had a baby daughter named Mary, but little Henry IX never appeared. Henry VIII grew more and more worried. A girl couldn't inherit his throne. He needed a son! [1]

When Catherine became too old to have any more children, Henry VIII was desperate. What would he do? He could only have a son now if he had another wife. He even picked out the wife he'd like to have—a beautiful young lady-in-waiting at the court, Anne Boleyn. But no one got divorced back in those days, so Henry VIII could only marry Anne if Catherine died. And Catherine was perfectly healthy.

So Henry VIII thought of another solution. He had only been able to marry Catherine in the first place because the pope gave him special permission to marry his dead brother's wife. If the pope would only say that the special permission didn't count, he could act as though he and Catherine had never really been married.

But the pope put his foot down and refused to take his permission back. Henry and Catherine had been married for eighteen years. It was too late for Henry to announce that he'd never really been Catherine's husband! Nothing Henry could say would change the pope's mind.

So when Henry heard the new ideas of Martin Luther, he was delighted. After all, Martin Luther said that the pope was wrong to allow indulgences. Henry was quick to agree. And then, Henry announced that if the pope was wrong about indulgences, he was just as likely to be wrong about Henry's marriage. As a matter of fact, the pope might be wrong about all sorts of things. So Henry declared that English Christians no longer had to obey the pope! Instead, they had to obey Henry, who was not only the king of England, but also the Supreme Head of the Church in England!

---

[1] Catherine actually had several stillbirths, several miscarriages, and one baby boy who lived for only six weeks.

As the Supreme Head of the Church in England, Henry VIII decided that he could declare his own marriage over. Naturally, the pope was furious. But powerful English noblemen supported Henry. They didn't want to see another civil war over the English throne! And they were willing to say that Henry was the head of the English church if that would get Henry an heir to the throne.

So Henry sent Catherine away and married Anne Boleyn. In order to get his way, he created a whole new church, the Church of England. From now on, the Church of England would be separate from the Catholic church of Rome.

Anne Boleyn and Henry VIII lived together happily—for a little while. Soon, Anne Boleyn had a baby. But her baby was a girl, named Elizabeth. Now Henry had two daughters, but still no sons! He hoped that Anne would have a baby boy. But when she didn't, Henry had her head chopped off.

Two weeks after Anne was beheaded, Henry married another girl, Jane Seymour. A year and a half later, Jane Seymour had a little boy, named Edward. Henry finally had his son! But he no longer had a wife. Jane Seymour died not long after her baby was born.

Henry VIII didn't mourn his wife for very long before he decided to get married again. He sent artists all around Europe to paint the pictures of the princesses he might marry. When he saw the picture of a beautiful German princess named Anne of Cleves, he pointed to it. "Bring me this woman!" he said. "I'll marry her!"

Anne of Cleves arrived in England on a cold, grey, winter day. Henry rushed out to meet her. But when he saw her, he realized that the painter had made her picture far too pretty. Anne was nothing like her portrait. "She looks like a horse!" Henry exclaimed.

But the wedding had already been planned. Henry was afraid that Anne's relatives would be angry with England if he didn't marry her, so he went through with the marriage. Afterwards, though, he announced that he would never live with her. Since he was the Supreme Head of the English church, he could declare that his own marriage was over—and he did. Anne left Henry's castle very happily. After all, Henry VIII wasn't exactly a handsome prince any more! He had gotten older, and he was extremely fat.

Three weeks later, Henry married a young girl named Catherine Howard. Would you like to guess what happened to Catherine Howard? Henry had *her* beheaded too.

Less than a year later, Henry VIII got married for the last time. Now he was an old man, and often sick. His new wife, Catherine Parr, was a good nurse. She took care of him when he was ill, and watched over his three children. She was still alive when Henry VIII died.

Today, Henry VIII is best remembered for his six wives: Catherine of Aragon, Anne Boleyn, Jane Seymour, Anne of Cleves, Catherine Howard, and Catherine Parr. There's even a little verse to remind you what happened to each wife:

Divorced, beheaded, died,
Divorced, beheaded, survived.

Chapter Thirty-Five
The Renaissance

A New Way of Thinking

Do you remember the magic carpet that you imagined, in the very first chapter of this book? That magic carpet took you back in time to the days of the Roman Empire. We call those long-ago days *ancient times*. In ancient times, great empires—Assyria and Babylon, Egypt and Greece—spread over vast expanses of the world. The last great ancient empire, Rome, was the largest of all. Wide, paved Roman roads ran all through this huge empire. Traders, soldiers, and ordinary people could travel from one end of the empire to the other. All of the people who lived within its borders followed the same laws. Most spoke the same language.

When barbarians invaded Rome, the last great empire began to fall apart. Cities were destroyed; roads became dangerous. People no longer traveled to distant places or learned the language that had once united the old, fallen empire. They lived in separate villages, speaking their different languages. And they no longer read the old books, written in Latin and Greek. They spent their days trying to grow enough food to stay alive and worrying about the next barbarian attack.

For hundreds of years after the fall of Rome, the history of Europe seemed to follow the same pattern: A great warrior, ruler of a small kingdom, would lead his army against the other small kingdoms around him. He would conquer them, and unite them all into a larger empire. His descendants would rule this empire for a little while—and then the empire would fall apart into small kingdoms again. Then another great warrior would start to gather an army, and the pattern would repeat itself. As these empires rose and fell, Christianity and Islam struggled with each other. We call the centuries after Rome was destroyed the Middle Ages.

But around the time that Martin Luther and Christopher Columbus lived—a thousand years after the fall of Rome—the pattern that had gone on for hundreds of years started to change. Countries such as England, France, Spain and Italy managed to build strong armies that protected them from invasion for years at a time. The people who lived in these countries didn't have to worry constantly about barbarian invasion. They had time to think, read, and study—instead of looking for a place to hide from the next rampaging army!

What did they read? Well, when the Ottoman Turks conquered the city of Constantinople and turned its great cathedral into a Muslim mosque, hundreds of Eastern Orthodox Christian scholars left the city and traveled west, into Europe. They brought with them scrolls written in Greek. Some of these scrolls were copies of books of the Bible. Others were writings of great Christians who had lived hundreds of years before. The Eastern Orthodox church had kept these manuscripts safe for centuries.

When the Eastern Orthodox scholars settled down in Europe, they taught others to read these Greek writings. Slowly, men and women who enjoyed reading and study began to be interested again in the old Greek and Latin books that had been ignored for hundreds of years. Many of these writings were translated into the languages of Spain, Italy, England, and France. More and more people began to hear about the ideas, the art, and the history of ancient Greece and Rome. Artists began to try to make their sculptures and paintings look like Greek art, which was *realistic* (more like a photo-graph). Sculptures began to look more and more like real people with real muscles and skin. Painters tried to make their landscapes look like real landscapes, and the light in their paintings look like it was really shining from the sun. Builders designed their buildings with Greek columns and Roman arches. Scientists studied Greek and Roman explanations for the movements of the stars and planets. Philosophers thought about Greek ideas.

We call this time the *Renaissance*. Renaissance means "rebirth." In a way, Greek and Roman ideas "died," during the Middle Ages, because so few people could read Greek and Latin books. Then, during the Renaissance, Greek and Latin ideas were "reborn" as these books were read again.

But the Renaissance wasn't just a time when people relearned old ideas. It was also a time of new discoveries. For the first time, ships were sailing all over the world. Explorers were realizing that their old ideas about the world (like boiling seas in the south and water that poured forever off the edge of the world) were wrong. So during the Renaissance, men and women began to make new theories about the world. They compared their new theories with the old Greek and Roman ideas. They started to ask, "Which ideas about the world are right? Let's go try to find out for ourselves."

When Prince Henry the Navigator sent ships south to see the southern waters, rather than just accepting the old stories about boiling seas, he was thinking like a Renaissance man. When Columbus insisted on going to India by sailing west, instead of trying to go around Africa like everyone else, he was acting like a Renaissance man. When Martin Luther told the people of Wittenberg that they should look at the Bible for themselves, instead of believing everything that the Church told them, he was talking like a Renaissance man.

During the Renaissance, men and women began to believe that they could find out truth by *looking* at the world and figuring out how it worked. After all, they argued, God had created the world. Why couldn't man, who was also created by God, look carefully at this world and understand it? So they *observed* the world: the sky, the earth around them, the people who lived on the earth. They drew conclusions from what they observed.

Today, we call this the *scientific* method of getting knowledge. When you observe something and try to draw conclusions from your observations, you are thinking *scientifically*. This way of thinking had its roots in the Renaissance.

Gutenberg's Great Invention

Think about the Middle Ages—knights in armor, horseback, stone castles, food cooked over open fires, long journeys on horseback, silk and spices from India. Now think about the world today—cars, airplanes, telephones, computers, Legos, movies. What invention did the most to change the world?

The answer might surprise you. The printing press! Without printed books, the Renaissance might never have happened. And our modern world would look very different.

Before the printing press was invented, books were written by hand. Do you remember reading about the medieval monks who copied out manuscripts in their monasteries? They had to make paper called parchment out of animal skins. Then they had to mix up ink, sharpen a feather into a pen, and write out each letter of

342

each book. One book might take years to finish. When it was done, it was put in the monastery library and chained to the shelf so that no one could take it away! Only kings and very rich men could afford to have books in their homes. There were no picture books, no magazines, no newspapers, no printed instructions or directions.

During the Middle Ages, merchants trading with China learned how to make *paper* from the Chinese. This paper was made by soaking bark, straw, or old rags in water, pressing it into sheets, and drying it. Paper was much easier and quicker to make than animal-skin parchment. Now, these merchants could keep records of how many pieces of silk or pottery they had sold. But they still had to write all of their facts and figures by hand. There were still no books!

Imagine for a moment that you live in a world without printed books, instructions, or directions. You want to play a new board game that came with five different sets of playing pieces, a spinner, two dice (one black and one yellow), and a funny metal chain with triangular links. And there are no instructions! How will you figure out what to do with all of those game parts? Eventually you might figure out how to play a game with the board and the parts. But your rules probably won't be like anyone else's. If you visit friends who have the same game, you won't be able to play with them until they explain all *their* rules.

Pretend that you're a scientist who wants to study the stars. But you don't know what other scientists have already discovered about the stars, because you don't have any science books. All you have are your eyes and the sky. After years and years of study, you figure out some basic facts about the stars. But it takes you so long to learn these simple facts that you never discover much more! All over the world, other scientists do exactly the same thing. So no one gets very far in his study of the stars. If only all of you had books! Then you could each learn the basic facts in just a few months of study.

Suppose that you are a Christian who wants to find out what the Bible says about right and wrong. But you don't have a Bible. There's a huge Bible chained to the pulpit of the church in your village, but it's written in a language you can't read. So you ask your priest what the Bible says. He doesn't read very well either, so he tells you what *his* priest told him years ago when he asked the same question. He might be right—or he might be wrong.

That's what life was like in Europe during the Middle Ages. Because there were so few books, scientists didn't make very many new discoveries. Historians couldn't find out much about the past. Doctors knew very little about the human body. And Christians had to find out what the Bible said by asking their priests. They had to trust their priests to give them the right information!

Then, everything changed.

A young man in Germany, the country of Martin Luther, was learning how to be a goldsmith. His name was Johannes Gutenberg. As he melted his gold and silver and poured the metal into molds, Johannes Gutenberg began to wonder whether he could also mold letters out of metal. He thought to himself, "I could fit the letters together to form a metal page. Then I could dip this metal page down into ink and press it onto paper. I could make hundreds of paper copies in no time at all! And then I could rearrange the letters to make another page."

Gutenberg experimented with finding just the right kind of metal for his pages. It had to be soft enough to press down on a page without shattering, but hard enough to stay in shape. He had to make molds for each letter, pour the letters in, wait for them to cool, and then remove them. His ink had to be just the right thickness—thick enough to cling to the metal when he dipped it in, but thin enough to come off the metal onto the paper. He had to find a way to lift the metal page up and press it down over and over, on sheet after sheet of paper.

After years of experimenting, Gutenberg made a printing press from an old wine-press that had been used to squeeze grapes. He made metal letters out of a mixture of tin, lead, and a poisonous metal called *antimony*. He made a new kind of ink with oil in it. And he began to work on his great project: a Bible. It took him several years to set all the metal letters into place for the pages. But once the pages were set, Gutenberg and twenty helpers printed 450 Bibles in one year. If twenty monks had tried to write out these Bibles by hand, it would have taken them ninety years each.

Others borrowed Gutenberg's technique. An English merchant named William Caxton got interested

 not just in printing books, but in translating them into the languages that people could actually read. He printed books of history and poetry in English. He also printed a book about how to play chess—the first printed set of directions!

As time went on, more and more books were printed. Books became cheaper and cheaper. More and more people could buy and read them! Now ordinary, everyday men and women could read about the past glories of Greece and Rome. Explorers could find out what other explorers had discovered in their journeys. Scientists could read what other scientists were learning and doing in other countries. And Christians could read their own Bibles written in their own languages.

Reformation and Counter Reformation

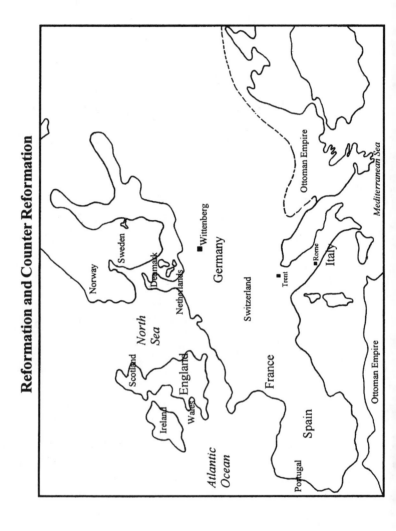

Chapter Thirty-Six
Reformation and Counter Reformation

The Spread of the Reformation

Do you remember Martin Luther and his new ideas about sin and forgiveness? Martin Luther said that God didn't require *penance* (acts to show repentance) to forgive sins. And he criticized the Catholic church for *selling indulgences* (allowing people to pay money to get out of doing penance). Martin Luther's Ninety-five Theses were printed by printing presses and passed around to thousands of people.

The Ninety-five Theses and other essays that Martin Luther wrote started a huge argument all across Europe. The argument wasn't really about sin and forgiveness. It was about the Catholic church. You see, when Martin Luther criticized indulgences, he was saying, "The Catholic church is telling Christians to believe the wrong things. The Catholic church doesn't know what God wants."

This was an incredible thing to say! For hundreds and hundreds of years, millions of Christians had trusted the church and its priests to tell them what God wanted. The Catholic church believed that the pope could speak for God, and that when he spoke for God he would never be mistaken. Now this German monk was saying that the pope and the church were *wrong!* He was claiming that Christians could read the Bible for themselves and could find out what God was saying to them without having a priest to help them. Every man could teach himself directly from the Bible—and now that printing presses were making hundreds of Bibles, ordinary people could have Bibles of their own for the very first time. Throughout Europe, Martin Luther found followers who wanted to read the Bible for themselves rather than accepting the teachings of the Catholic church. Their slogan became, "Every man his own priest!" These followers of Luther were called *Reformers,* because they wanted the church to change, or *reform.*

The Catholic church was horrified. If every man was his own priest, every man could come to his own conclusions about God. What would happen to the truth? What would happen to the Christian church? It would splinter into a hundred different pieces, and then *no one* would know which "church" had the truth about God. And the church was also worried about the new Bibles that were being printed in England, in Germany, and in other countries. These Bibles were being translated into English, German, and other languages. But how could anyone know whether these translations were *good* translations or not? An Englishman might translate the Bible into English—and get part of it wrong. Then Englishmen reading this English Bible would be misled about God.

So the church spoke out strongly against the Reformation. The pope condemned many Reformers as *heretics*—men who no longer followed the truth about God. But the Reformation continued. One of Martin Luther's followers, a scholar named Philip Melanchthon, wrote down the teachings of the Reformers in a document called the Augsburg Confession. This *Confession,* or statement of faith, gave Reformers a chance to think of themselves as one group, with one set of ideas about the Christian faith. They became known as *Protestants,* because they *protested* against the practices of the Catholic church.

350

From now on, the church would be divided into two groups. *Catholics* would continue to listen to the pope and to the Catholic priests and to follow the official teachings of the Catholic church. *Protestants* would insist that every man could read the Bible and interpret it for himself. Today, we still talk about Christians as Catholics and Protestants. Protestant churches (including Lutherans, Presbyterians, Baptists, Episcopalians, Methodists, and Pentecostals) are separate from the Catholic church because of Martin Luther's Reformation, five hundred years ago.

For hundreds of years, Catholics and Protestants argued about how to understand and obey God. Both Catholics and Protestants wanted to follow God and obey him. Protestants thought that men and women should be able to read the Bible and find out what God wanted for themselves. Catholics thought that the Bible could only be interpreted properly with the help of the church.

But during the Reformation, Protestant teaching also spread for reasons that didn't have anything to do with obeying God. "Every man his own priest" was a good slogan for Renaissance times, because many Renaissance men and women just didn't like the idea of accepting someone else's teachings without question. They wanted to make up their own minds about God, just like they wanted to make up their own minds about the shape of the earth.

And many countries didn't like the idea that a pope who lived in Italy could tell English, German, and French Christians what to do. When Henry VIII became a Protestant by setting up his own English church, he wasn't trying to obey God. He was telling the pope, "I am an English king, and I can do whatever I want, no matter what an Italian pope says!" So the disagreement between Catholics and Protestants also had to do with *politics*—the ways in which earthly rulers controlled their kingdoms. Being Catholic or Protestant meant *more* than simply belonging to different churches. Arguments between Catholics and Protestants sometimes turned into wars between countries. And sometimes Catholics and Protestants in the same country fought civil wars with each other.

The Council of Trent

Twenty-eight years after Martin Luther posted his Ninety-five Theses on the church door at Wittenberg, the pope called for a *council* (an official meeting of the Catholic church's leaders). "Our faith says that there must be one church," the pope announced. "But our unity has been torn apart by division and quarrelling. So we must gather together to consider what we should do next."

The pope ordered all of the leaders, or *bishops,* of the Catholic church to meet on the first of November, in an Italian city called Trent. This *Council of Trent* was supposed to discuss the beliefs of the Catholic church and how they differed from Protestant beliefs. The leaders of the church wanted to write out a statement that would tell everyone exactly what the church taught about every important area of belief.

This took eighteen years!

For eighteen years, the church leaders held meetings at Trent. They discussed forgiveness of sins, the Bible, penance, the authority of the pope, and hundreds of other issues. Sometimes the discussions got a little bit rowdy. According to one story, two bishops who were arguing about Martin Luther's teachings on faith got so angry with each other that one grabbed the other by the beard and shook him! When the king of Spain heard about this, he wrote the Council of Trent and told them that if they didn't quiet down a little, he would come throw a few bishops into the river to cool them off. [1]

Finally, after eighteen years, the Council of Trent wrote down a number of different statements on Catholic belief. These statements became the official doctrines of the Catholic church. But the bishops who met at Trent went even further. They insisted that the teachings of the church were all true and that the church had not misled any Christians about their faith. But they also admitted that the church's priests and bishops had sometimes *acted* wrongly.

You see, during the Middle Ages, the church had built many cathedrals, started many schools, and bought a lot of land. As a matter of fact, by the end of the Middle Ages, the church owned more land than any king or emperor. This meant that bishops and priests did more than preach and take care of people's spiritual needs. They also had to act like landlords and mayors. Some of these priests and bishops got more interested in making money than in preaching about Christ. Archbishops (bishops who had authority over a number of other bishops) had even been willing to sell priesthoods. They would make a rich man a bishop in return for a large payment of money. This meant that the church had bishops who weren't really interested in spiritual matters! These kinds of problems had led many of the Reformers to speak out against the Catholic church.

The Council of Trent agreed that some of the church's practices had been wrong. So when the bishops made their statements about the Catholic

---

[1] Will Durant tells this story in *The Reformation* (Volume 6 of *The Story of Civilization*).

church's beliefs, they also wrote out ideas for fixing these problems From now on, no one could buy their way into being a bishop. Everyone who wanted to be a priest had to go to a special school called a *seminary.* There, priests would be trained and taught all of the Church's doctrines.

The Council of Trent *reformed* the Catholic church so that it would be even stronger. We call the years after the Council of Trent the *Counter Reformation,* because during this time the Catholic church changed some of the practices which Martin Luther and the other Reformers had criticized.

But the Counter Reformation didn't bring peace between Protestants and Catholics. Protestants and Catholics still fought with each other. Protestant kings and queens often ordered Catholics who lived in their countries to be arrested, put in jail, and sometimes even put to death. And Catholic kings and queens did the same to Protestants.

Chapter Thirty-Seven
The New Universe

The Revolution of Copernicus

During the Renaissance, young artists studied ancient art. Young philosophers read ancient philosophy. And young scientists read ancient books about the sky and earth. One of these young scientists was named Nicholas Copernicus.

Nicholas Copernicus grew up in the part of Europe that we now call Poland. When he was eighteen, he began to study science at the university in the big, busy city of Cracow. Copernicus had always been interested in the stars, and at the University of Cracow he studied *astronomy,* the science of the stars. He learned how to read *star maps* (charts that show where each star is at different times of the year) and how to measure the positions of the stars in the sky. He also learned that the earth stood at the center of the universe and was surrounded by clear spheres, like balls made out of glass. Each ball was bigger than the next, and each had a planet attached to it. The stars were on an enormous sphere that surrounded all the rest. And each sphere turned at a different speed.

This idea about the universe was based on the writings of the Egyptian astronomer Ptolemy, who had lived hundreds of years ago. Ptolemy's theories, found in his famous book the *Almagest,* explained why the planets seemed to move around the sky at different speeds, sometimes coming closer to certain stars and sometimes moving farther away. It also explained why the sun appeared to move across the sky from the east to the west.

355

But when Copernicus used his instruments to measure the positions of the stars and planets, and then compared his findings with the *Almagest,* he discovered that Ptolemy was sometimes wrong. He was startled! He had always been taught that Ptolemy's book was the most accurate book about the universe that could possibly be written.

Copernicus began to read the writings of other scientists and found that he was not the first astronomer to notice problems with Ptolemy's explanations. Others tried to solve the problems by suggesting Ptolemy's sphere theory needed more spheres.

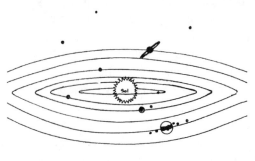

Copernicus thought that the earth and other planets revolved around the sun.

Perhaps there were more than eighty spheres surrounding the earth, each speeding up and slowing down as it turned!

Copernicus didn't see why the explanation for the movement of the stars and planets needed to be so complicated. He knew that another ancient writer, the Greek astronomer Aristarchus, had once suggested that the earth moves around the sun, rather than the other way around. Could this explain the difference between Copernicus's findings and Ptolemy's? It might. And it might also explain some other puzzling things he had noticed. For example, he had seen that the planet Mars was brighter at some times of the year, and dimmer at others. Maybe Mars was circling the earth in an *oval*

356

shape. Then, it would be brighter when it was closer to earth, and dimmer when it was farther away. But Mars couldn't move in an oval if the other planets were attached to spheres—Mars would run into the round spheres around it! On the other hand, if Mars moved around the *sun,* sometimes Mars would be closer to the earth, and sometimes it would be farther away.

Copernicus thought that this new, simple idea was much more likely than the complicated system of spheres described by scientists of his day. He knew that simple, clear explanations were likely to be correct. And Copernicus realized that almost all of his observations would be explained if the earth and the other planets all circled the sun.

This meant that the stars were much, much further away than anyone had ever thought—so far away that it was hard even to measure the distance. If Copernicus's new theory was correct, the universe was much larger than anyone had imagined! He thought that this new idea showed that God had created the universe to be more magnificent than man could imagine.

But Copernicus was a devout Catholic. And for centuries, the church had taught that, since man was the most wonderful part of God's creation, man's home (the earth) must be at the *center* of creation. Copernicus was afraid that the leaders of the Catholic church might not approve of his theory. So at first he only put his ideas into a little, handwritten book called the *Little Commentary on the Movement of Celestial Orbs.* A few scientists read the *Little Commentary* and told him that he needed to print his ideas in a book that more people could read.

Copernicus worked for years on a book that would explain how he had come to his conclusions. Finally he published *On the Revolutions of the Heavenly Spheres.*

Copernicus died the same year that *On the Revolutions of the Heavenly Spheres* was printed. The first copy was put into his hands on his deathbed! But after his death, the church *did* condemn this new idea. Many priests were afraid that Copernicus's new ideas would be interpreted by others to mean that man was no longer at the center of God's plan in making the world. Even Martin Luther thought that Copernicus must be wrong.

But slowly, Copernicus's theories were accepted by more and more people. Other scientists saw that if the earth revolved around the sun, the different motions of the stars and planets made sense. Today we call Copernicus the *Father of Astronomy*, because he was the first to explain the movement of the planets and stars in a way that made sense.

Galileo's Strange Notions

Twenty-one years after Copernicus died, a little boy named Galileo Galilei was born in Italy. Like Copernicus, Galileo learned Greek and Latin so that he could read the works of ancient scientists. He also learned *logic* (how to argue for the truth of an idea by showing how the evidence supports it). As a matter of fact, Galileo didn't do very well at school because he argued with his teachers so much. They nicknamed him "The Arguer" because he spent so much time disagreeing with them!

Galileo was never content to accept an explanation until he had figured it out for himself. This curiosity led him to ask all sorts of odd questions. Once, he was sitting in church. But instead of paying attention to the sermon, he was watching the big chandelier above his

358

head. It swung back and forth, first in long sweeping strokes and then in shorter and shorter movements. Why did the chandelier slow down? What force was pulling on it?

Another day, Galileo went up to the top of a famous tower in Pisa, Italy. The tower leaned to one side, so it was called the Leaning Tower of Pisa. He dropped two weights from the top of the tower. One weight was heavier than the other, and according to old theories about the way the universe worked, this heavier weight should have landed first. But both weights landed at about the same time. Why?

Galileo thought that perhaps the same force was working on the chandelier and on the weights. He was right! Today we call this force *gravity*. Galileo's experiments led a later scientist, Isaac Newton, to make a theory about gravity and how gravity works.

Galileo spent much of his time trying to figure out how things worked. He threw balls and measured how far they flew. He swung pendulums back and forth and tried to understand what laws made them move in certain directions. He moved objects of different weights with levers of different lengths and measured how much force was needed to move each one. He shot cannonballs and figured out the angle of each cannonball's trip through the air. He dripped water from one cup into another and timed how many seconds it took each drop to form and fall. He spent years experimenting and making scientific instruments (such as the thermometer, which he invented when he was thirty-two). Galileo was one of the first *modern scientists,* because he used the *experimental method* to find out how the world worked. Rather than trying to decide whether or not his ideas lined up with philosophy, Galileo made theories about the world and then tested them through doing experiments. "Measure what is measurable," he once said, "and if something cannot be measured, figure out how it *can* be."

When Galileo was almost fifty, he discovered a brand new scientific instrument invented by Dutch scientists: the telescope. Telescopes had two lenses in them that made far away objects seem very close. As soon as Galileo got his hands on a telescope, he pulled it apart and began to make it better. He made a telescope more powerful than any scientist had seen before. When he looked at the sky with his new telescopes, he discovered hundreds of new stars! And around the planet Jupiter, he saw something that no one had ever seen before: Tiny moons, going around and around and around the planet. This proved that Copernicus's theories could be true. Planets and stars *could* rotate around something other than the earth.

To tell the world what he had discovered with his new telescope, Galileo wrote a book called *The Starry Messenger*. He traveled to Rome to show his new telescope to the pope. Soon, though, Galileo found himself in trouble. He was suggesting that Copernicus might have been right. But Copernicus's book *On the Revolution of the Heavenly Spheres* had been placed on a list of books that good Catholics should not read. The church insisted that the idea of the Earth revolving around the Sun denied man's place at the center of God's created order.

Galileo was ordered to repent of his mistaken ideas. And he wanted to obey the church. So he agreed to say that the sun could be going around the earth. Even though he believed the church to be wrong, he was unwilling to say in public that the leaders of his faith were making a mistake. But he did write a book about three imaginary scientists having an argument. One insisted that the earth was at the center of the universe. The second insisted that the sun was at the center. And the third scholar listened to both and asked questions.

When this book was published, church leaders asked Galileo, "Why are you supporting the theory of Copernicus?" Galileo protested, "I'm not! I didn't say which theory was *true*. I just described each one!" But his book was also added to the list of books that Catholics should not read.

Galileo, who loved the church, was deeply saddened by this condemnation of his book. He didn't believe that his ideas proved any part of the Bible to be untrue. Instead, he thought that the priests who condemned his writings were misinterpreting the Bible. So he put all of his ideas into a new book called *The Two Sciences*.

Galileo died not long after *The Two Sciences* was published. He did not live to see his theories accepted by the world. But today, his discoveries are part of the study of *physics*. Physics is the study of why objects (like swinging chandeliers, falling weights, and orbiting moons) behave as they do. Because of Galileo's curiosity, the great modern scientist Albert Einstein called Galileo the *Father of Modern Physics*.

England under Elizabeth I

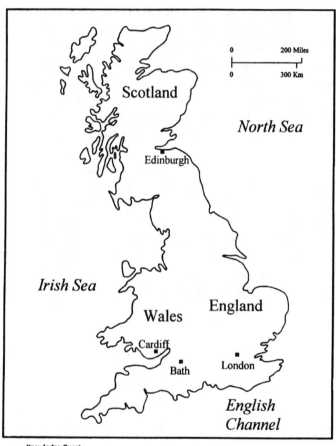

Scotland

North Sea

Edinburgh

Irish Sea

Wales

England

Cardiff

Bath

London

English Channel

0   200 Miles

0   300 Km

Chapter Thirty-Eight
England's Greatest Queen

The Queen Who Almost Wasn't

Do you remember Henry VIII, the English king who had six wives? He kept getting married because he wanted to have a son. And then, when his third wife Jane Seymour finally gave birth to a baby boy, he hoped for another one. Back in the early days of the Renaissance, people often died of illnesses that wouldn't really be very serious today. So Henry VIII wanted another son in case anything happened to his oldest boy, little Prince Edward.

But Henry VIII never had another son. When he died, Prince Edward became King Edward VI of England. Edward was only nine years old, so his uncles helped rule England for him. And Edward wasn't in very good health. He kept coughing, and he was very thin.

As Edward got older, he became even weaker. By the time he was sixteen he was forced to stay in bed. Physicians tried every cure they knew. One cure was to put leeches on the young king to suck out some of his blood. Another was to have him swallow a live spider covered in molasses! But none of these cures worked. Soon, everyone knew that the king was dying.

But who would rule England next? Edward had no brothers, only two sisters. Mary, the oldest sister, was the daughter of Henry VIII and his first wife Catherine, the princess of Aragon. Elizabeth, the younger sister, was the daughter of Henry VIII and Anne Boleyn, who had been beheaded. Even though England had never had a woman on the throne before, one of these two sisters would have to become queen. Their followers argued over who should have the throne. Mary's powerful supporters won the argument! Mary was declared the first queen of England. She rode through the streets of London to the Tower of London to be crowned. And her little sister Elizabeth knelt down and promised to be faithful to the new queen.

Elizabeth was very careful to say only kind things about her sister. In public, Elizabeth acted humble and loving to Mary. But the truth was that Elizabeth was frightened! She and Mary had never been good friends. Mary had been declared Princess of Wales, heir to the English throne, when she was born. Until she was a teenager, Mary had been treated like a queen in waiting. She had her own coat of arms, her own private apartments, and 160 servants to wait on her. She traveled in a velvet litter carried by servants and ate her meals beneath a special canopy that showed how important she was. Everywhere she went, people bowed to her and called her "Princess."

But then her father, Henry VIII, married Anne Boleyn, and Elizabeth was born. The minute that Elizabeth drew her first breath, a herald announced to all the people that Elizabeth, not Mary, was now Princess of Wales and heir to the throne. Henry VIII ordered Mary's coat of arms to be stripped from all her clothes and given to Elizabeth. He sent all of her servants away and told Mary that she had to be her little sister's maid of honor. Now the baby Elizabeth was carried around on the velvet litter. Mary had to ride or walk behind her. Elizabeth was given the household of servants, the special place to eat, and beautiful clothes made out of satin and silk. Mary had to eat down at the foot of the table and live in an uncomfortable room in the palace.

How do you think Mary felt about Elizabeth then? It would be hard to love your little sister if your parents took everything that belonged to you and gave it to her, and then told you that you had to be her servant! Mary refused to admit that Elizabeth was now the princess. "That is a title that belongs only to me!" she told her father. But he ordered her to accept her new place. Elizabeth was the Princess of Wales; Mary was just a lady-in-waiting.

But exactly the same thing happened to Elizabeth only a few years later. When Elizabeth was four years old, little Prince Edward was born. Immediately, the herald announced that Edward, not Elizabeth, was now the heir to her throne. Henry took away *Elizabeth's* coat of arms, her servants, her velvet litter, and her special place to eat. She was sent to live in a house away from the castle. Her governess wrote a letter to the palace, complaining that the little girl hadn't been given enough money to live on. "She doesn't even have a decent nightgown or handkerchiefs!" the governess objected.

Now that Elizabeth and Mary had *both* lost their positions as Princesses, Mary was kinder to her little sister. But she never forgot how Elizabeth had taken her place. When she became queen, she passed a law saying that Elizabeth had never really been the Princess of Wales. Then she accused Elizabeth of plotting against her. She ordered her sister imprisoned in the Tower of London!

When soldiers came to arrest Elizabeth and take her away, Elizabeth was afraid that she would be killed. She cried out, "Give me a minute to write my sister a letter!" And then she scrawled on a piece of paper, "I never talked or thought about any such thing as taking your throne away! May I die a shameful death if I did such a thing! Do not condemn me!" But Mary refused to even read the letter.

Elizabeth spent months in the Tower of London, expecting every morning that soldiers would drag her away and behead her. Mary couldn't find any evidence that Elizabeth had plotted against her, though. So finally, Mary let her sister go and live in a small, dingy house in the country. Here, Elizabeth was surrounded by servants chosen by Mary and by soldiers who searched her house constantly for any signs of treason. She wasn't even allowed to go for a walk without special permission from Mary.

Four years after Elizabeth's arrest, she was sitting under a tree reading the Bible in Greek. A soldier nearby watched her every move. She heard galloping hooves and lifted her head to watch the road. A messenger came into sight, wearing the royal colors. Was he coming to tell her jailers that Mary had finally condemned her to death? Elizabeth stood up and watched the man dismount from his horse. But instead of speaking to the soldier behind her, the messenger fell on his knees in front of Elizabeth. "Mary, queen of England, is dead," he said. "You are now queen of England. God save the Queen!"

Good Queen Bess

Elizabeth was now queen of England. When the people of England heard that Mary was dead, they sang and danced in the streets. Mary had been very unpopular. As queen, Mary wanted to bring England back to the Catholic faith that her father Henry had rejected. So she had sent men throughout England, demanding that her people swear allegiance to the Catholic church. Three hundred men and women who refused were burned at the stake! Mary's subjects had begun to call her "Bloody Mary" because of her cruelty.

So when Elizabeth rode into London with a thousand men behind her, the streets were lined with cheering people. Elizabeth arrived at the castle and took charge of it. She replaced all of Mary's servants and ladies-in-waiting with her own and fired most of Mary's advisors. And she planned a great ceremony in which she would be crowned queen. When the day came, Elizabeth was carried to Westminster Abbey, London's most important church, on a litter covered with gold

Queen Elizabeth

cloth. Her gown was also made of gold cloth. Over it, she wore a velvet cape with ermine fur on its edges and a heavy necklace of rubies and pearls. A heavy gold crown was placed on her head. A minister put holy oil on her head, and she was given a scepter, a globe with a cross on it (called an orb) and a special ring to show her power. Elizabeth was now Elizabeth I, queen of England. She would remain on the throne for forty-five years. These years became known as the *Elizabethan Age*. Under Elizabeth, England would become peaceful, rich, and more powerful than ever before.

Elizabeth didn't want to make the same mistakes that Mary had made. She wanted her people to love her, not loathe her! So although she announced that England would now be a Protestant country again, she did not force her people to swear that they were Protestants. No more Catholic church services were allowed, and Elizabeth wanted her advisors to be Protestants. But she didn't ask her subjects what they were doing in private. She told her advisors that she didn't intend to make "windows into men's souls."

This was an unusual attitude for a Renaissance ruler to take! Many other European rulers were busy making sure that all of their subjects swore allegiance to either the Catholic or Protestant faiths. But Elizabeth was more worried about whether or not her subjects were loyal to *her*.

Elizabeth was also determined not to marry. Mary had married a Spanish prince who convinced her to send English soldiers to help with Spanish battles. The English didn't like this prince, whose name was Philip. They thought he was arrogant and selfish—and above all, a foreigner! They didn't want English soldiers to go fight in foreign wars. And when Philip started to help Mary make laws for England, many of Mary's people ran through the streets, yelling, "We will have no for-eigner for our king!"

All of Elizabeth's advisors expected her to get married as soon as possible. As a matter of fact, when Elizabeth called her first *Parliament* (the group of representatives who would help her to pass laws), Parliament told her, "We can't talk about laws until we've arranged a wedding for you!"

But Elizabeth knew that if she got married, her husband would be the real ruler of England. Back in those days, most people thought that men were always wiser, smarter, and stronger than women. If Elizabeth married a prince, more and more of her power would go to him. Elizabeth had no intention of giving up *any* of her power!

Parliament insisted. They didn't think that a woman could do a good job of ruling England. (Mary certainly hadn't!) Elizabeth needed a man to help her. And she needed to have children! What if she died without an heir? Who would be king after her?

Philip, Mary's husband, offered to take on the job of marrying Elizabeth. He had enjoyed the power that came with the throne of England, and he wanted it back! Of course, he didn't say, "I want to marry Elizabeth so that I can be king of England again." He put it in much grander words. "I have decided," he wrote to Parliament, "to render this service to God and offer to marry the queen of England. It would be better for herself and her kingdom if she would take a *consort* [a husband] who might relieve her of those labors which are only fit for men."

But Elizabeth put her foot down. She took off the ring she had been given when she was crowned and held it up in front of all of those men. "Behold," she said, "the pledge of this my wedlock and marriage with my kingdom. Every one of you, and as many as are Englishmen, are children and kinsmen to me." Elizabeth's words meant that she was "married" to England. She had no room for a husband; the job of being queen would take up all of her time.

And Elizabeth *did* put all of her time into ruling England. She worked hard, making alliances with other countries, sending explorers out to claim undiscovered lands for England, and defending her land against invasion.

Thirty years after she became queen, Elizabeth encouraged her soldiers before a battle by shouting out, "[I am] resolved, in the midst and heat of the battle, to live and die amongst you all; to lay down for my God, and for my kingdom, and my people, my honour and my blood, even in the dust. I know I have the body but of a weak and feeble woman; but I have the heart and stomach of a king, and of a king of England too!"

Elizabeth was right. She was the best ruler England ever had! Her people called her Good Queen Bess.

Chapter Thirty-Nine
England's Greatest Playwright

William Shakespeare

Elizabeth worked hard ruling her country. But sometimes she took time off to enjoy herself. She loved music, and she kept a fifty-person choir and full orchestra at court. She paid composers to write songs for her choir. She even sang herself, playing the lyre (an instrument with strings) as accompaniment. She liked poetry, and wrote a few verses herself. Most of all, she enjoyed seeing a good play—especially a play written by William Shakespeare, England's most famous playwright.

Shakespeare was born six years after Elizabeth became queen. When he was young, he acted in a traveling company that went from town to town, performing plays in wooden theatres and in the courtyards of inns. When he grew a little older, Shakespeare and several friends formed their own band of actors. Shakespeare acted parts, helped choose costumes, ran rehearsals, found props—and wrote plays. He wrote *comedies* (funny plays) such as *The Taming of the Shrew,* about a hot-tempered woman who has to marry a man she doesn't like, and *A Midsummer's Night Dream,* about fairies who play tricks on people who wander through the woods. He wrote *tragedies* (sad plays) such as *Hamlet,* about a prince who has to avenge his father's death, and *Romeo and Juliet,* about a boy and girl who fall in love even though their families hate each other. And he wrote *historical plays* based on the lives of great men and women in the past. *Richard III* tells the story of the English king who took the throne from the Princes in the Tower; *Henry V* is about the Battle of Agincourt, in France.

In all, Shakespeare wrote more than forty plays. They have been performed over and over again for the last 450 years! Shakespeare's plays have been translated into almost every language. They have been made into movies, written about in books, and studied in schools. Some of the most familiar phrases in English come from Shakespeare's plays. Have you ever heard someone say, "Something is rotten in the state of Denmark" or "To be or not to be—that is the question"? Both lines are from *Hamlet*. "A horse, a horse! My kingdom for a horse!" is from *Richard III*. Has your mother ever said, "You're going to eat me out of house and home!"? Shakespeare first used that expression in *Henry IV, Part 2*. And if you've ever heard jealousy called "the green-eyed monster," you've heard a line from *Othello*.

One of Shakespeare's most famous plays, *Macbeth,* tells about a nobleman who wants to be king. Here is the beginning of the story:

Macbeth

Scotland was at war. White-haired King Duncan, afraid that a band of rebels would throw him from his throne, sent his cousin Macbeth and Macbeth's trusted friend Banquo to fight the rebels. He waited anxiously to hear the outcome of the battle. Finally, a soldier arrived, covered with blood, straight from the battlefront. "Macbeth faced the enemy with brandished steel!" the soldier gasped. "He fixed their leader's head upon the battlements! He and Banquo have fought like cannons overcharged with double cracks!"

"Valiant cousin!" King Duncan cried out. "Great happiness!" And he decreed that Macbeth would receive a new, noble title: Thane of Cawdor. (Thane is a Scottish word for a warrior who fights for the king.)

Meanwhile, Macbeth and Banquo were trudging home across a blasted heath (a bare, barren field), through fog and wind. Suddenly, they saw three weird women, crouched around a fire. "Hail!" the weird women cackled. "Hail, Macbeth, Thane of Cawdor, King of Scotland to be! And hail, Banquo; you will not be king, but you will be *father* to kings!" And then they disappeared.

"Where'd they go?" Banquo asked. "Have we gone insane? I'm not the father of kings! And why did they call you Thane of Cawdor and King of Scotland? You're neither!" But just then, messengers arrived. "Macbeth!" they said. "We have brought you word from King Duncan! He has made you Thane of Cawdor!"

When Macbeth heard this news, he was dis-

Macbeth ponders the message of the weird women.

turbed. The words of the weird women had already begun to come true. But how could he become King of Scotland, as well as Thane of Cawdor? His cousin Duncan was king.

Then Macbeth realized that he could become king if he turned traitor, and had Duncan murdered. But he thrust the thought away from him. "Let not light see my black and deep desires!" he muttered to himself.

But the idea stayed with him. He wrote a letter to his wife, Lady Macbeth, who was still in their castle back home. He told her about the weird women and their words. At once, Lady Macbeth seized onto the idea of Duncan's death. If her husband became king, she would become queen! But she thought to herself, "Macbeth is too full of the milk of human kindness to murder his cousin."

Just as she finished reading her husband's letter, Lady Macbeth heard a messenger approaching the castle. The messenger wore the royal colors. "The King comes here tonight!" the messenger announced, sliding from his horse. "Macbeth is with him. They are returning from the battlefront. Make everything ready!"

At once, Lady Macbeth decided that she and Macbeth would murder King Duncan that very night. She paced the room, convincing herself that she was brave enough for such a deed. "Spirit of courage and ambition, fill me from the crown to the toe, top-full of direst cruelty!" she growled to herself. "Make thick my blood! Let no regret or conscience shake my purpose!"

As she spoke these horrible words, Macbeth came into the room. "Duncan is with me!" he said. Lady Macbeth put her hand on his arm. "He must be provided for," she said, with great meaning. But although Macbeth knew what his wife meant, he turned away from her. The idea of becoming king was more and more wonderful to him—but he was not yet ready to kill his cousin, King Duncan.

Just then the king himself entered, with Banquo and other noblemen. At once, Lady Macbeth was all smiles. "Your majesty!" she cried. "You load our house with honor! Our servants are yours! Come to the hall,

374

where a great feast has been laid for you!" And she led the king from the room.

Macbeth remained, fretting to himself. "If I were going to do it," he mumbled, "I would need to do it quickly, not wait. But oh, what a dreadful deed it would be! He is here both as my king and as my cousin. I am his host; I should shut the door against murderers, not bear the knife myself! Oh, I do not have enough determination to do this thing!"

When Lady Macbeth returned, having taken Duncan and others to the dining hall, Macbeth said stern, "Lady, we will go no further with this dreadful plan. He has just given me a great honor! How can I do this?"

"What?" Lady Macbeth snapped back. "Are you afraid? You'll have to live with your cowardice the rest of your life! Be a man! Screw your courage to the sticking place. When Duncan is asleep, I'll give his guards drugged wine, so that they sleep like pigs. And then we'll say that his guards did it."

"But will they believe us?" Macbeth asked nervously.

"Of course they will," Lady Macbeth said. "We'll be weeping so hard over Duncan's death that they'll never suspect us!"

What do you think Macbeth will decide to do when the story continues?

Macbeth's Decision

In another part of the castle, Banquo was getting ready for bed. He took off his sword and handed it over to his servant, and then glanced out at the starless night. "There's good housekeeping in heaven," he murmured to himself. "All their candles have been put out! I should put my candle out as well, but I'm too restless. I feel that something terrible may happen tonight."

As he said these words, Macbeth knocked on the door. "Do you have everything you need?" he inquired.

"I do," Banquo said, "but I'm too restless to sleep. I've been thinking over the words of the weird women. They said that you would be Thane of Cawdor, and you are. But when they said you would be King…"

"Let's talk about that later," Macbeth interrupted, "when you have the time. For tonight, sleep well."

While Macbeth and Banquo were talking, Lady Macbeth took drugged wine to Duncan's guards. Soon they were slumped outside the king's door, snoring. She took their daggers gently from their belts and crept into the king's room. Duncan too slept. But as Lady Macbeth stared down at him, she realized that he looked like her father. "I cannot do it!" she whispered to herself, backing from the room. But she laid the daggers before the doorstep. "Macbeth will see them when he comes by," she thought, "and perhaps he will do the deed."

After Macbeth left Banquo, he wandered up and down the hall in a frenzy of uncertainty. As he grew more frantic, he began to see things. "I think I see a dagger, hanging before me in the air!" he cried. "Is it my imagination? Is it a vision, telling me to carry out this dreadful plot? Here is a real dagger in my belt. Will I draw it? Yes, I will. I have made up my mind! Duncan, this night you will go to heaven or to hell." And he made his way towards the stairs.

Lady Macbeth waited for her husband in their rooms. When she heard his step, she opened the door. There he stood, his face white. "I have done it," he whispered. "But I think I will never sleep again. I thought I heard a voice cry, 'Sleep, no more! Macbeth doth murder sleep! Macbeth shall sleep no more.'"

"Pull yourself together!" Lady Macbeth told him. "Go wash your hands! Put on your night clothes, and we'll tell everyone we were asleep when it happened."

When Duncan's guards discovered that the king was dead, Macbeth and his wife came yawning from their room, pretending to be shocked and horrified. Lady Macbeth even fainted! They played their parts so well that Duncan's followers decided to make Macbeth, the dead king's cousin, the next King of Scotland. But although Macbeth had gotten away with murder, he was afraid that Banquo would be the next to plot for the throne. Hadn't the weird women said that Banquo would be the father of kings? Maybe Banquo was planning to put his children on the throne in Macbeth's place!

So Macbeth hired three murderers to follow Banquo on his morning's ride—and kill him. Now Macbeth was truly safe. But as he sat at dinner that night, Macbeth saw Banquo's ghost. He shouted, "Hence, horrible shadow"—startling his other guests, who could see nothing.

As time went on, Macbeth and Lady Macbeth felt more and more guilt. They had nightmares. "We sleep in the affliction of these terrible dreams that shake us nightly," Macbeth complained. "Duncan sleeps peacefully in his grave. He is better off than we are." And Lady Macbeth started to walk in her sleep, rubbing her hands together over and over as if she were washing them. "Out, out, bloody spot!" she would whisper, until someone woke her up.

Finally Macbeth decided to go find the three weird women again, and ask them whether his throne was safe. He discovered them in a cave, huddled around a cauldron, chanting "Double, double, toil and trouble. Fire burn and cauldron bubble!" One of the women, hearing Macbeth approach, said, "By the pricking of my thumbs, something evil this way comes!" And in came Macbeth.

"Answer me this question!" he said to them. "How long will I be king?"

"Till the forest walks up to your castle," the women answered him.

"That will never be!" Macbeth exclaimed. "Who can command the trees to unfix their roots from the earth?" And he went home, comforted.

But when he arrived at his gate, he saw his servants weeping. "Your lady is dead!" they told him. Lady Macbeth had died of a guilty conscience. And worse was to come. Macbeth's lookouts began to shout that they could see a forest, approaching the castle! When Macbeth ran up to the wall, he saw an enormous army moving towards his castle, each man carrying in front of him a branch cut from the woods so that the defenders in the castle could not tell exactly how many soldiers were coming. Duncan's relatives were at the front of the attack, ready to fight for the throne! Soon the avenging army broke into the castle. Armed men ran towards Macbeth.

Macbeth realized that his life was over. He shouted, "Out, out, brief candle! Life's but a walking shadow, a poor player that struts and frets his hour upon the stage, and then is heard no more. It is a tale told by an idiot, full of sound and fury, signifying nothing!" And then he drew his sword, plunged into the fight—and was killed.

Macbeth is a tragedy. At its end, Macbeth and Lady Macbeth and a number of other characters are all dead! But Queen Elizabeth probably enjoyed this play. After all, it showed that a nobleman who plotted treason against a ruler would come to a bad end!

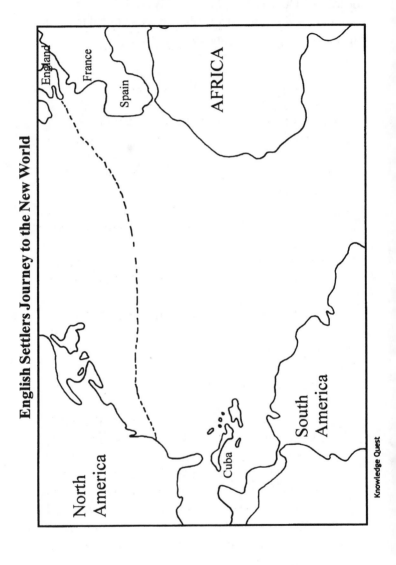

English Settlers Journey to the New World

Knowledge Quest

380

Chapter Forty
New Ventures to the Americas

Walter Raleigh and the New World

During Elizabeth's reign, the Spanish were busy building an empire. Philip, the Spanish prince who had married Mary (and who had offered to marry Elizabeth) had inherited the throne of Spain. He ruled not only over Spain itself, but over parts of Italy and Europe. And Spain's empire stretched over to the Americas as well. Spanish settlers had built colonies in Central and South America. Now, the Spanish were beginning to move into North America too. Two Spanish adventurers, Hernando de Soto and Francisco Vásquez de Coronado, had already explored parts of what is now the United States. And a Spanish colony had been built in the land that now belongs to Florida.

If the Spanish took over both North and South America, the Spanish Empire would become the largest and most powerful in the world. Elizabeth didn't want Spain to become more important than England. So she gave English pirates permission to attack Spanish ships headed for the New World. And she began to plan English expeditions to North America. England needed to build its own colonies in North America before Spain claimed it all!

Who would be in charge of the English attempt to explore North America? Elizabeth decided to give the job to one of her favorite knights, Sir Walter Raleigh.

Walter Raleigh was a tall, handsome, hot-tempered man, always getting himself involved in tavern fights and arguments. But he was also a poet who swore eternal devotion to the queen. One story tells us that Raleigh was walking with the queen when the two came to a muddy spot in the road. Raleigh whipped off his velvet cloak, threw it across the mud with a flourish, and invited the queen to walk on top of it.

This sort of behavior charmed the queen! She gave Raleigh land, money, and a special position at court. And she told him that he could organize the expedition to North America. That meant that Raleigh would arrange for ships, provisions, and sailors. In return, Elizabeth promised to give Walter Raleigh plenty of land in North America for his own.

Raleigh had tried to get to North America before. When he was a young man, he had gone with his brother on an attempt to land in the New World. But their ships never made it across the ocean. First, a Spanish fleet attacked them and drove them back. And then a storm forced them to return to land. Later, Raleigh's brother tried once more to make it across the Atlantic. But his ship was lost at sea—and he was never seen again. This time around, Elizabeth ordered Raleigh to stay in England while the ships tried to reach North America She didn't want her favorite knight to drown or be killed by the Spanish!

So Raleigh filled two ships with provisions and men and sent them off. The sailors had orders to explore the coast of North America, find the best place for a colony to settle, and then return. The ships were gone for over a year—a long year for Sir Walter Raleigh. Finally, the ships were sighted on the horizon. They had returned safely!

Raleigh ran down to the docks to hear their news. When the ship's captains came down the gang-planks, they were full of stories and enthusiasm. They had landed on the east coast of North America and found rich, fertile land, perfect for growing crops. The native Indians were friendly; two had even agreed to return to England on the English ships. The sailors had brought back pearls, soft beautiful animal skins, and two new plants: potatoes, and tobacco. They told Raleigh that the Indians put tobacco into clay pipes, lit it, and then blew smoke from their mouths. They had never seen anyone smoking before!

Raleigh decided to try out this new tobacco for himself. One evening, he sat in his rooms, trying to figure out how his new pipe worked. He blew and puffed and choked. Finally, he managed to breathe the smoke into his lungs. Just then, his manservant came into the room. When he saw smoke coming out of Raleigh's nose, he thought Raleigh was on fire! Yelling for help, he grabbed a bucket of cold water—and dumped it over Raleigh's head. Now Raleigh had to find colonists who would be willing to build a new town in the New World. Eventually, 107 men and women agreed to go to America. Raleigh filled their ships with seed, salt, livestock, and building tools and sent them off. He told them to name their new colony *Virginia* in honor of Elizabeth, who was known as the "Virgin Queen."

The settlers landed safely in Virginia and began to build homes, fences, and gardens. But after a year, they begged to be allowed to come back to England. The Virginia winters were freezing cold. The ground wasn't as fertile as the first explorers had told them; they had so little food that they had been forced to eat their dogs! And the Indians were growing more and more unfriendly. Finally a ship brought the unhappy colonists home.

Walter Raleigh was determined to try again. He sent another ship full of settlers to Virginia, but this attempt failed as well. And in the meantime, Raleigh started to have troubles of his own in England. He had fallen in love with one of Elizabeth's maids of honor, a beautiful girl named Bess Throckmorton. But he knew that Elizabeth would be angry if she found out. She wanted Raleigh to be dedicated only to her service! So he and Bess Throckmorton married in secret, and Bess went on living at the palace.

But then Bess discovered that she was going to have a baby. When the queen found out what had happened, she arrested both of them and threw them into the Tower of London. She didn't like secrets at her court!

After a month, Elizabeth let both of her prisoners out. But she banished them from her court and told them to go away and live in the English countryside. The year after his release, Raleigh wrote a poem that began, "Like truthless dreams, so are my joys expired," and went on, "My lost delights...have left me all alone in unknown ways." Walter Raleigh's days as the queen's favorite were over.

Although Raleigh lived for many more years and had many adventures, his story ends sadly. He never sent another expedition to North America. When Elizabeth died, there was still no English colony in the New World. And the king who inherited her throne charged Raleigh with treason and threw him in the Tower of London for twelve years. Finally, the king let Raleigh out and told him that he could go free as long as he went to South America and found gold for England. Raleigh tried—but when he returned empty-handed, he was beheaded.

The Lost Colony

Do you remember the first Virginia colonists, who grew so hungry that they begged to come home? They had settled on an island called Roanoke Island. (Today, that island is part of North Carolina.) Storms from the sea often blew across the island, and the Native Americans there had begun to threaten the English settlers. So when the colonists went back to England, they left fifteen soldiers behind to guard their little town.

When Raleigh's second band of colonists set out for Virginia, they decided to abandon Roanoke Island. Instead, they planned to land further north, near the Chesapeake Bay. But they did convince the commander of their ships to stop at Roanoke Island to pick up the fifteen soldiers who had stayed behind. The ships anchored in the water nearby, and the colonists rowed over to the island in small boats. But the fifteen soldiers had disappeared! The settlement was deserted, the houses overgrown by vines and weeds. Deer wandered through the village, poking their heads into windows. The colonists searched, but found only the skeleton of a single soldier. "They've all been killed by Indians!" the colonists muttered. "Let's get out of here!"

But the commander who was in charge of the colonists' ships was tired of having the colonists on board. They were seasick all the time, and they complained about how uncomfortable the ships were. And the commander had already argued with John White, the colony leader. So he ordered the ships to leave the colonists on Roanoke Island and go back to England!

The colonists were horrified. They had only a few boats, so they couldn't get off the island. It was July in Virginia—hot and very muggy. Bugs were everywhere, and the settlement was falling down around them.

But the colonists did their best. They cleaned out the abandoned houses and fenced in the deserted gardens. They tried to make friends with the Native Americans again, and for a little while, friendly Native Americans helped them to trap fish and grow corn and beans. Less than a month after the colonists were stranded on Roanoke Island, John White's daughter Eleanor had a baby girl. She and her husband, Ananias Dare, named the little girl Virginia. Virginia Dare was the first English baby born in the New World. For a little while, it seemed that the Roanoke Island colony might survive.

But then the colonists attacked a group of friendly Native Americans because they thought that the Native Americans were dangerous. They were wrong! But after this disastrous mistake, the Indians refused to help the colonists find any more food. The colonists were afraid they would starve when winter came.

So the colony voted to send John White back to England in one of the small boats. If he could make it back alive, he could get help: food, supplies, and more ships. If he left right away, perhaps he could even be back before winter was over! Then the colonists could go to the Chesapeake Bay, as they had originally planned.

John White didn't want to leave his daughter and granddaughter on Roanoke Island. But the other colonists insisted. So John White began the long, rough journey back across the Atlantic Ocean. Three months later, he arrived in London. At once, he asked to see Sir Walter Raleigh, and told the great man what had happened.

Raleigh began to collect supplies and ships to help the colonists. But his efforts took time. The winter dragged slowly by. Finally, in early spring, the ships were ready to sail. John White could only hope that the colonists had survived the winter.

But then disaster struck. England and Spain declared war on each other. Spanish ships sailed up and down the Atlantic, threatening any English ship that passed. And Queen Elizabeth took Raleigh's ships to help fight the Spanish. John White couldn't get back to his colony for three more years!

Finally, he begged to be taken aboard a warship which was headed to South America to raid Spanish colonies. John White spent months on this ship, waiting for it to head north. Finally, the ship made its way up to the Virginia coast to Roanoke Island.

John White hoped to be greeted by the colonists at the shore. But the island was empty and still. He walked warily along the overgrown paths, towards the settlement. But when he arrived, he found only gardens filled with weeds and the foundations of the houses. The wood, windows, and doors were completely gone. The colony had disappeared.

John White was frantic with worry. But he saw no signs of fighting, and no bones or bodies. And since there were no ruins, it seemed clear that the colonists had taken the houses down and moved them to another place. If they planned on building a new settlement, they would need the materials from their old homes. But where were they?

John White searched the whole island. He had told the colonists to carve a cross in a tree if they began to get into trouble, to serve as a message. But there was no cross anywhere. Finally he found his only clue: the word "Croatoan," whittled into the thick trunk of a tree at

the settlement's edge. Perhaps the settlers had gone to nearby Croatoan Island, using their small boats to travel across the water a few at a time. But Croatoan Island was too small for the whole colony, and when his ship had passed it just days earlier, he had seen no sign of life.

Still, John White planned to go search Croatoan Island. But as his ship set out for the island, a hurricane blew up from the south and almost drowned everyone on board. For days, wind and rain lashed the ship, which almost sank. When the wind finally died down, the ship's captain insisted on going back to England right away.

Back in England, John White tried to convince Walter Raleigh to send another expedition to find out what had happened. But Raleigh couldn't find anyone willing to go. It was twenty years before another Englishman set foot on Roanoke Island. By then, the traces of the settlement were fading, and Croatoan Island was empty.

Many years afterwards, other English settlers heard different stories from the tribes near Roanoke Island. Some said that the colonists had been killed (although no bodies were ever seen). Others claimed that they had gone to live with nearby Native Americans. Rumors started that a blond-haired child had been seen living with a tribe near the Chesapeake Bay. But no one has ever solved this mystery for sure. The "Lost Colony" will always remain a puzzle.

First Discoveries in Canada

Arctic Ocean

North Atlantic

Greenland

Hudson Bay

Newfoundland

Gulf of St. Lawrence

St. Lawrence River

St. John's

Micmac territory

Huron territory

NORTH AMERICA

Chapter Forty-One
Explorations in the North

The New-Found Land

After Columbus and Amerigo Vespucci sailed across the Atlantic, other Europeans followed. The Spanish and Portuguese planted their colonies in Central and South America. The English did their best to settle in Virginia. And further up north in North America, another colony began to form on the island of Newfoundland. This colony wasn't Spanish, Portuguese, or English. It was filled with settlers from all different nations! It had many different names, in many different languages, but like the English "New-found-land," these names all mean "New land." Today, Newfoundland is part of the country of Canada.

The colony on Newfoundland (which was often known by its French name, *Terre-Neuve*) got its start when a merchant named John Cabot sailed north from England and bumped into the North American coast. John Cabot was a little bit like the people who would follow him to Newfoundland—he was from several different countries! He was born in Italy, tried living in Spain, and then came to England. Here, he convinced the English to help him pay for a journey of exploration. Like Columbus, John Cabot wanted to find a quick way to get to India. He thought that if he sailed north, he might find the fastest possible route to the East.

Five years after Columbus landed in America, John Cabot began his own journey into the North Atlantic. He had only twenty men and a single small ship, the *Matthew*. But his journey was even shorter than he had expected! Before too many weeks had passed, Cabot sighted land ahead of him. An island, rocky and fog-shrouded, rose out of the ocean. Cabot sailed around the island's shores and found that beyond it lay a huge, forested mass of land. He could glimpse grassy meadows beyond the beaches. Silver streams trickled through the meadows, down to the sea.

As Cabot's ship cruised along this new coast, his men leaned over the ship's rail, their mouths open with astonishment. The water was filled with large fish, leaping around the ship's bow. "Quick!" one said. "Lower a basket down!" They tied a rope to a nearby wicker basket and dragged it through the water beside the ship. When they pulled it up, it was full of codfish—perfect for eating. This was the easiest fishing they had ever done!

John Cabot beached his ship, climbed ashore, and announced, "I claim this land for England!" Then he sailed back to England and reported, "I have found the shortest route to the northeast coast of Asia. There are so many fish in the water that England's fishermen could feed the whole country! Now I want to return with more ships and look for the spices of the east."

Of course, John Cabot hadn't reached Asia. He had landed on the northern part of North America. But he was sure that he had accomplished his goal. The following spring he left England with five ships, ready to finish his journey to the East.

Months later, one of the ships limped back to England, tattered by storms. It had never reached North America. Winds had driven it off course, and its captain had decided to give up the journey. John Cabot and the other four ships had disappeared entirely. No one ever saw or heard from them again.

Probably the ships sank in the North Atlantic. But even though Cabot never made it back to his new land, English fishermen had heard stories about the swarms of fish in Cabot's new-found land. They set out with their own boats to follow John Cabot's route.

When these fishermen came back with the holds of their ships stuffed full of fish, word spread quickly! Other fishermen from France, Spain, Portugal, and other European countries followed them. They fished around the island of Newfoundland and even ventured into the rivers that ran through the vast expanse of land that lay just beyond the island. Many fishermen built huts on the island of Newfoundland and stayed all summer long. They built wooden platforms called *flakes* where they salted and dried the fish so that their catch wouldn't spoil. Little fishing villages sprang up around Newfoundland's best harbor. Merchants came to Newfoundland to sell food, ropes, iron hooks and harpoons, clothes, shoes, and medicines to the fishermen. This fishing settlement became known as St. John's. It was the first European colony in the country that we now call Canada.

But the colony of St. John's wasn't exactly like the other colonies in North and South America. The fishermen who lived in St. John's only stayed in their colony during the spring and summer. When the breezes that blew across the island began to grow colder, St. John's settlers started packing their fish, their tools and clothes, and all of their fishing tackle into their ships for the journey home. No one tried to stay all winter on the island of Newfoundland! Icy winds would blow across St. John's, sucking the warmth from the little wooden huts. Fog would descend on the settlement, so thick that one colonist couldn't see another across the street. Snow would cover the houses, the flakes, and the merchants' shops. The nights would grow longer and longer. Huge, unpredictable storms would sweep down from the north and cover the island, lashing at the harbors and shores. Cakes of ice would form in the waters surrounding Newfoundland. Ships still anchored off Newfoundland's shore would be frozen into the water.

St. John's was a fantastic place to fish—but not to live. For many years, no one would stay on this northern island all year long. The first settlement in Canada would remain a warm-weather colony!

Jacques Cartier's Discoveries

Spain, Portugal and England were all building colonies in the Americas. The king of France decided that he didn't want to be left out! When he learned about the fish-filled waters around Newfoundland, he ordered a French explorer named Jacques Cartier to go find out more about this new land.

So Jacques Cartier set off to claim some of the "New Land" for France. But Cartier had another plan in mind as well: He still wanted to find a way to China. He hoped that he could sail through the North Atlantic Ocean, find a river that cut right through the whole continent of North America, come out the other side, and then sail straight to the Chinese coast.

Cartier got a good start to his adventure. His journey to North America took less than three weeks! When he arrived at Newfoundland, he sailed around the island and drew a map of it. Then he explored and mapped the smaller islands nearby. Now it was time to look for the river that would take him all the way across the continent!

Cartier sailed past Newfoundland, into the waters that we now call the Gulf of St. Lawrence. He discovered that these waters ended in a river that seemed to wind straight into North America. Could this be the river that flowed through the continent? Perhaps it was!

But before Cartier could explore this river, he had to make friends with the Native Americans who lived nearby. He didn't want to sail down his newly-discovered river with hostile tribes on either bank, ready to attack him as soon as he landed!

So Cartier and his men landed on the North American shores and made friends with the people who lived there—the Micmacs. The Micmacs had learned how to survive the cold northern winters. They lived in *wigwams,* cone-shaped huts made of animals skins stretched over wooden timbers. These wigwams could be taken apart and moved. So during the warm summers, the Micmacs moved their villages to the coast, where they would fish and swim in the waters. In the fall, when the wind began to grow cold, the Micmacs took their wigwams apart and journeyed back into the deep woods away from the ocean. Here, the trees would protect them from the cold northern winds.

When Cartier asked the Micmacs, "What is this land called?" they thought he was asking them the name of their small summer settlement on the coast. "We call it 'the village'!" they answered him. In the Micmac language, "the village" sounds like "canada." So Cartier called all of the vast expanse of land before him *Canada.* We still call it Canada today.

As Cartier explored the Micmac land, he met a hunting party from another tribe who lived further away, along the river that Cartier hoped would lead him to China. This tribe was called the Hurons. Their chief,

Donnacona, and his two sons were part of the hunting party. When they described their home to Cartier, he wanted to sail down the river at once to see it!

But winter was coming, and Cartier knew that his men might not be able to survive the Canadian cold. He decided, reluctantly, that they would return to France and come back again in the spring. But he wanted to show his new discoveries to the French king. So he asked Donnacona, "Can I take your sons back to France with me?"

Donnacona didn't want his two boys to disappear into the mysterious waters beyond Newfoundland. But finally he agreed to let his sons go. They waved goodbye to their father and boarded Cartier's ship, which sailed away and vanished over the horizon.

Donnacona waited and waited. An entire year went by, with no sign of his boys. Would his sons ever return?

Finally, Donnacona heard reports that the strangers had landed again on the coast of Canada. He gathered a party of warriors with him and hurried towards the ships. When the Hurons arrived, they saw Cartier and his men, preparing to journey into Canada along the river. And they also saw Donnacona's sons! They were taller and stronger. "The Frenchmen want to sail down the river, towards our homeland," they told their father.

Donnacona was grateful to have his boys back. He welcomed Cartier and treated him as a friend. So Cartier and his men began their journey down the river, which we now call the St. Lawrence River. They sailed farther and farther down the St. Lawrence River, closer and closer to Huron land. And soon Donnacona began to get nervous. How far would these strangers go? What would they do to the Huron people when they landed?

When Cartier came ashore at the Huron village where Donnacona lived and announced, "I claim this land for France!" Donnacona decided that they had gone far enough.

"No further!" he ordered. "I am the king of this land, and I command you to stop here!" And three of Donnacona's priests, or *medicine men,* dressed up like devils to frighten Cartier. "Go no further!" they warned. "Or disaster will come upon you!"

Cartier ignored Donnacona *and* his priests. He boarded his ships again and went on. But soon the river began to grow shallower and narrower. Cartier watched the shores nervously. If the St. Lawrence went all the way to the Pacific, it would grow wider and deeper again! Before long, Cartier saw rapids ahead—places in the river where the bottom is so shallow that huge rocks jut up into the air through the water. The water bubbled and frothed around this rocks. Cartier knew that the river was coming to an end. The St. Lawrence would not lead him to China.

But he didn't want to return to France empty-handed. And he had heard the Hurons tell tales about a rich land filled with gold and jewels, farther north. So Cartier went back to Donnacona's village and kidnapped the king of the Hurons. He took him back to France to tell these tales of treasure to the French king. Donnacona died in France without ever seeing his native country again.

When the French king heard the stories of a rich, mysterious northern land, he sent Cartier back for a third trip. This time, Cartier found another river, lined with sparkling stones all along its banks. He was sure that he had discovered the land of jewels.

But when he arrived back in France with his boatload of "treasure," the French laughed at him. The stones were worthless, common quartz! And the stories of the Hurons had just been fairy-tales.

Cartier, disgusted, never returned to Canada. But his journeys to Canada had shown other explorers and traders that there was much more land to discover beyond the Gulf of St. Lawrence. Soon Canadian merchants were making regular journeys to Canada, trading with the Indians for rich skins and other goods. Seventy years later, the French established the first year-round colony in Canada. Today, many people who live in Canada speak French, because of the French-speaking settlers who came to live in this new land.

The Spanish and English Collide

Scandinavia

North
Sea

England

London

Plymouth

Southern path of
English fleet

Germany

*English
Channel*

Northern path
of Spanish fleet

France

Switzerland

Portugal

Spain

Rome

*Mediterranean
Sea*

North Africa

Chapter Forty-Two
Empires Collide

Spain and England's War

Now four countries had claimed land in the Americas. France claimed part of Canada. England claimed the coast of what is now the United States. Portugal had colonies along the coast of South America.

But Spain had more settlements in the Americas than anyone else. Spanish cities had been built all through South America and Central America. Spanish explorers had even journeyed up into North America. One adventurer, named Hernando de Soto, had sailed up the Mississippi River. Another explorer, Francisco Vasquez de Coronado, discovered the Grand Canyon. While the English and French were struggling to build tiny villages in North America, Spain was building an enormous empire. Spain was so huge and powerful that it was called "Mistress of the World and Queen of the Ocean."

But Spain had a problem: English adventurers kept getting in its way. And soon this problem would lead to one of the most famous sea battles of all times.

Philip, the king of Spain, had once been the king of England. Do you remember Philip? When he was still just a prince, he married Elizabeth's older sister Mary and became king of England. Two years later, Philip also inherited the throne of Spain. For a brief time, Philip was king of England and king of Spain.

But then Mary died. Elizabeth inherited the English crown. And Philip lost the title "King of England." He offered to marry Elizabeth to get it back—

but when she said no, Philip realized that he would have to learn to live without his English crown.

Philip didn't really need an English crown. His empire was so big that he was already having trouble running it properly! But Philip became more and more annoyed by English ships that insisted on sailing into Spanish waters. English traders were making money by selling slaves to the West Indies. English explorers were trying to settle land in North America that Philip wanted for himself. And sometimes English ships stopped Spanish ships, loaded with gold, and robbed them. Finally Philip sent Elizabeth a message: "Keep your English ships out of Spanish waters, or Spain will declare war on England!"

Elizabeth didn't want to risk a war with Spain. She wasn't sure that England was strong enough to defeat the Spanish! So she sent Philip a peaceful, humble message in return. She promised that the English would leave Spanish territory and Spanish ships alone.

But secretly, Elizabeth gave her sailors permission to go on robbing the Spanish. English pirates knew that they could steal Spanish treasure and sink Spanish ships with no fear of punishment from the queen! And meanwhile, Elizabeth kept right on sending English ships on journeys of exploration. England grew richer and richer and stronger and stronger. And soon Philip realized that Elizabeth's promise had been a big lie. He decided that it was time to prove, once and for all, that Spain—not England—was the most powerful country in the world.

Philip began to build the biggest fleet of warships ever. Shipbuilders labored over huge galleys (warships rowed by oarsmen down in the ship's belly) and galleons (enormous sailing ships, filled with men and supplies). Philip planned to crush the English navy with these huge

Spanish fighting ships

ships. Then they could unload their soldiers on England's shores. Smaller, quicker ships were built as well; Philip planned to send these ships inland, down England's rivers. Once England was filled with Spanish soldiers, Philip could force England to stay out of the New World.

And Philip had another reason for invading England. Philip was a Catholic king, and he knew that Catholics were not allowed to worship openly in England. Once he had conquered England, he planned to make England a Catholic country again. He thought that his conquest of England would be a great service to God!

Finally, Philip assembled over 130 ships into a great floating army called the Spanish Armada. When the Armada was ready to sail for England, the Spanish commander gave their soldiers very strict orders. They were to act in a Christian manner at all times. Catholic priests would accompany every ship and would hold church services on board. All of the sailors were expected to attend! And the soldiers were not allowed to swear, even while fighting. Philip wanted his Armada to be a holy army, taking England back for the Catholic church.

Meanwhile, the English were frantically preparing for invasion! Queen Elizabeth put her cousin Lord Howard in charge of the English navy—but she made her most experienced sailor, Sir Francis Drake, second in

403

command. At first, Howard and Drake decided that the English ships should sail south and attack the Spanish Armada before it could even leave the Spanish port! But strong winds blew the English navy back to the north. The ships anchored at Plymouth, on the south coast of England, and waited for the Armada.

Philip's huge fleet sailed slowly north. Finally, a small English ship keeping watch in the Channel glimpsed the masts of Spanish galleons on the horizon. Its captain sped back to Plymouth Harbor, leaped from his ship, and ran to find the fleet's commanders.

Sir Howard and Sir Francis Drake were having a friendly game of lawn bowling on a smooth grassy field near the harbor. Drake was just getting ready to toss his own ball down the grass when the captain arrived.

"Sir Francis!" the captain gasped. "Come at once! The Spanish are in sight!"

Sir Francis Drake aimed his ball down the smooth grass. "Don't worry," he said. "There is plenty of time to finish the game and beat the Spaniards too."

But Drake and Howard didn't spend much time finishing their game! They ordered the English ships to sail into the English Channel and wait for the Spanish Armada there. When the Spanish ships arrived, they found the English navy ready to fight. The battle for England was about to begin!

The Spanish ships were huge and filled with soldiers, because the Spanish planned on winning by "grappling and boarding." A Spanish ship would sail up beside an English ship, throw hooks over onto its deck, and pull the two ships together. Then Spanish soldiers would pour over onto the English ship and take it over. But the English had a different strategy in mind. Their ships were small and quick, with guns along each side. Rather than boarding the Spanish ships, the English just tried to shoot them full of holes so that they could no longer fight.

The English strategy worked! Even though the Spanish navy was twice as large, the English won. Seventy Spanish ships were destroyed. Twenty thousand Spanish soldiers had been killed. Spain, the "Mistress of the Seas," had been defeated in a sea battle.

The defeat of the Spanish Armada changed Spain and England forever. Spain would remain a powerful country—but it would never be quite as strong again. From now on, the English empire would begin to grow. And soon England, not Spain, would rule over an empire that stretched all across the world.

The World at the End of the Sixteenth Century

Back at the beginning of this book, you pretended to be riding a flying carpet that took you all over the Roman Empire. The Romans thought that they ruled the whole world. They didn't even know about North and South America, or about Australia or New Zealand, or about Japan. Your flying carpet didn't take you to any of these countries. Maybe it was a Roman carpet and didn't know any better!

The Spanish Armada tried to invade England eleven hundred years after the fall of Rome. In those eleven hundred years, the world has changed! It looks very different than it did in the days of the old Roman Empire. So let's take another little trip around the world and see just how different it is.

But you won't need a flying carpet any more. You can board a fast sailing ship and skim around the world by sea!

Let's set sail from Plymouth, where the English navy has just defeated the Spanish. A good wind catches your sails and sends you south. As you pass France, you cross the path of a merchant ship headed for North America. Its owner is hoping to get rich, soft skins from the Native Americans of Canada and bring them back for French ladies to wear! As you continue south, you also pass a battered group of Spanish ships, limping back to port after their humiliating defeat by England. The sailors are pumping water out of the ships' holds. The Spanish galleons are leaking, because the English navy shot them full of holes!

You could turn to the east now and sail through the Straits of Gibraltar, into the Mediterranean Sea. But you decide to keep on sailing down the coast of Africa. You know that you can sail around the southern tip of Africa and back up towards India—Vasco da Gama already did, nearly a hundred years ago!

As you sail down the coast of Africa, you see Portuguese, Spanish, and English ships, anchored at African ports. Some of these ships are loading up gold. Some are filling their holds with ivory. But you also hear wails and cries. African captives are being herded onto slave ships to begin the long trip across the Atlantic. They will work in the New World—and never come home again.

You stay on your southern route. Soon the trading ships are behind you. The southern African coast is thick, green, and mysterious. Past the coast, deep in the heart of the African continent, tribes roam the grassland and the jungles, hunting and fishing. You don't know anything more about these tribes; the rest of the world hasn't yet explored into the center of Africa!

You round the tip of Africa, the Cape of Good Hope, and start north. Now you're in the Indian Ocean.

And after hundreds of miles of ocean have passed beneath your ship, you see the Arabian peninsula ahead of you. The Ottoman Empire, which captured Constantinople and changed its name to Istanbul, ruled over much of Arabia—until a few years ago, when its great emperor Suleiman the Magnificent died. Now the Ottoman Empire is beginning to shrink, and its people are casting a wary eye east, at the Persians who live between Arabia and India. It looks as though war may break out between the Persians and the Ottomans! You don't want to run into any fighting, so you stay safely out to sea. You head your ship east—and soon see the coast of India.

You're no longer alone! Other ships are headed for Indian ports too. Portuguese, Spanish, and English ships are hoping to trade for Indian spices. India, ruled by a strong Moghul emperor, is at peace; Hindus and Muslims live side by side, and the whole country prospers because of trade with Europe! You're half-tempted to drop anchor and go ashore, to see the beautiful Indian buildings and smell the rich scent of spices at the ports— but you decide to keep on.

You make your way carefully through a maze of islands into the South China Sea. South of you lies the huge island of Australia, where Aboriginal nomads hunt kangaroos, dig water-frogs out of the ground, and tell their stories of the Dreamtime. Even farther south lies the smaller islands of New Zealand, where the Maori skim along the coastal waters in their fishing canoes. But explorers haven't yet made their way to these islands, and so you turn north, towards China, and sail along the eastern coast of this huge, mysterious country. Once, China had its own ships and traded with the outside world. But now the Ming dynasty rules over China. The Ming emperors have forbidden sailors to set

407

out into the ocean. They have built a secret palace in the center of China's capital, where the Emperor lives, far away from foreign eyes. You'd like to land your ship and explore—but you're afraid that you won't be welcome!

So you sail on. North of you lies the islands of Japan, where the samurai are fighting with each other for control of their country. The emperor isn't strong enough to stop them! The famous samurai warrior Oda Nobunaga has just captured the capital city of Japan. For now, he is the strongest leader in Japan!

You turn your ship right and head east again, out into the Pacific Ocean. You know that since the earth is round, you'll eventually run into the west coast of North America! And after months of travel, land finally comes into view. There are no colonies on this coast yet, but when you turn and sail south, down along the coast of Central America, you begin to see Spanish settlements where Aztec cities once stood. Past Central America, down along the South American coast, you see the ruins of Incan temples and broad Incan roads, high on the mountains that rise up from South America's beaches. The wind grows stronger. You are reaching the southern tip of South America! You could take a shortcut through the Straits of Magellan—but you're afraid your ship will run aground in that rough, choppy water! So you go all the way down to Cape Horn, sail around it, and head back up north. Now you begin to see Portuguese settlements. And you have to tack quickly out of the way when a Portuguese ship sails by on your left, firing at a Spanish ship approaching on your right. The Portuguese and Spanish are still arguing over that South American land!

Eventually you sail around the broadest part of South America and head up through the Caribbean, toward North America. Spanish colonies dot Florida, but as you keep on sailing north along the coast, the land grows wilder. You glimpse a hunting party of Native Americans, silently stalking a herd of deer, but when they see your ship they disappear into the forest. As you reach the middle of the continent, you sail past a wind-swept island a little off the coast. A couple of water soaked planks lie on the beach. When you squint, you can see the ruins of a fence, with deer grazing content-edly on the watermelons that grow in an old garden, overgrown with weeds. The remains of the Lost Colony still stand on Roanoke Island.

You skim on up the coast, feeling the air turn cooler. Far, far north, you see an island up ahead of you, with a busy fishing settlement on its shores. French, English, Portuguese, Italian, Spanish, and Dutch fishing ships circle the island, dragging fishing nets behind them. Smoke rises up from the chimneys of dozens of small houses. Drying fish lie on stands all along the shore. It's the height of the fishing season in Newfoundland, and the colony of St. John's is busy! By fall, the ships will be gone and the island will be empty.

It's time to turn to the east once more and sail back toward England, where you began your trip. You've managed to make a journey all around the world—and back again.

Timeline

In order to keep the narrative coherent, I have occasionally told the story of one culture or country before going back in time to begin the story of another.

200	(BC/BCE) Ajanta caves begun (Chapter 5)
70	The Temple in Jerusalem destroyed by Rome (20)
300	Yamato dynasty established in Japan (9)
300	The approximate beginning of the Three Kingdoms period in Korea (9)
320	Beginning of the Gupta dynasty of India (5)
395	The Roman Empire divides permanently into two (1)
410	Rome sacked and burned by Visigoths (1)
449	Anglo-Saxon invasion of England (2)
455	Beginning of Skandagupta's reign (5)
467	End of Skandagupta's reign (5)
485	Clovis begins his reign over the Franks (11)
510	Clovis ends his reign over the Franks (11)
527	Justinian comes to the Byzantine throne (4)
535	End of the Gupta dynasty of India (5)
565	Justinian dies in the Byzantine empire (4)
570	Muhammad born (6)
581	Beginning of the Sui dynasty in China (8)
590	Yang Chien completes the unification of China (8)
597	Augustine begins his Christian mission to England (3)
600	Peak of classical Mayan civilization (32)
618	End of the Sui dynasty and beginning of the Tang dynasty in China (8)
622	Muhammad flees to Medina (the Hegira) (6)
632	Muhammad dies (6)
650	Ajanta caves deserted (5)
690	Charles Martel born (13)
711	Tariq invades Spain (12)
732	Battle of Tours (Battle of Poitiers) (13)
741	Charles Martel dies (13)
771	Charlemagne comes to power (13)
790	Viking raids on Europe begin (14)

1608   The first French settlement in Canada is established in
        Quebec (41)
1609   Galileo invents the telescope (37)
1616   William Shakespeare dies (39)
1924   The last Chinese emperor leaves the Forbidden City
        (22)

Index

K

L

M

N

Also available from Peace Hill Press

The Story of the World, Volume 2
Activity Book

This comprehensive activity book and curriculum guide contains all you need to make modern history come alive for your child!

Don't just read about history—experience it! Designed to turn *The Story of the World*, Volume 2 into a complete history program, this activity book provides comprehension questions and answers, sample narrations, maps and geography activities, coloring pages, lists of additional history and literature readings, and many hands-on learning activities, all designed for students reading Volume 2 of *The Story of the World*!

"I am not a crafty or creative person, so all the crafts my children do come directly from the Story of the World Activity Book. My older child is excellent at narrations and is an avid reader, so the book lists help me to quickly obtain quality library books for him to read. My younger child struggles with narration and only recently became a reader, but he loves doing projects from the Activity Book. I have discovered that after completing a project—like when we made Henry Hudson's boat or Robin Hood's arrow quiver—my younger son could then tell Dad all about what we learned. Thanks to the Activity Book, our history is enriched to meet both my boys' needs."
— Carole M. • Middletown, DE

Available at www.peacehillpress.com and wherever books are sold.

ISBN 0-9714129-4-4

$29.95

Blackline maps from Knowledge Quest Maps were used in this book. You can obtain maps for coloring by contacting:
Knowledge Quest Maps
7722 SE 282nd Ave.
Gresham, OR 97080

or by visiting the website:
www.knowledgequestmaps.com

Blackline Maps of World History

The Ancients 5000 B.C. to 500 A.D.

The Middle Ages 500 to1500 A.D.

The Age of Exploration 1492 to1850

The Modern World 1850-Present

Notes

Notes

Notes

Notes

Notes

Notes